THE REINDUSTRIALIZATION OF AMERICA

THE

McGraw-Hill Book Company

*New York   St. Louis   San Francisco   Auckland   Bogotá   Hamburg
Johannesburg   London   Madrid   Mexico   Montreal   New Delhi
Panama   Paris   São Paulo   Singapore   Sydney   Tokyo   Toronto*

REINDUSTRIALIZATION OF AMERICA

by

The Business Week Team

Seymour Zucker

Claudia H. Deutsch

John Hoerr

Norman Jonas

John E. Pearson

James C. Cooper

Library of Congress Cataloging in Publication Data
Main entry under title:

Reindustrialization of America.

Includes index.
1. United States—Industries. 2. United States—
Economic policy—1971– I. Business Week (New
York)
HC106.7.R35   338.0973   81-8360
ISBN 0-07-009324-5   AACR2

THE REINDUSTRIALIZATION OF AMERICA

1 2 3 4 5 6 7 8 9 0   DODO   8 9 8 7 6 5 4 3 2 1

This book was set in Century Schoolbook by University
Graphics, Inc. The editors were William Sabin and Earle
Resnick; the designer was Elliot Epstein; the production
supervisor was Thomas G. Kowalczyk. R. R. Donnelley
was printer and binder.

CONTENTS

Introduction   1

PART ONE   **HOW AND WHY AMERICA LOST ITS ECONOMIC LEADERSHIP**   5

1   The Decline of U.S. Economic Vitality   7

2   How Government Has Stifled Growth   29

3   How Inflation Has Crippled Savings and Investment   39

4   How Business Has Hobbled Itself   47

5   Where Labor and Management Went Wrong   63

PART TWO   **CREATING THE CLIMATE FOR GROWTH**   73

6   Forging a New Social Consensus   75

7   Building a New Partnership in the Workplace   87

8   Putting the Future into Business Decisions   101

PART THREE   **A BLUEPRINT FOR REINDUSTRIALIZATION**   113

9   Laying Four Cornerstones of National Policy   115

10   Setting Our Own Directions   141

11   Capitalizing on America's Assets   159

12   Two Stages of an Industrial Policy   181

Index   187

INTRODUCTION

In the early spring of 1980, a group of *Business Week* editors met with editor in chief Lewis H. Young in his office on the thirty-ninth floor of the McGraw-Hill Building in New York City. The purpose of the meeting: to plan a special issue of the magazine that would assess the economic malaise affecting the United States and offer the nation a method for setting itself back on the track to prosperity. From that meeting was born the most successful issue in *Business Week's* 51-year history. The combined effort of some fifty editors and reporters, "The Reindustrialization of America," dated June 30, 1980, generated more controversy and letters from readers than anything *Business Week* had previously done. It became the subject of interviews on national television, and literally hundreds of newspapers and magazines devoted articles to it. It won a host of awards: the Deadline Club Award, the 1981 National Magazine Award, and the John Hancock Award. Reindustrialization became the subject of intense debate in both the legislative and executive branches of government, and it was even to play a role in the 1980 presidential election.

Less than 2 months after the issue appeared, the AFL-CIO executive council adopted a statement urging the government to "take the lead in developing a new partnership with labor and business" to reindustrialize America. The AFL-CIO called for the creation of a "national reindustrialization board" to carry out this policy. A few days later, on August 28, President Carter issued a white paper detailing his proposed "economic renewal program." Carter announced he would establish an economic revitalization board, with representatives of industry, labor, and the public, to advise him on the "broad range of issues involved in the ongoing process of revitalization."

Since the election of Ronald Reagan, who hopes to stimulate the economy with a general cut in taxes rather than specific policies aimed at rebuilding the industrial base, an industrial policy has never gotten off the ground. But the idea is proving difficult to hold down. At a symposium held in Philadelphia to mark the hundredth anniversary of the Wharton School on March 22–24, 1981, for example, the need for specific policies to rebuild American industry was supported by economists, business executives, and labor leaders from a wide ideological spectrum. And reindustrialization has won over no less a Reagan supporter than business lobbyist Charls Walker, who played an active part in Reagan's election campaign and who is calling for the creation of a public corporation to help ailing companies.

With the debate once again stirring and certain to gain momentum, the editors decided that what was needed was a book in which we could explore in depth the concepts that were originally presented in *Business Week* but, because of the inherent limitations of weekly magazine publishing, were not fully developed. We wished to incorporate important new material that had emerged, to update the statistics, and to evaluate what the Reagan economic policies might accomplish in revitalizing the American economy. The task was assigned to a team of six *Business Week* editors chosen from the original fifty and led by senior editor Seymour Zucker.

In the pages that follow, we document how the standard of living of most Americans is shrinking. We show that the United States has lost its competitive leadership, both at home and abroad, and examine what has happened to such bedrock industries as autos, steel, apparel, and consumer electronics. The data that we have developed indicate that overall the loss of competitiveness has been an economic disaster. In the last 10 years alone, it has cost the country some 2 million industrial jobs and almost $125 billion in lost production. The Northeast and the industrial Midwest have been particularly hard-hit, and a good part of the unemployment in these regions, especially among blacks and semiskilled workers, can be traced to the loss of America's manufacturing muscle.

The combination of misguided government, shortsighted management, and a creaking collective bargaining system is responsible for much of the decline of U.S. industrial might, we will argue. Government has not only taken a hostile position in its regulation of business, but its overall policies and tax structure discourage savings and investment, inhibit productivity gains, and stifle innovation.

Management, for its part, runs U.S. industry with an emphasis on short-run planning and an eye on the next quarter's profits. Labor and management both get bad marks for holding to outdated adversary positions rather than moving toward more cooperation to reflect the new realities of international competition.

We offer a blueprint for reindustrialization. As a first step, the nation must forge a new social consensus involving all elements of society: government, business, labor, minorities, and public-interest groups.

These diverse elements of society have to recognize that the country must commit itself to returning to the path of strong economic growth. The adversary relationships of the past worked because the economic pie was growing; so even the losers got a piece. Continuing economic decline means that no group in society will achieve its aspirations.

The commitment to growth must be followed by specific actions. For example, we will explain how companies can lengthen their planning sights and encourage innovation to foster faster growth and how the U.S. workplace can change to spur a more collaborative relationship between labor and management.

We will explore the strengths of the U.S. economy upon which may be built the reindustrialization of America: how the vitality of U.S. high technology can be effectively applied, how the nation can capitalize on its energy assets, how government can tailor the tax system to encourage innovation and investment, how trade policy can be redirected to enable the United States to regain its former position in international trade, which industries should be encouraged and which should be allowed to shrink, and what this country can learn from industrialization efforts in Europe and Japan.

In short, we will show you why America must change or shrivel. And we will tell you how it has to change.

PART ONE

HOW AND WHY AMERICA LOST ITS ECONOMIC LEADERSHIP

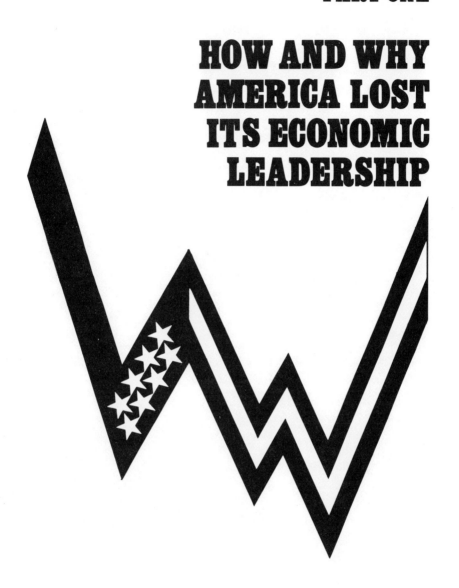

THE DECLINE OF
U.S. ECONOMIC VITALITY

"A chicken in every pot, a car in every garage."
—1928 Republican campaign slogan

During the 1980 presidential campaign, Ronald Reagan kept asking Americans if they were better off in 1980 than in 1976. The answer was recorded in voting booths across the land and resulted in the humiliating defeat of Jimmy Carter. President Reagan maintains that America can once again be great if only the size of government is reduced. But whether the Reagan administration can reverse the erosion of America's economic strength and the losses in economic well-being suffered by the American people really depends on how well it grasps the dimensions of the problems facing this country and whether it then institutes the appropriate actions to help solve them.

Just how badly has the nation's economic might been crippled?

The Shrinking Standard of Living

The American people had to endure a great depression and fight a world war before the 1928 promise of affluence could be realized—and then spectacularly transcended.

For three decades after the end of World War II, Americans enjoyed an ever-rising standard of living. Each successive year, with few exceptions, found people working less and earning more. It became not only two chickens in every pot but for many American families two cars in every garage, not to mention the TV sets, hi-fi systems, wall ovens and blenders. The appetite of the U.S. consumer for more and more goods made this country's factories hum, as well as those of Europe, Japan, and the third world, creating more than a quarter century of unprecedented economic growth.

But the golden age of growth is over. The U.S. standard of living is shrinking. Living standards are being battered by a combination of sagging productivity, rip-roaring inflation, the transfer of more than $80 billion of income a year from the pockets of U.S. consumers to the oil-exporting countries, and the severe decline of U.S. competitiveness. In the wake of these blows, the American credo that each generation can look forward to a more comfortable life than its predecessor has been shattered.

Shattered, too, is the optimism about the future that uniquely characterized the U.S. economy. Not only did parents believe that their chil-

How U.S. manufacturing's market share has been shrinking at home...

Manufacturing sales in U.S.

▲ Percent sold by U.S. manufacturers

Data: Commerce Dept., BW

dren would have more opportunities than they did, they were convinced that they themselves would be better off this year than last.

Yet so deeply ingrained is the American promise of "more" that many economists and business leaders refuse to accept the idea of a shrinking standard of living. They point out that by some measures the economic well-being of Americans appears to have improved in the 1970s, although not at the heady rates of the 1960s. For example, the nation's disposable income, adjusted for population and changes in the consumer price index, rose 20 percent in the past decade, compared with 30 percent in the 1960s.

But this is an illusion born of that streak of optimism in the American psyche that colors the future brighter than the past. It fails to consider that the world changed drastically in 1974, when the Organization of

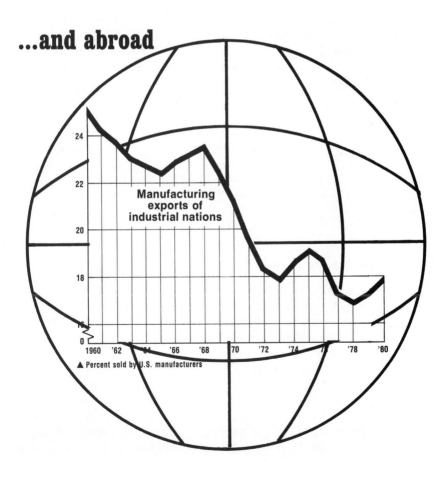

...and abroad

Manufacturing exports of industrial nations

24

22

20

18

0

1960   '62   '64   '66   '68   70   '72   '74   '78   '80

▲ Percent sold by U.S. manufacturers

Petroleum Exporting Countries (OPEC) quadrupled oil prices. In order to pay for rising oil bills, the industrial rivals of the United States, especially the Japanese and Germans, embarked on a policy of pushing exports—particularly into the huge U.S. market. And only when we separate the data into pre-OPEC and post-OPEC periods can the real extent of the damage to the U.S. standard of living be assessed.

Between 1966 and 1973, disposable income per person adjusted for consumer inflation increased by 21.5 percent; over the next 7 years, the gain fell to a meager 1.5 percent; and, beginning in 1978, the numbers actually turned negative. The picture is even bleaker for production and nonsupervisory workers. Their average paychecks, adjusted for inflation, fell 3.4 percent in 1979 and 5.5 percent in 1980. The story gets even more dismal when one looks at what is left over from income after taking into account spending on basic necessities such as food, fuel, and shelter. Unlike the 1950s and 1960s, the last decade has seen the prices of essentials skyrocket. So the nation's total real discretionary income increased only 16.7 percent over the last 10 years, compared with a 78 percent increase during the 1960s, according to calculations by Chase Econometrics, the economic consulting firm. In 1980 the nation's total discretionary income was actually 1.2 percent below the 1973 level.

In fact, when one adjusts the nation's total discretionary income for inflation and the huge increases in employment to reflect the sweat that goes into producing that income, one finds that discretionary income per worker over the past 7 years declined by 14.3 percent, compared with a 12.8 percent increase in the previous 7 years. Leonard A. Rapping, an economist at the University of Massachusetts, puts it this way: "Everybody is working harder to maintain their standard of living, but most of them are not making it."

Industries under Fire

U.S. industry's loss of competitiveness over the past two decades has been nothing short of an economic disaster and goes a long way toward explaining the shrinking standard of living. Even in 1960, well after the economies of Europe and Japan had been reconstructed, the United States accounted for more than one-fourth of the manufacturing exports of the industrial nations while supplying 98 percent of its domestic market. Since then, not only has the United States been losing market share both at home and abroad, the decline has actually been accelerating.

In the 1970s the United States lost 23 percent of its share of the world market, compared with a 16 percent decline during the 1960s. U.S. manufacturers' share of the domestic market also fell more in the most recent decade than it had earlier. The losses in the 1970s are particularly telling, because they came in the wake of a 40 percent depreciation in the value of the dollar, which made U.S. exports cheaper and foreign imports more expensive. The decline in the U.S. position in the 1970s alone amounted to some $125 billion in lost production and a loss of at least 2 million industrial jobs.

Everywhere, American products and American know-how are being challenged, even in product lines in which U.S. superiority has long been taken for granted. More and more, the competition is coming from rivals as big and well-financed as the U.S. giants. The U.S. auto industry, overtaken by both European and Japanese car makers in quality and productivity, suffered the additional humiliation in 1980 of being far surpassed by Japan's industry in numbers of cars built: 11 million vs. 8 million.

Japan, having flattened U.S. competitors in products ranging from steel to motorcycles and challenging the United States in fast-growth, high-technology industries such as semiconductors, is mounting a determined drive to capture an early lead in the industries of tomorrow, from industrial robots to bioengineering. Foreign rivals, after perfecting their products and honing their competitive edge in the fierce scramble for worldwide market shares, are carving off larger and larger slices of the once-invulnerable U.S. market.

Even sectors in which the United States still racks up tremendous trade surpluses have been steadily losing their share of the world market. The aircraft industry, for example, exported more than $12 billion worth of products in 1980, while only $2 billion worth of planes and parts was imported. Yet U.S. domination is by no means as complete as it once was. America's 52 percent share of world airplane exports in 1980 represented a significant decline from the 66 percent share of a decade ago. Further erosion is almost inevitable. Europe's Airbus Industrie, having captured 21 percent of the world's commercial aircraft market in the 6 years since it turned out its first plane, boasts that it will double production and overtake Boeing as the world's number one aircraft builder within the next few years.

Other research-intensive industries in this country are also having trouble holding their own, although the depreciation of the dollar in the 1970s improved their price competitiveness. The U.S. share of plastics exports, for example, dropped from 27.8 percent in 1962 to 13 percent in 1980. In organic chemicals, where the U.S. position actually improved in the 1960s, U.S. exports accounted for only 15 percent of world trade in 1980.

The U.S. drug industry, once a technological trailblazer, is now well on the way to becoming a producer of standard products, because the task of bringing a new drug to market, made arduous by regulation, has considerably reduced the payoff from research and development. Its 27.6 percent share of world exports in 1962 dropped to just 15 percent by 1980. And while the United States still exports more drugs than it imports, the difference is shrinking rapidly.

The U.S. computer industry has maintained its position over the last two decades, but the United States may soon be making way for the Japanese. U.S. production is currently three times Japanese production, and the value of U.S. exports is higher than Japan's both in total and as a percentage of domestic output. Japanese exports, however, have increased over the past 7 years at an annual rate of 35 percent, which is about double the U.S. rate of growth. The ratio of exports to production in Japan, currently at about 9 percent, will be increasing through the 1980s. The government there has targeted a 16 percent ratio by 1985, and that ambitious target may prove to be far too conservative—Japanese computer firms have goals of almost twice that percentage. These goals are not to be taken lightly. Xerox, for example, long the kingpin of copying machines, has been caught off guard by Japan's Minolta and Ricoh and by other foreign manufacturers who have captured the major share of the low-priced U.S. copier market in just 5 years.

The U.S. trade surplus in machinery is still impressive, reaching a record $23.9 billion in 1980. Yet agricultural machinery already is under siege, not only in the world market but in the domestic market as well. The U.S. share of world exports slipped from more than 40 percent in 1962 to less than 25 percent in 1980. One problem is that the industry increasingly has concentrated on making big and expensive equipment that is appropriate only for the U.S. market. The United States no longer makes any farm tractor under 45 horsepower, which means, among other things, that it has now largely excluded itself from developing countries. Moreover, imports of farm machinery are growing by leaps and bounds, increasing some 40 percent from 1978 to 1980. Canada is the largest exporter of farm machinery to the United States, and imports from there rose by 38 percent over those same 2 years. Imports from West Germany increased by 70 percent, and from Britain by some 60 percent. The entire domestic market for small tractors is now supplied from abroad, primarily from Japan, which exported about 50,000 tractors to the United States in 1979.

America will continue to be the world's biggest exporter of construction machinery for some time to come. Yet increased demand abroad, both in industrial nations and developing economies, has spurred considerable foreign competition. The United States still maintains its technological advantage in construction machinery, but its lead has been eroded over the past few years by foreign firms.

The textile machinery industry, which used to be a strong trade performer for the United States, has now moved into the deficit category.

The U.S. share of world exports of textile machinery is about 7 percent. It was more than 15 percent in 1962. Meanwhile, U.S. manufacturers supplied only 53 percent of the domestic market for textile machinery in 1980, in sharp contrast to the 93 percent share they held in 1962. Ironically the technological upgrading of the U.S. textile industry, one of this country's few successful responses to competitive pressures, has been accomplished largely by using foreign equipment.

In metalworking machinery, the United States has been overwhelmed by West Germany. The two countries were neck and neck in the early 1960s, with each having about one-third of world exports. Now the U.S. share is down to 25 percent, while Germany's is close to 40 percent. Much of the problem seems to stem from reluctance on the part of the fragmented U.S. industry to build enough capacity to serve the market in periods of peak demand.

Meanwhile, the failure of the U.S. machine tool industry in its own market has been dramatic. Over the last decade, the domestic manufacturers' share of the U.S. market for metal-forming machine tools has dropped from 93 percent to 76 percent, while their share of metal-cutting machine tools has gone from 89 percent to 71 percent. The equivalent figure for both categories was 97 percent in 1960.

The U.S. steel industry was still putting up open-hearth furnaces in the late 1950s, while the Japanese were building modern steel plants that used the basic oxygen process. Ironically, the basic oxygen process was a U.S. invention. "The U.S. steel industry is still living with the consequences of its own conservatism," says economist Walter Adams of Michigan State University. And only the protection of "voluntary" quotas and trigger-price mechanisms has allowed it to retain its 83 percent share of the domestic market.

Detroit's failure to build sufficient small-car capacity was largely responsible for the surge in imports in 1979 and 1980 that gave foreign auto producers nearly 30 percent of the U.S. market on the basis of units sold. But the competitive problem of the auto industry is a long-standing one. Imports, which were negligible in 1960, captured nearly 15 percent of auto sales only a decade later, mainly because American companies chose to ignore the fact that many customers were returning to the idea of simple and efficient transportation that Henry Ford pioneered. This gave foreign companies an opening that they were able to exploit when oil price increases made the big American car obsolete. The result has been not just to produce $4 billion worth of losses for Detroit in 1980 and bring Chrysler to the brink of oblivion but to shrink the market for the supplier industries.

The most obvious area in which U.S. manufacturers have ceded their own market is consumer electronics. In 1960 about 95 percent of radios,

Key industries hardest hit in the U.S. market...

	Ranked by total sales of industry Percent of market		
	1960	1970	1980
Autos	95.9%	82.8%	72.9%
Steel	95.8	85.7	83.4
Apparel	98.2	94.8	90.1
Electrical components	99.5	94.4	78.9
Farm machinery	92.8	92.2	80.7
Industrial inorganic chemicals	98.0*	91.5	76.2
Consumer electronics	94.4	68.4	53.1
Footwear	97.7	85.4	66.6
Metal-cutting machine tools	96.7	89.4	71.0
Food processing machinery	97.0*	91.9	84.2
Metal-forming machine tools	96.8	93.2	76.2
Textile machinery	93.4	67.1	53.1
Calculating and adding machines	95.0*	63.8	57.1

Data: Commerce Dept., BW

...and in world markets

	Ranked by size of U.S. exports Percent of world exports		
	1962	1970	1980
Motor vehicles	22.6%	17.5%	11.4%
Aircraft	70.9	66.5	52.2
Organic chemicals	20.5	25.7	15.3
Telecommunications apparatus	28.5	15.2	15.0
Plastic materials	27.8	17.3	12.6
Machinery and appliances (nonelectric)	27.9	24.1	16.6
Medical & pharmaceutical products	27.6	17.5	14.9
Metal-working machinery	32.5	16.8	24.0
Agricultural machinery	40.2	29.6	24.9
Hand or machine tools	20.5	19.1	13.5
Textile & leather machinery	15.5	9.9	7.2
Railway vehicles	34.8	18.4	12.2
Housing fixtures	22.8	12.0	7.8

Data: Data Resources Inc., BW estimates   *Estimated

television sets, and the like were supplied domestically. By 1980 imports had captured almost half the market. The U.S. no longer even makes radios, and black-and-white TV sets are now almost all manufactured abroad. Not only are U.S.-made color television sets now assembled largely from foreign-made components, an increasing number come from Japanese companies that have set up U.S. plants to escape the impact of the "orderly marketing agreements." The Japanese captured the TV market not because of lower labor costs but because of superior management and technology. The videotape recorder has become something of a symbol for the waning entrepreneurial spirit of American industry. Although the videotape recorder was invented in the United States, it was left to the Japanese to devise the techniques of mass production. Not surprisingly, despite the strong market for consumer electronic products, employment in the industry has been declining steadily for more than a decade. Over the past 6 years it has declined by 5 percent a year.

For some industries, of course, the decline in American competitiveness was inevitable. In labor-intensive industries such as apparel or shoes, there is simply no way that U.S. manufacturers can hold back the import tide. Only the existence of quotas and orderly marketing agreements has allowed domestic companies to retain 90 percent of the U.S. apparel market. But production has shifted to the newly industrializing countries of Asia and Latin America, where labor is even cheaper. Other labor-intensive industries inevitably will move in the same direction. This shift in world trade will have relatively little effect on other industrialized countries, in which unskilled labor is now in short supply. But the United States has large numbers of unskilled workers who still depend on relatively unsophisticated industries for employment.

The Skewed Economy

The implications for the American economy and the nation's standard of living would have been bad enough had the decline of U.S. industrial power been distributed equally across the nation. But because the decline has been centered in the densely populated areas of the North and Midwest, the impact has been disastrous. It has produced a skewed economy, in which some economic sectors and geographic regions are surging ahead while others are in a state of free fall. And if this decline is not reversed, the country may soon be divided into areas of the haves and the have-nots.

Dynamic economic growth, to be sure, is often a process of what the late Harvard economist Joseph A. Schumpeter called "creative destruction," in which rapidly growing industries inflict distress on declining industries and ultimately replace them. If this process takes place within a more or less homogeneous region, displaced labor and capital can be diverted fairly easily into the new industries and there are relatively few growing pains. But when this growth process crosses state and even regional boundaries so that one region is growing at the expense of the other, economic and sometimes political conflicts are sure to ensue. Population, production, and employment are booming in the South and West, while they are declining or stagnating in the Northeast and Midwest. As long as the migration of population and employment was gradual from what at one time was a rich Northeast to a poor South, it probably helped unify the country. But with the decline of U.S. competitiveness in world markets, which has hit the nation particularly hard in its industrial heartland, the pendulum has swung to the other side and the North is in serious trouble.

In addition, while the North remains oil-poor, the coffers of states such as Texas and Louisiana are bulging with oil tax revenues.

Near Depression in Basic Industries

The nation's basic goods-producing industries, such as steel, autos, and tires—located mainly in the North—have been in the throes of what amounts to a near depression. For example, while gross national product (GNP)—the country's total output of goods and services—in the fourth quarter of 1980 increased by a snappy 5 percent, following a 2.4 percent increase in the third quarter, December unemployment in Michigan stood at 14 percent, and in highly industrialized Illinois it reached almost 10 percent. Yet such industries as computers, semiconductors, and oil drilling are booming. High-technology companies worry about how to get workers to fill new jobs. It is little wonder that unemployment in December 1980 in Texas was less than 5 percent, significantly below the national average of 7.4 percent.

The surging growth of the South and West and the concurrent decline of the North and the Midwest is evident from an examination of the employment trends in manufacturing industries over the past decades, even if 1980 is excluded in order to adjust for the sharp decline in automobile sales and the extensive layoffs that resulted in that industry. The combined regions of New England, the Mid-Atlantic, and the Midwest all showed employment gains from 1959 to 1969. From 1959 to 1969 manufacturing jobs in New England increased 6.2 percent; over the next decade they declined 1.4 percent. The Mid-Atlantic region saw a rise from 1959 to 1969 of 6.5 percent; from 1969 to 1979 employment fell by 15.5 percent. In the industrial Midwest (Illinois, Indiana, Ohio, and Michigan) employment increased 19.9 percent from 1959 to 1969, but during the next 10 years it declined 5.5 percent. In the meantime, manufacturing employment in the South increased by 20 percent in the 1970s, and in the West the rate of gain was a robust 21 percent.

The Northeast and Midwest did, at least in part, share in the national trend of employment growth in service industries, such as banking and retail trade. Service employment in the 20 years from 1959 to 1979 doubled in the North. But it tripled in the South and West. Clearly, the growth in service employment depends to some extent on manufacturing employment. And this means that service employment growth, which has already begun to slow in the North, will continue that downward trend.

Moreover, service employment depends critically on population growth, and population growth has been evident mainly in the South and West. Indeed, there has been a population transfer taking place largely from the North and East to the South and West. Between 1970 and 1978, the South gained 2.8 million people and the West 1.1 million. Meanwhile, the North Central states were losing some 3 million inhabitants and the Northeast nearly 2 million. For the first time in history, the South and the West have more than half the U.S. population. And the Report of the President's Commission for a National Agenda for the Eighties, issued in January 1981, noted that "these regions are expected to continue to grow at the expense of the population in other regions."

High Unemployment in the Cities

Unemployment in the Northeast and Midwest has been well above the national average, especially in the large cities. In 1979—a nonrecession year—the nation's jobless rate was 5.8 percent. It reached 7.1 percent in New York State but in New York City unemployment hit 8.7 percent; it was 6.9 percent for all of Pennsylvania but 11.8 percent in Philadelphia; 5.9 percent in Ohio and 9.6 percent in Cleveland; and 7.8 percent in Michigan with 14.8 percent in Detroit.

Blacks, who are concentrated in the large cities, have been especially hurt by the loss of industrial jobs in the North. Unemployment among blacks in 1979—even before the 1980 recession hit—was 11.9 percent in New York City, 19 percent in Philadelphia, 11 percent in Chicago, and 18.8 percent in Detroit. Experts attribute the rise in black teenage unemployment—from 29.1 percent in 1970 to 37 percent in 1979—to the loss of entry-level industrial job opportunities in the North.

Not only were the Northeast and the industrial Midwest losing jobs in the 1970s, their industrial plant was being run down. Investment data for individual states are available only through 1976. Yet the trend is undeniable. Capital spending on new plant and equipment for the New England, Mid-Atlantic, and Midwest regions increased in real terms during the 1960s by an average of 9.2 percent a year. For the next 7 years capital spending declined by 0.3 percent a year in these regions. In contrast, the South showed an average rate of increase in real investment of 13.9 percent in the 1960s and 8.5 percent during the next 7 years.

As factories and equipment in the North have deteriorated, the movement to the South and West has accelerated. The migration of industry, jobs, and population becomes a self-sustaining process. The migration itself shifts incomes, accelerating market growth in the new region. As new markets spring up, the region begins to attract a broad array of industries—from manufacturing to all of its financial, advertising, wholesale, printing, and other support services. This rapid growth of taxable eco-

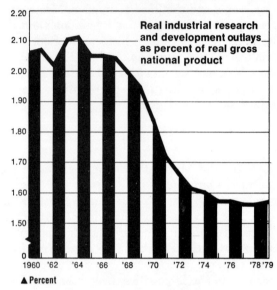

The slump in industrial R&D spending

Real industrial research and development outlays as percent of real gross national product

Data: National Science Foundation, BW

nomic activity ensures more than adequate revenues for maintaining and even improving public services without increasing tax rates. So the lure of the West and South, especially the Sunbelt, has intensified.

Meanwhile, the declining regions of the North have been experiencing a declining tax base, which has led to higher tax rates or a cutback in public services or, in some cases, even both. Fast growth, slow growth, and decline all have a tendency to snowball. The West and the Sunbelt will continue in relative affluence. And if the United States fails to reindustrialize, the nation can look forward to continued economic decline and fiscal crisis in the cities and states of the North, especially those which provide the broadest range of public services for the poor.

A Declining Payoff from Innovation

American industry has produced a dazzling array of technological innovations that have radically altered the lives of most of the world's population. In this century alone, U.S. technology has spawned the computer, television, and the airplane.

But there is frightening evidence that the ability of U.S. industry to innovate—to convert ideas to commercial products and processes—is slipping. Even while potent new technology such as genetic engineering waits in the wings, the flood of new products is dwindling, and there is fear that the United States may be reaching the bottom of its technological cornucopia. "It is abundantly evident that U.S. technological innovation and productivity are on the decline," says Allen H. Skaggs, director of the research center of the Aerospace Industries Association of America.

A study of innovation between 1953 and 1973 for the National Science Foundation (NSF) produced these statistics: In the 1950s the United States was the first to market 82 percent of all major innovations. By the late 1960s, though, the share had dropped to 55 percent. If anything, that share has since deteriorated even further.

One explanation of the apparent downturn, says Robert M. Coquillete, executive vice president at W. R. Grace, is that U.S. industry has been living off technology conceived during the Depression, when there was scant incentive to exploit new knowledge, and World War II, when the emphasis was on military applications. Jacob E. Goldman, senior vice president and chief scientist at Xerox, sees a similar pattern. Most of the major technological forces that are shaping today's world, he observes, stem from discoveries made before 1970—the whole microelectronics revolution, color TV, a host of new drugs, the Polaroid camera, and of course xerography. To drive home his point, Goldman notes: "One is hard put to compile a list of innovations in the last few years that matches any equivalent span of time in the 1950s or 1960s."

U.S. industry is liquidating its technological capital at the same time that companies are stressing short-term, applied research instead of longer-range programs that are more likely to produce scientific breakthroughs.

The evidence shows that small companies account for the major share of innovations. Companies with fewer than 1000 employees accounted for nearly half the technological innovations introduced between 1953 and 1973, according to the NSF. And perhaps even more significant, companies with twenty or fewer employees created two-thirds of all the new jobs in the economy from 1969 to 1976.

But the number of new small firms that have had adequate capital financing has declined over the past decade. In 1969 small companies made 698 offerings of equity securities. In 1972, 568 initial public offerings were sold. By 1973 the number fell to just 100. It skidded to fifteen in 1974 and by 1979 recovered to only eighty-one. Even in 1980, with the much-publicized wave of new issues, the number reached only 250. More important, the amount of capital raised in 1980 was $1 billion, compared with $2.8 billion in 1972. And the 1980 figure, adjusted for inflation to put it on a comparable basis with 1972, comes to $600 million.

Even successful companies find it increasingly difficult to be innovative. "The door closes to innovation as a company grows successful on the foundation of past technology," says Jay W. Forrester, a professor at the Massachusetts Institute of Technology's Sloan School of Management. "Very few corporations plan for the replacement of technologies." That kind of corporate planning requires an investment in fundamental research and a serious commitment from top management to pursue long-term projects. Without it, companies standardize and fine-tune existing products and processes to the point of diminishing return. William J. Abernathy, a professor at the Harvard Business School, is critical of the "perverse shortsightedness" of American managers that has had "a deleterious impact on U.S. firms' inclination and capacity for innovation."

The most disturbing aspect of the decline in innovation has been the sag in research and development (R&D) spending since the mid-1960s. It is R&D that largely provides the invention of products and processes and brings those inventions to the point of commercialization. But R&D spending, in constant 1972 dollars, reached a peak of $29.8 billion in 1968 and then hovered between $29 billion and $27 billion annually until 1976. In 1979 it reached an estimated $31.2 billion, still only 5 percent above the 1968 highpoint.

Potentially more serious, industrial R&D spending peaked in 1969 at $21.1 billion in constant dollars. It did not exceed that amount again until 1978, and then by only $900 million. In 1979 it crept up to an estimated $22.7 billion—a meager 8 percent above the 1969 level. From a 1964 high of 2.1 percent of the U.S. gross national product, spending slumped to 1.6 percent in 1978.

Meanwhile, foreign competitors of the United States have been devoting increasing shares of their gross national products to R&D. Germany and Japan, for example, have both increased their share of total output that is applied to research and are edging up on this country. Furthermore, those nations allocate almost none of their R&D budgets to defense spending. In the fiscal 1981 budget, defense accounted for some $17 billion of U.S. R&D dollars, or about 45 percent of total federal research spending.

Those raw figures tell only part of the story. While spending has only barely stayed ahead of inflation, there has also been a dangerous de-emphasis on basic research. Inflation, shortsighted management, and government regulation have conspired to spur companies to put their money into short-term applied research projects rather than exploring basic science, which could open up new possibilities. Between 1960 and 1974 industry cut that portion of its R&D spending which is devoted to basic research from 8 percent to 4 percent, and there it has remained ever since.

Indeed, the number of patents filed by U.S. inventors—a clue to the state of basic research—declined from more than 76,000 in 1970 to 64,000 in 1975. And the share of U.S. patents granted to foreign nationals has been on the upswing—from 13 percent in 1966 to 28 percent in 1975.

The growth of technical labor power has also slowed dangerously. NSF figures peg the annual growth rate of scientific and R&D personnel between 1954 and 1969 at 5.9 percent. Some 556,000 employees were involved in technical work in 1969, but the number slid to 517,000 in 1973 and then grew to only 610,000 by 1979—a rate of only 2.8 percent annually.

The great fear is that short and misdirected funding may exact a penalty far into the future. And America may lose its technological edge.

The Stunted Growth of Productivity

Sagging spending for research and development, along with lackluster investment in plant and equipment, has reduced the growth in U.S. productivity almost to a grinding halt. From 1960 to 1968 output per hour worked in the total business sector (excluding agriculture) increased at an average annual rate of 3.4 percent. From 1968 to 1973 the annual increase was cut exactly in half, to 1.7 percent. And from 1973 to 1980 the yearly increase fell to a minuscule 0.3 percent. The faltering growth has been partly due to the huge increase in employment in the service industries, especially in health and social services, where productivity gains are harder to come by.

But productivity growth has been abysmal in the industrial sector of the economy, too. Mining, construction, and utilities have shown absolute declines in output per worker, largely as a consequence of government regulation and skyrocketing energy costs. Manufacturing employment has risen only modestly in recent years; nonproduction workers employed by manufacturing companies have accounted for 80 percent of these gains. And in manufacturing, the rate of productivity growth has fallen sharply. From 1967 to 1973 output per worker-hour increased at a compounded annual rate of 2.9 percent. From 1973 to 1979 the gains dwindled to 1.3 percent a year, and in 1980 output actually fell. Moreover, U.S. manufacturing has fared worse than that of its foreign competitors.

In Japan, productivity growth in manufacturing has slowed from the 10.4 percent annual rate racked up from 1967 to 1973, but it slowed to a tidy 6.9 percent a year from 1973 to 1979. France's 6.1 percent annual gain slowed only slightly, to 4.9 percent. And in Germany there was hardly any interruption in the upward sweep of industrial productivity growth: both periods registered annual gains of slightly more than 5 percent a year.

Unit labor costs in manufacturing have increased throughout the industrial world. But the rise in this country has been particularly sharp. U.S. unit labor costs accelerated fourfold—from 1.8 percent a year during the period 1960-73 to 7.9 percent a year from 1973-79—as a consequence of gains in hourly wages coupled with the sharp productivity slowdown. In contrast, unit labor costs in Germany increased only 0.1 percent over the two periods, from 4.4 percent to 4.5 percent, and in Japan they went from a 4.5 percent annual rate of gain to a 5.5 percent rate.

While some sectors of U.S. manufacturing have recorded good gains in productivity, such as the 3.9 percent annual increase in autos and equipment from 1973 to 1978, other industries have performed dismally. Output per worker-hour actually declined from 1973 to 1978 in the following key manufacturing industries: household furniture, folding paperboard boxes, soaps and detergents, ready-mix concrete, motors and generators, primary aluminum, and steel.

Economists have not been able to fully explain the rapid deterioration in U.S. productivity. In part it is a consequence of tough environmental and safety regulations, which have necessitated increased spending by

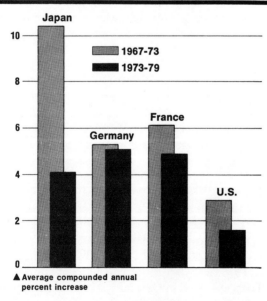

How U.S. productivity lags in manufacturing

■ 1967-73
■ 1973-79

Japan

France

Germany

U.S.

▲ Average compounded annual percent increase

Data: Bureau of Labor Statistics

business with no real increase in the nation's output. Perhaps about one-sixth of the recent sag in productivity is due to this factor, according to Edward Denison of the U.S. Commerce Department. Vastly more significant is the fact that the United States has simply not been adding enough capital equipment to enable its workers to be more productive.

On the face of it, business investment looks relatively healthy. Investment in plant and equipment in the United States as a share of the gross national product in the 1970s averaged 10.4 percent a year, compared with 9.9 percent in the 1960s. But the figures on business investment as a percentage of GNP are no longer a good measure of the adequacy of capital investment. "What is really relevant to economic growth is net investment, not the gross figures," says Dale Jorgenson of Harvard University, a leading expert on capital theory. Jorgenson explains that since a good part of gross investment is earmarked for replacing worn-out plant and equipment, the key to determining whether the capital stock is increasing sufficiently is to look at what is happening to net investment.

Economists calculate net investment simply by subtracting depreciation from gross investment. When the ratio of investment to GNP is adjusted for depreciation, the numbers paint a far less robust picture. From 1972 to 1979 the net investment ratio averaged 4.7 percent, well below the 6.1 percent average of the 1960s. Moreover, the composition of investment, starting in the late 1960s, shifted from structures to relatively short lived equipment. And this trend intensified in the 1970s as the investment horizons of business managers shortened, largely because of the uncertainties generated by accelerating inflation. As the average lifetime of the capital stock decreased, the share of total investment that went to replace worn-out capital increased, explains J. Randall Norsworthy, Director of Productivity Research for the Bureau of Labor Statistics.

But even on a gross investment basis, the United States is investing relatively less than its major world competitors, especially the Japanese. Japan is plowing back about 17 percent of its GNP into new plant and equipment, compared with 11 percent for this country.

The disparity in investment rates means that U.S. output is coming from increasingly obsolete plants, compared with those of its major competitors. The average age of industrial plants in Japan is just 10 years, compared with 12 years in Germany and about 20 years in the United States. By the end of 1980, 63 percent of U.S. industry plant was less than 10 years old; just 2 years earlier 69 percent was less than 10 years old. To make matters worse, the rising volume of output by Japanese and European producers is gradually giving them the advantages of large-scale production that once gave U.S. producers a crucial competitive edge over smaller foreign rivals.

The Capital/Labor Ratio

Not only is the amount of new capital investment crucial in determining the economic viability of a nation; so, too, is the relation between the amount of capital the country possesses and the number of workers who use that capital. Indeed, the key determinant of a nation's productivity—and ultimately its cost-competitiveness in world markets—is the amount of capital it has invested per worker. By this criterion the United States has been rapidly falling behind its rivals. For decades the average annual increase in the ratio of capital to labor in this country has been about 2.5 percent. Since 1973, according to economist Michael J. Boskin of Stanford University, "there has been no increase whatsoever in that ratio." A Labor Department study estimates that in Korea and Japan, for example, this ratio has risen at about 12 percent and 10 percent a year, respectively, in recent years.

While net investment in the United States in the 1970s averaged 1.4 percentage points below the 6.1 percent annual rate of gain in the 1960s, the increase in employment in the past decade was far greater than in the 1960s. From 1960 to 1970 total employment increased by 12,500,000 workers, or 19.5 percent, but over the next decade some 18,650,000 were added to the job rolls. Little wonder that productivity in this country is on the wane.

To be sure, the United States still remains the most productive nation in the world economy, but the rest of the industrial world—especially Germany and Japan—is fast closing the gap. In 1950 the real gross domestic product per employee in Japan was only 16 percent of that of the United States, and Germany's was 40 percent. In 1973 the average Japanese worker was producing 55 percent as much as a U.S. worker, while in Germany the ratio moved up to 74 percent. By 1979 those ratios increased to 66 percent for Japan and 88 percent for Germany.

Put very simply, there has been virtually no growth in GNP per employee—a key measure of economic growth and living standards—in the United States since 1973. From 1963 to 1973 the annual rate of increase in GNP per worker was 1.9 percent. From 1973 to 1979 it fell to 0.1 percent. While all industrial nations experienced declines in this measure, as a consequence of the rapid increase in energy prices, the drop in this country has been sharper than that of its major competitors. In France, GNP per worker from 1973 to 1979 increased at an annual rate of 2.7 percent, in Germany it increased at a 3.2 percent rate, and in Japan it increased at a 3.4 percent rate. Unless there is a radical change in U.S. productivity, Germany will exceed the United States in output per employed person by mid-decade and Japan will be coming close.

Facing a New Kind of World Competition

Perhaps belatedly, with a sense of bewilderment and shock, American officials, business managers, and workers are awakening to the harsh realities of ruthless global competition. Not only are individual U.S. industries increasingly vulnerable to this new competition, the entire position of the United States as the world's number one industrial power is being challenged, especially by the Japanese. Although this country's GNP is roughly double that of Japan, a big share of U.S. production is not in industrial goods but in services, from motels to banking. In industrial output, where the primary international competitive battles are being waged, Japan is already about two-thirds as big as the United States and growing much faster. Its GNP after adjustment for inflation, heavily concentrated in manufacturing, expanded an average of 5.1 percent annually in the past 5 years, compared with 3.7 percent for the United States. And Western Europe, too, has been catching up with the United States. The combined GNP of the ten countries that make up the European Economic Community climbed to $2.1 trillion in 1980, compared with this country's $2.6 trillion.

But the really big challenge is coming from Japan. Underlying that country's dazzling industrial achievements is a broad economic strategy known as export-led growth. The technique is to use the global market, far larger and far less volatile than that of any market in any single country, as the engine of Japanese economic expansion. Although European countries, traditionally concerned about their balance of payments and the strength of their currencies, are also aggressive exporters, the Japanese have organized their entire industrial structure to achieve success in exports. In doing so, they have reaped fabulous benefits, in the form of rapidly rising wages and living standards, for Japanese workers and consumers. Now "new Japans" such as Taiwan, Singapore, and South Korea are following Japan's lead. "Exports have played a key role in each of these success stories—each has been able to achieve a high or rapidly rising market share in the world trade of manufactures," says Bruce R. Scott, a professor at Harvard's Graduate School of Business Administration.

Export-led growth, in fact, has become the "dominant consideration abroad in fashioning both domestic and foreign policies," according to Penelope Hartland-Thunberg, Director of Economic Research at the Georgetown Center for Strategic and International Studies in Washington, D.C. Most Americans, by contrast, have never heard of the concept—and that is one reason why the United States is losing its industrial leadership. Instead, U.S. policy has continued what Hartland-Thunberg describes as the "postwar pattern of favoring imports and obstructing exports under the illusion that the domestic economy was autonomous and independent of the rest of the world."

At the heart of export-led growth strategy is a simple concept: by aggressively pushing exports, industries are able to continue expanding, even if domestic demand for their products slows down. If these industries are competitive enough to enlarge their world market share, they can keep growing even amid economic slowdowns in key foreign markets. The business activity and jobs created within Japan by these export industries thus help cushion the Japanese economy against the ups and downs of business cycles. A dramatic illustration was Japan's economic performance in 1980. While most major industrial nations had little or no growth, Japan's GNP expanded by a robust 4.8 percent in real terms. But 3.3 percent of that increase came from production for booming exports, and only 1.5 percent came from output to supply sluggish domestic demand.

Export-led growth has also protected Japan against other troubles, such as the impact of high energy costs. After the big jump in oil prices in 1973 and 1974, Japan quickly earned enough additional revenues to pay for its huge oil import bill by means of a massive export drive, backed up by heavy investments in new factories. Among the best customers for the outpouring of Japanese goods were the newly rich oil-producing countries themselves. Now, to offset the 1979 and 1980 oil price rises, the Japanese are repeating this performance. In effect, the export strategy has enabled Japan to turn successive "oil shocks" into new opportunities to expand and modernize its industry. One measure of its success is the rise in the value of Japan's currency, the yen, over the past decade.

The strategy requires, of course, a long-term commitment to exports. Japanese corporate managers give priority to exports over domestic sales not only in their day-to-day operations but also in their long-range planning and investments, while the Japanese government encourages overseas sales by means of export credits, tax incentives, cheap loans to export-related industries, and other aids. Underpinning the strategy is a national export-or-die psychology: labor unions avoid strikes or other actions that would jeopardize overseas sales, and even grade school textbooks emphasize the importance of exports to the nation's strength and well-being.

Setting their sights on global markets also requires that Japanese business leaders think big. In fast-growing export industries, managements regularly plan investments in new capacity far in excess of what the domestic market can absorb, with the expectation that much of the new output will be sold abroad. What has enabled Japan's auto industry to grow bigger than that of the United States is the shipment of more than 50 percent of its production overseas. By contrast, most U.S. managements plan additions to capacity that will be just large enough to supply the modest projected growth in the U.S. market, with exports virtually an afterthought. The plight of the U.S. steel industry, compared with Japan's, shows the results of these differing mentalities: Japanese steel plants are the world's newest, biggest, and most efficient, while the stagnant U.S. steel industry, saddled with aging plants and high costs, has had to ask for government protection against imports.

The problem now facing U.S. industry is that the success already achieved by Japan and other industrial rivals, using the export-led growth strategy, will breed still more success. The high sales volume achieved by producing for export is providing the revenue base for expanded research to develop even better products and processes and will justify even heavier investments in new plants that incorporate the latest technologies. Those are the important reasons why Toyota's Kanigo plants turn out nine engines per employee per day, compared with an average of only two at Ford's best facilities. With the competitive edge that many other Japanese industries now have, they seem likely to conquer still bigger global market shares and thus become still more competitive.

What this signifies, especially in advanced technologies, is that Japanese companies may be moving ahead of U.S. rivals on the "learning curve." This is crucial in the competitive race, because the cost of producing a manufactured item declines as the total number manufactured increases; the accumulated production experience yields improvements in manufacturing processes and organization. What Japanese and Europeans understand—and many American managers do not—is that export volume is critical in an increasing number of industries in order to gain the benefits of such production experience. Japanese business managers have "learned the profound effect of global share on unit costs," says former Secretary of Commerce Peter G. Peterson, who is now chairman of investment bankers Lehman Brothers Kuhn Loeb.

Too many American corporate managers, though, are still concerned only about their share of the U.S. market. Such a focus on domestic sales could succeed only as long as the U.S. economy dwarfed all others, and only for a shrinking range of products. Ironically, because Japan is now investing more than the United States in plant and equipment, the advantage of having the biggest home market for many types of machinery and other capital goods is shifting to Japanese manufacturers.

In the future, more and more of such investment will go into high-technology products, such as industrial robots for the fully automated assembly lines of the years ahead. And in such fast-growth industries, the Japanese are determined to grab an early lead; already some 120 Japanese companies are turning out half the world's robots. That lead is likely to become unbeatable if Japanese manufacturers combine domination of their big and expanding home market with their traditional prowess in capturing global market shares.

The consequences of industrial decay for America go far beyond the loss of jobs and income. The economic growth that has been forfeited because American industry is increasingly unable to compete abroad and at home is limiting the nation's ability to support a strong military capability and exert political leadership in the Western alliance.

American influence in world affairs, moreover, does not depend solely on military might and the direct economic leverage that the United States brings to bear through programs such as direct economic foreign aid. In international financial institutions and trade negotiations, this nation's muscle reflects in good part the volume of its international trade and financial transactions. The worldwide activities of U.S. business executives, engineers, and bankers also assert U.S. influence. By their presence and the products and services they supply, these people serve as important symbols of American power and prestige around the globe.

More than a decade ago, foreign perceptions of U.S. might were embodied in popular notions of an almost unbridgeable technology gap between U.S. industry and that of the rest of the world, of global domination by U.S. corporations. Now, weak U.S. exports, coupled with the relinquishing of an increasing share of its domestic market to overseas competition, suggest to foreigners that the United States is a diminishing factor in the world. Such perceptions are serving everywhere to curtail U.S. political influence. In contrast, the prestige of successful industrial rivals such as Japan and Germany continues to rise.

2
HOW GOVERNMENT HAS STIFLED GROWTH

For years, business criticism of the federal bureaucracy could be easily dismissed as a smoke screen to hide business's own shortcomings. But today many economists, members of Congress, academics, labor leaders, and even concerned officials at federal agencies are joining business managers in pinning on Washington a large share of the blame for the deterioration of American industry and the resulting decline in national economic vigor and trade competitiveness. And the landslide victory of Ronald Reagan in the presidential election can be read in no small measure as a mandate to Reagan from the general public to deliver on his campaign promise to "get government off the backs" of American businesses and investors.

The Government's Contribution to Economic Stagnation

Business executives, of course, have never doubted that Washington bears much of the blame for the problems of American industry. "Government has got to wake up to the fact that it is abusing the industrial base of this country," says Robert E. Coleman, chairman of South Carolina-based Riegel Textile. In a comment typifying the views of business leaders, James E. Burke, chairman and chief executive officer (CEO) of Johnson & Johnson, considers government to be "probably the root cause" of the nation's stagnating productivity. Irving S. Shapiro, former chairman of Du Pont, holds government largely responsible for "decapitalizing" industry with tax, regulatory, and other policies that discourage capital formation. And Reginald H. Jones, former chairman and CEO of General

29

Electric (GE), asserts that "regulatory pollution" by the government is "clogging the streams of investment."

Government is beginning to plead guilty to some counts in these indictments. Increasingly, the economic and tax committees of Congress are recognizing that government policies and the existing tax structure discourage savings and investment, limit productivity gains, and stifle innovation. The result is a massive drag on industrial modernization, economic growth, and trade competitiveness. GE's Jones recalls trying to make this case as long ago as the early 1970s. But he did not get much attention in Washington until 1974, when he was invited to appear at a "pioneering, one-man hearing" by the sympathetic but then junior Senator Lloyd M. Bentsen Jr. (D-Tex.).

In the intervening years—years of pernicious inflation, sagging production, and eroding U.S. economic leadership—the push for a redirection of tax policies began picking up more and more adherents. Under Bentsen's leadership as chairman, Congress's Joint Economic Committee (JEC) in 1979 and 1980 abandoned its long-standing support for Keynesian demand-oriented policies and converted to supply-based policies, plugging hard for a tax cut that would provide new incentives for capital investment.

Gaining impetus from the JEC's hearings and studies, the powerful Senate Finance Committee drafted a strongly pro-capital tax reduction bill in 1980. The measure, partly authored by Bentsen, emphasized a 40 percent speedup in the tax schedules by which business can write off the depreciation of plant and equipment. And the Kemp-Roth tax bill, sponsored by Representative Jack Kemp (R-N.Y.) and Senator William V. Roth (R-Del.), which is designed to cut marginal tax rates for individuals by 30 percent over 3 years, is the centerpiece of President Reagan's long-range economic program. Given the markedly pro-capital formation mood of the new Ninety-seventh Congress, the legislation emerging from these proposals strongly favors savings and investment. But concern over the way government impedes industrial growth ranges far beyond tax matters. The list includes policy inadequacies, inconsistencies, and failures in such other areas as federal spending, regulation, trade, natural resource development, antitrust enforcement, and industrial promotion.

The Government as Adversary

Underlying all these concerns is a growing apprehension that as Washington intervenes ever more deeply in the conduct of business, government and business are becoming increasingly bitter adversaries. If President

Reagan hopes to reverse the development of this adversary relationship, he not only will have to stem the tide of government regulation that business views as overly burdensome but will also have to deal with the charge of J. Clayburn LaForce, dean of the Graduate School of Management at the University of California at Los Angeles, that Washington has "politicized the economy of this country." Business has been forced to make its decisions less on the basis of economics and more on the social and political priorities set by the government.

"We've got to halt this tendency [of government] to horsewhip industry," says H. Jack Meany, CEO of Norris Industries. Harry J. Gray, chairman and CEO of United Technologies, ascribes much of the problem to the "overbearingness" of federal regulators. A recent study by the Conference Board comes to a similar conclusion. Those surveyed, it reports, view "a great number" of regulators as "pecksniffs—untrained, self-important, pious in the public service, overly concerned with detail, jealous of turf, and suspicious of all business."

More and more, the response from the corporate boardroom has been to dig in industry's heels and engage in a no-holds-barred fight over virtually every new regulation, sharply increasing the amount of litigation both at the agency level and in court. This growing business animosity toward government has led to a "steady decline in voluntary compliance" with federal mandates, says New York lawyer Bayless Manning, former dean of the Stanford University Law School.

The Huge Cost of Regulation

Industry is convinced that the heavy burden of environmental, safety, health, equal employment, energy efficiency, and other regulations imposed by government over the past 15 years has diverted a vast but imprecisely measured number of dollars from the basic function of producing goods, financing growth, and nurturing innovation. Estimates of the diversion vary widely because there is no commonly accepted method for computing either the costs of regulation or its benefits.

One respected but limited study, conducted by the leading accounting firm of Arthur Andersen for the Business Roundtable, examined the direct incremental costs that forty-eight companies experienced in complying with the regulations of just six federal agencies in 1977. The total came to $2.7 billion, the equivalent of 16 percent of net income (23 percent for the industrial companies surveyed) and 43 percent of spending for research and development.

Economist Murray L. Weidenbaum of Washington University in St. Louis and chairman of President Reagan's Council of Economic Advisers, estimates that, on the average, each dollar that Congress appropriates for regulation imposes an additional $20 in costs on the private sector. On that basis, he figures that the administrative and compliance costs of regulation currently exceed $100 billion—and the annual total keeps rising with inflation. Many economists dispute this figure, but Stephen D. Bechtel Jr., chairman of the Bechtel Group, thinks the actual cost "is well beyond that amount—perhaps as high as 10 percent of the gross national product."

Whatever the precise bill for regulation may be, to the extent that regulatory costs exceed benefits or that agencies insist on unnecessarily expensive means of compliance or set regulatory goals unrealistically high, the costs are excessive and remove capital from productive use.

The Conference Board survey found that the 300 executives it polled accept the underlying need for "virtually every" federal regulatory program on the books. But these executives believe strongly that some mechanism must be devised to judge how all the regulations being issued by Washington cumulatively affect costs and prices and how they affect particular industries. Beyond that, they say that the regulatory system as a whole is poorly managed and marred by jurisdictional overlaps and conflicts, duplicative or overly detailed reporting requirements, and lengthy delays in setting standards and issuing rules and permits.

Even the Carter administration accepted these as valid comments. It launched major reforms to reduce the regulation of airlines, railroads, trucking, and banking, and President Reagan has pledged to continue and even expand this deregulation effort. In addition, the Carter administration established a regulatory council to improve the management of eighteen agencies under the direct control of the executive branch and required the agencies to make economic analyses of major regulations for review by a panel headed by the chairman of the Council of Economic Advisers. A similar review system that will weigh the economic effects and cost-effectiveness of regulation has already been created under the Reagan administration, and Reagan has even spoken of freezing the issuance of new regulations for a year or so, or at least until a thorough review of existing regulations can be completed. Furthermore, the new Congress is expected to consider a request made by Carter in 1979 to require so-called independent agencies (bodies responsible to Congress rather than to the executive branch) to participate in the regulatory review process. How effective this procedure has been so far is a matter of debate. But it has had one clear-cut effect: it has slowed the pace at which new regulations are being issued.

The Contradictions of Policy

One major objective for the Reagan administration will be to eliminate a host of contradictory regulations and procedures that currently confuse and hobble industry. The many ways in which regulation works at cross-purposes include the following:

- The Environmental Protection Agency (EPA) is pushing hard for stringent air pollution controls, while the Department of Energy, which President Reagan would like to dissolve or pare down, is pushing companies to switch from imported oil to coal, which is a far dirtier fuel and requires much more costly emission controls.

- The Occupational Safety and Health Administration (OSHA) chooses the lowest level of exposure to hazardous substances technically feasible short of bankrupting an industry, while the EPA uses more flexible standards for comparing risk levels with costs.

- The Department of Energy tries to keep down rail rates for hauling coal, so as to encourage plant conversions from oil, while

How Washington's contradictory policies hobble U.S. industry

On the one hand...	...on the other
The Environmental Protection Agency is pushing hard for stringent air pollution controls	The Energy Dept. is pushing companies to switch from imported oil to dirtier coal
The National Highway Traffic Safety Administration mandates weight-adding safety equipment for cars	The Transportation Dept. is insisting on lighter vehicles to conserve gasoline
The Foreign Corrupt Practices Act imposes stiff penalties on U.S. businessmen for bribery abroad.	The law is vague on what kinds of payments are illegal, and the Justice Department is reluctant to give guidance.
The Occupational Safety & Health Administration chooses the lowest level of exposure to hazardous substances technically feasible short of bankrupting an industry	The Environmental Protection Agency uses more flexible standards for comparing risk levels with costs
The Energy Dept. tries to keep down rail rates for hauling coal, to encourage plant conversions	The Transportation Dept. tries to keep coal rail rates high, to bolster the ailing rail industry
The Environmental Protection Agency restricts use of pesticides	The Agriculture Dept. promotes pesticides for agricultural and forestry uses

the Transportation Department attempts to keep coal rail rates high to bolster the ailing railroad industry.

- The National Highway Traffic Safety Administration mandates weight-adding safety equipment for automobiles, while the Transportation Department insists on lighter vehicles to conserve gasoline.

- The EPA restricts the use of pesticides, while the Department of Agriculture promotes pesticides for agricultural and forestry uses.

- The Justice Department and the Securities and Exchange Commission, responsible for enforcement of overlapping aspects of the Foreign Corrupt Practices Act, have been at odds on their interpretation of the law.

Other Impediments to Business Growth

Other major worries that critics have about government are focused on the following areas, in which government fails to help business and actually impedes it.

Spending Policy. For more than a decade, government spending has exceeded the tax base, causing large deficits not only during recessions but during recoveries as well. Thus the government engages in what economist Robert M. Dunn Jr. of George Washington University calls massive "dissaving" of its own. This drains funds away from the private sector, raising borrowing costs and reducing the financial capital available for productive physical investment. President Reagan has promised to cut the growth of federal spending by 7 percent to 10 percent below the levels currently projected by fiscal 1985 and to balance the budget by fiscal 1984.

Natural Resources. As Alexander B. Trowbridge, former Secretary of Commerce and now president of the National Association of Manufacturers, points out, government prohibits or severely restricts resource exploration and development on its vast holdings of public lands at a time when dependence on foreign raw materials is rising. And it has yet to set a clearcut policy on whether protection of the environment or energy development should be a higher national priority. During the presidential campaign in 1980, President Reagan promised a variety of actions to encourage resource development by U.S. companies and was especially firm on the need to open more federal holdings on the continental shelf to offshore oil exploration and drilling.

Antitrust Policy.   Government antitrust authorities impede business efficiency when they attack industry giants that have won market dominance not by illegal deeds but by being first with the best, says law professor Richard A. Posner of the University of Chicago. The same holds true when antimerger litigation is aimed not at protecting competition in a specific market but at combating bigness in itself. A broad spectrum of business executives and members of Congress also have the impression that the Justice Department is balky about clearing joint ventures of American companies trying to compete with monopolistic or government-backed foreign sellers in trade deals. The Justice Department insists that this is not the case. Nevertheless, Congress proposes to clarify the application of antitrust laws to overseas activities and to permit banks to own shares in export trading companies. "The real antitrust arena is a global one," says former Senator Adlai Stevenson of Illinois. "We should be moving to develop international antitrust codes to protect the world from price-fixing and the allocation of markets."

Industrial Promotion.   The United States "clearly stands out as an example of a country that hasn't tried to conduct a coherent national policy for economic development," says John D. Ong, chairman and president of B. F. Goodrich. It is only now beginning to debate whether to adopt policies actively favoring dynamic industrial sectors or to continue makeshift policies of propping up financially troubled companies and industries with such ad hoc programs as loan guarantees for Chrysler and "trigger price" protection for the steel industry. Senator Roth of Delaware, and other members of the Senate's "Export Caucus" have sought to promote aggressively U.S. industries and products overseas through the creation of a cabinet-level department of trade. Although President Reagan favors the expansion of U.S. markets abroad, he opposes a move that he fears would create a new bureaucracy in Washington. And senior Reagan advisers voice strong doubts about having government encourage specific industries.

The Trade Policy Vacuum

No area of U.S. economic life besides exports has been so neglected by government, which has been held hostage to a huge number of other national priorities, ranging from human rights to white-collar crime. The government's export policy, where it exists at all, is at best inconsistent. Perhaps mirroring the lack of export thrust from business, export policy is so far from being the central concern of Washington that responsibility remains divided among dozens of agencies and thousands of bureaucrats. This is so even after a major reorganization under the Carter administration and a major export drive by America's industrial rivals.

So bad is Washington's attitude toward exports that the most recent efforts to improve the U.S. trade position have focused on attempts at simply eliminating existing government disincentives rather than building new incentives to sell more goods and services abroad. Yet the cost to the United States is anywhere from $5 billion to $10 billion in lost exports annually as a direct result of government restrictions, according to Abraham Katz, former Assistant Secretary of Commerce for international economic policy.

Policymakers make choices on national goals in a vacuum, with little thought to the actual cost to the United States in terms of exports. Decisions on nuclear proliferation and human rights that curb U.S. exports overseas are made as though the United States were the only source of goods around the world. Europe and Japan are far less interested in imposing their views of morality internationally than is this country. They are more than willing to step in and sell nuclear reactors or military aircraft or grain to countries the United States has decided to embargo.

The major competitive strength of the United States is still in its high-technology products. The single most glaring failure of Washington trade policy is its inability to guarantee that foreign markets remain open for those products in which the U.S. still has an edge. The new, more subtle forms of protectionism now spreading around the world are precisely those directed at high-technology industries, and it is here that U.S. policy is weakest. At the General Agreement on Tariffs and Trade talks that concluded in 1980 in Geneva, Washington officials were able to negotiate an antisubsidy code with member trading partners that would set up international enforcement machinery for dealing with trade distortions that result from government aid to industries. But the negotiations took 7 years, and the code remains vague and untested. The United States with great difficulty pressured the government-owned Japanese national communications corporation to stop its policy of buying only made-in-Japan technology. And in France the government has come out with a plan that puts six major new industries basically off limits to U.S. participation: electronic office equipment, industrial robots, consumer electronics, bioindustries, offshore submarine work, and energy-saving equipment. Behind a wall of protectionism, France and other nations hope to build their own high-technology industries, aided by government subsidies and contracts.

So far, the United States has done little to prevent this new form of protectionism from spreading around the world. In the only successful negotiation on high technology during the Tokyo round of trade talks in 1980, Washington was able to pressure Europe into cutting its subsidies to the Airbus—a major competitor to U.S. commercial planes around the world—in exchange for chopping off tariffs on planes imported into the United States. But that occurred after the major expenditure of European government money on the development of the Airbus had already taken place. Says John L. Nesheim, treasurer of National Semiconductor, "The American policy is the savior policy, whereas in the rest of the world they adopt the winner policy."

Of course, the United States has other objectives in its relations with the rest of the world besides promoting exports, and at times they are bound to conflict. But in establishing priorities among diverse goals, U.S. policymakers have consistently put exports, and their crucial role in creating jobs and healthy economic activity, at the bottom of the list.

A classic example was the partial shutoff of grain sales to the Soviet Union that President Carter imposed in retaliation for the Soviet invasion of Afghanistan in 1980. Carter chose the measure as a means of registering disapproval of the Soviet intervention without risking a serious U.S. confrontation with Moscow. Politically, though, the grain curb was little more than a weak gesture which served to highlight the inability of the United States to respond with more effective actions. Economically, although the supply pinch forced Soviet consumers to tighten their belts a notch and eat less well—something that they had often done before—it also imposed a real cost on the U.S. economy in lost sales and lower economic activity throughout the farm belt, as well as inflationary storage costs and government price supports for the unsold grain. The beneficiaries of the U.S. action were countries such as Argentina which rushed to export more grain to the Soviets at high prices.

It is doubtful therefore that the grain cutback—which President Reagan subsequently rescinded—served the broad interests of the United States. What the episode demonstrates, though, is a mindset of U.S. policymakers that prompts them to sacrifice America's economic interests whenever that seems the easiest course in foreign affairs.

For America's successful competitors such as Japan, Germany, and France, almost the reverse is true. They have been all too willing to sell nuclear equipment and fuel, products that create global environmental hazards, and other sensitive goods and technologies that the United States has decided to place under export restrictions. We must exert strong leadership and persuade our allies to join in curbing exports that create perils for themselves and the rest of mankind. But first, America must rethink its own priorities in trade to recognize the crucial importance of a strong economy for U.S. influence in world affairs.

3
HOW INFLATION HAS CRIPPLED SAVINGS AND INVESTMENT

Ever since World War II, U.S. policymakers, under the influence of John Maynard Keynes, have treated savings as a fact of life that is somehow beyond their control or even interest. They have assumed that savings—both by individuals and by businesses—represented a fairly constant share of national income that would grow in step with the economy and would always equal what Americans wanted to put into investment. By this formulation, the policymakers felt that they had to focus only on the management of demand to spur consumer spending and create the huge markets that in turn would generate business investment.

But now it is becoming increasingly evident that this emphasis on consumption at the expense of savings is a key factor in the declining ability of the United States to compete in the world marketplace and is causing losses in productivity and growth. Furthermore, the nation's chronically high inflation rate is exacerbating the erosion of savings and severely distorting the profit picture upon which businesses must base their investment plans, since most companies depend heavily on internally generated funds for financial capital.

"We have lived high on the hog and failed to modernize our plant and equipment," says Nobel laureate Lawrence Klein of the University of Pennsylvania. A leading Keynesian, Klein warns that "we must go from being a high-consumption economy to being a high-savings economy if we are to reindustrialize and improve our standard of living."

This, of course, will not be an easy job. Personal savings as a percentage of disposable income in the United States has been stuck for at least 15 years around a trend line of 6 percent, and during the inflation-fueled buying spree of late 1979 and early 1980 it plummeted as low as 3.4 percent. This is in stark contrast to average household saving rates of about

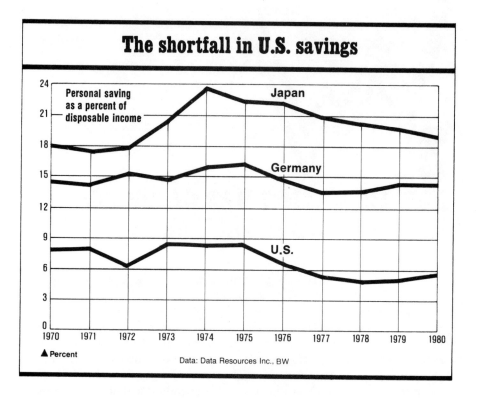

The shortfall in U.S. savings

Personal saving as a percent of disposable income

Japan

Germany

U.S.

1970 1971 1972 1973 1974 1975 1976 1977 1978 1979 1980

▲ Percent

Data: Data Resources Inc., BW

20 percent in Japan, 14 percent in West Germany, and similarly plump rates for other U.S. trade rivals. It is little wonder that in the same period, U.S. investment in plant and equipment as a percentage of gross national product averaged just 10 percent, while Japan topped 17 percent.

The nation's tax system may hold the key to the lag in savings. The income tax has an inherent bias against savings, and it rewards consumption. The tax rate on a dollar of income spent today is less than the rate on a dollar saved, because the interest earned on the savings continues to be taxed, diminishing the future reward that the saver should get for postponing consumption. Soaring inflation compounds the problem by reducing the purchasing power of the dollar saved and, at today's inflation rates, virtually offsetting the value of the interest, even before taxes.

"American savers have taken an awesome beating in recent years," says economist Robert M. Dunn Jr. of George Washington University, in a National Planning Association study. Dunn holds that "when inflation rates were low, the typical American saver probably viewed interest rates in nominal terms, that is, without mentally deducting the rate of inflation." But because of accelerating inflation, real after-tax rates of return on financial assets turned negative for much of the last decade. Thus Americans lost their "money illusion" and therefore their incentive to save, Dunn argues.

The Flight from Money

"During the long, sustained inflation, people became impressed with the idea of moving out of money and into goods," says economist F. Thomas Juster, director of the University of Michigan's Survey Research Center. "Now, Americans will try to get back to the old 6 percent savings rate, but it will be tough to do while income growth is slow and people are still dipping into savings just to maintain their living standards."

The shift away from money or, more broadly speaking, away from financial assets of all types and into tangible assets has been carefully documented by economist William Fellner in an American Enterprise Institute study. In studying changes in the composition of American household wealth in an inflationary period, 1965 to 1978, Fellner finds a flight from holdings of financial assets, such as stocks, bonds, and money itself, to tangibles, such as owner-occupied homes and durable consumer goods. Over the 14-year period, the ratio of the net financial wealth of households to their tangible wealth fell almost 50 percent, from 0.81 to 0.43. At the same time, says Fellner, the ratio of net financial household assets to disposable income per year fell from 2.15 to 1.26.

Fellner's empirical observations strongly confirm the long-held view of economists that financial wealth and holdings of durable goods are closely related substitutes in an economic sense, since much of the saving done by households is aimed at the eventual purchase of goods. Accelerating inflation of the kind that characterized the 1965-78 period forces consumers to speed up their purchasing schedule to beat continuing price increases. Furthermore, in an inflationary environment, physical assets actually become more valuable than current dollars. As Fellner explains, "Except to the extent that resale is contemplated, the expected real yield of these assets depends not on risky market prospects but on the untaxed use value accruing to the households themselves." Thus the result of persistently high inflation rates is what economists came to call the "buy now" psychology of the 1970s.

Juster notes that inflation may, at times, have the opposite effect if it is coupled with the fear of unemployment, pushing consumers to save now to pay their bills and maintain their life-styles if times turn bad. But he adds that "we now have an entire generation with no memory of a sustained period of bad times such as the Depression and therefore little motivation to boost saving." Dunn agrees that "the 'now generation' values of the 1970s probably have contributed to low saving rates." However, he considers "government programs to eliminate the possibility of rainy days for which people save" an even more important cause of the erosion of savings.

The growth of government income maintenance and retirement programs is striking. In the 1970s transfer payments of this type soared to almost half of federal spending from less than one-third at the start of the decade. And since 1960 these payments have rocketed from 8 percent of disposable income to 15 percent.

Harvard University economist Martin Feldstein has found that social security alone has reduced private saving by about 40 percent by diminishing the consumer's incentive to save. Although Social Security Administration economists have challenged Feldstein's work both on the basis of logic and because of an error in his original 1976 study, Feldstein's finding still has strong intuitive appeal to many economists. And a social security system in which the current year's contributions are no longer adequate to pay this year's pension costs clearly has become a source of dissaving for the economy as the trust fund is drawn down.

Government itself can be a major source of savings as well as investment for an economy, but not with the U.S. budget running deficits almost every year since 1969. Says Michael J. Boskin, a top economic adviser to President Reagan during the 1980 campaign: "Disinvestment by the government actually offset investment in the rest of the economy in 1979, causing a net investment loss for the United States of about $40 billion."

Curbs on Investment

The savings lag sets a critical limit on investment. Other factors that may bear heavy weight are low or negative rates of return caused by inflation, high marginal tax rates, the costs of regulation, and uncertainty over public policy.

The after-tax rate of return required for an investment decision—White House consultant Alan Greenspan calls it the "hurdle rate of return"—has become too high in the face of these disincentives. An increase in the personal savings rate would provide more of the wherewithal needed to revive lagging investment. In short, the incentive system of the U.S. economy must be restructured to induce Americans to consume less and save more.

No less important to U.S. investment prospects are the savings of business itself—the retained earnings that must finance much of industry's investment in plant and equipment, particularly in an era when high interest rates make the cost of borrowing increasingly prohibitive. Here, too, income taxes and inflation play hob with investment decisions.

In a recent study for the National Planning Association (NPA), Michael Boskin of Stanford, Mark Gertler of Cornell, and Charles Taylor of the NPA found that the distorting effects of inflation on inventory and capital cost accounting, along with other interactions of inflation and the tax code, had, "by 1977, imposed an extra tax burden of $32.3 billion on capital income from nonfinancial corporations.... These tax effects undoubtedly contribute to a fall in savings and investment."

Almost as devastating as the rise in the tax burden is the fact that until quite recently business had not been fully aware of the damage. The stagnation of U.S. industry has been largely camouflaged—particularly during the last decade—because inflation has made a shambles of the key corporate performance measure: reported profits. Traditional financial accounting has been providing disturbingly misleading signals about the growth and health of company earnings. Year after year, the glossy annual reports from corporate America boast of record sales and earnings, while in real terms profits are flat or even eroding.

What this means is that the ability to develop and market new products, finance essential investment in new plant and equipment, and, at the same time, pay handsome dividends to shareholders simply is not there, even though traditional accounting methods say that it is. For example, in its most recent financial report, a company's sales are stated in 1980 dollars because that is the year in which the company actually gets most of its money for the products it sells. But to arrive at a profit figure, it has to deduct from these 1980 revenues the cost of raw and semi-finished materials that may have been bought at lower prices in 1979 or even 1978. In addition, the company must make charges for the depreciation of its fixed assets, based on costs that may date back 20 years or more. Yet when the company replenishes its inventories and replaces its plant and equipment, it has to do so at far higher current or future prices. For this reason, many business analysts argue that such earnings reports show overstated or even illusory profits.

Noted management consultant Peter F. Drucker puts it succinctly. During inflation, "the figures lie." What bothers him most is that even the most knowledgeable executive falls victim to such illusions. "He may know that the figures he gets are grossly misleading," Drucker asserts, "but so long as these are the figures he has in front of him, he will act on them rather than on his own better knowledge. And he will act foolishly, wrongly, irresponsibly."

Phantom Profits

According to Commerce Department calculations, after-tax corporate profits based on traditional accounting measures rose 485 percent during the three decades from 1950 to 1979, a linear compound annual growth rate of 13.1 percent. But if earnings are calculated on a current-cost basis in each of the 30 years by making adjustments for underdepreciation and the higher replacement costs of inventories, annual profit growth is only 7.4 percent. According to the NPA study by Boskin, Gertler, and Taylor, just the failure to scale up depreciation allowances to correct for inflation cost corporations $3.2 billion in 1960, and this "excess tax liability" soared to $19.1 billion by 1977.

The current-cost earnings numbers do not begin to tell the whole story of inflation's toll. While 1955 profits may reflect 1955 costs and revenues, and 1970 profits are in 1970 dollars, the current-cost measure fails to take into consideration what has happened to the purchasing power of the dollar during the three decades. If each year's current-cost profits are translated into a common monetary measure—say, the dollar at its 1950 value—the earnings picture is sobering. It indicates that such "real" profits barely doubled over the three decades, achieving a minuscule annual growth rate of 2.6 percent, in stark contrast to the reported corporate earnings growth rate of 13.1 percent a year.

As long as inflation remains relatively low or uniform, the gap between reported and real profits is not particularly worrisome. But once inflation begins to accelerate, as it did during the 1970s, the performance measures become grossly misleading. During the 1950s, for example, when inflation was low, the growth of both reported and real earnings averaged about 2.5 percent. In the following decade, after-tax profits showed a 7.5 percent annual growth rate, or 6.1 percent in real terms. But during the 1970s, when reported profits appeared to soar 17.3 percent a year, real growth came to only 3.7 percent.

This anomaly in accounting for corporate profits generates another set of illusions and problems in the measurement of corporate income for tax purposes. The current corporate income tax contains a hodgepodge of ad hoc provisions that allow partial corrections for the effects of inflation but fall far short of eliminating the distortion.

For example, companies have the option of adopting last-in, first-out (LIFO) accounting for inventories, which permits them to reflect inventory costs at close to current price levels. LIFO thus reduces reported profits and current-year tax liabilities. But companies have no such option for plant and equipment, which also must be replaced at continually rising prices. Without that option, as inflation soars, companies fall further and further behind in their ability to replace capital facilities.

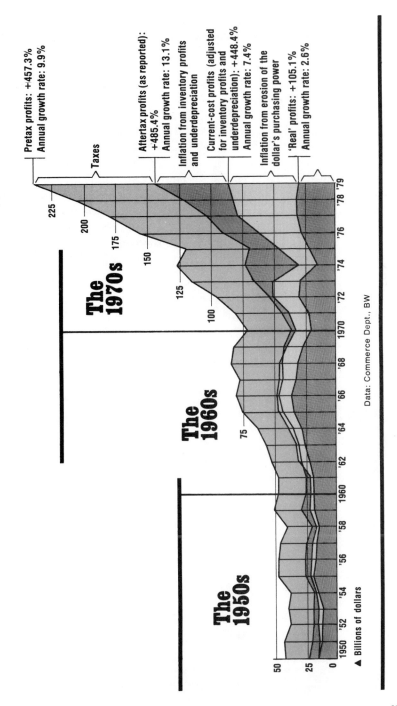

Pretax profits: +457.3%
Annual growth rate: 9.9%

Taxes

Aftertax profits (as reported):
+485.4%
Annual growth rate: 13.1%

Inflation from inventory profits
and underdepreciation

Current-cost profits (adjusted
for inventory profits and
underdepreciation): +448.4%
Annual growth rate: 7.4%

Inflation from erosion of the
dollar's purchasing power

'Real' profits: +105.1%
Annual growth rate: 2.6%

The 1970s

The 1960s

The 1950s

225
200
175
150
125
100
75
50
25
0

'79 '78 '76 '74 '72 1970 '68 '66 '64 '62 1960 '58 '56 '54 '52 1950

▲ Billions of dollars

Data: Commerce Dept., BW

Many corporate executives say that meaningful corporate tax relief and investment incentives can be achieved only through a current-cost or inflation-indexed depreciation deduction. Several major legislative proposals that would move the tax system at least partway in that direction have been gaining support in Congress in the past year and have the strong backing of President Reagan. But such an innovation faces major obstacles, since the mating of traditional accounting and rampant inflation has produced the illusion of "obscene profits" in the public eye.

Business itself has moved to eliminate the confusion over corporate profits by partial adoption in the past 2 years of new reporting requirements developed by the Financial Accounting Standards Board. But these standards, requiring parallel statements in constant and current dollars as well as in traditional terms, apply only to large companies and have left a major area of debate over the treatment of debt. Both business and Congress have their work cut out for them in the years ahead in dealing with the inflation-based problem of the great profit illusion.

4
HOW BUSINESS HAS
HOBBLED ITSELF

Item: Harry J. Gray, chairman and CEO of United Technologies (UT), points with pride to the "Spirit," his company's new commercial helicopter. He sees it as a truly new, maybe even revolutionary product. Although the Spirit was a drain on UT's profits for several years, Gray insists that its potential made the losses more than worthwhile. Yet apparently without seeing any contradiction in the two sentiments, Gray expresses equal pride in UT's current efforts to strengthen its chances of getting quick "economic payback" on future investments. From now on, Gray says, only investments with a potential 20 percent annual return will get the green light.

Item: H. Jack Meany, president and CEO of Norris Industries, likes to offer "proof" that he focuses squarely on his company's future. He notes that over the last decade Norris has spent "more on new facilities than the market value or net worth of the company," even when it has meant settling for 10-year paybacks. Yet managers working at Norris receive bonuses that are linked entirely to the company's annual financial performance.

Item: Fletcher L. Byrom, chairman of Koppers, describes himself as an "enabler"—someone who creates an atmosphere in which managers are encouraged to take risks, to make decisions now and defend them later as reasonable. Yet Byrom insists on a nonwaivable rule that new investments produce an average 25 percent return before taxes and interest during the first 5 years, as well as a maximum 5-year payback.

Using Shortsighted Strategies

There is a schizophrenia pervading American business today. It is a rare CEO who has not publicly expounded on the need for focusing on the future, usually in a speech castigating government or labor unions for their short-term policies. Yet the compensation systems in their companies, the financial requirements for investing in new projects, the criteria for management-by-objective goals and performance appraisals all point to an exceedingly short-term orientation.

The corporate landscape is dotted with visible examples of the inevitable economic chaos that results from a refusal to see beyond the next quarterly earnings statement. Chrysler's financial tribulations have become the butt of more bad jokes than some ethnic groups. And its sisters in the once-powerful American auto industry have not fared well, either. To a country whose people grew up on the cliché "As goes General Motors, so goes the nation," the sight of GM's losses in 1980 must have been horrifying. And the temptation has been overwhelming to blame such losses on OPEC pricing decisions, which have made gasoline an ever more precious commodity, or on government policies that have allowed small foreign cars to capture more than $15 billion of the U.S. auto market.

Yet on June 4, 1980, Thomas A. Murphy, chairman of General Motors, and the perennial optimist of the auto industry, made a speech that was uncharacteristically critical. "The 1970s were all but a disaster" for auto executives as well as for leaders of other sectors of business and government, Murphy declared. "We seem to have spent most of our time not making decisions but postponing them."

While they may be atypical for an auto executive, Murphy's comments are right on the mark. By May 1980 imported cars had gobbled up 28 percent of the U.S. market, up from about 15 percent in 1970. And the reception afforded Detroit's long-awaited fuel-efficient 1981 cars remained less than enthusiastic. This is threatening the death of Chrysler and has shaken GM, Ford, and American Motors. Murphy touched the heart of the problem: In a decade when the entire nation postponed the need to devise long-range solutions to its economic problems, the auto makers, too, postponed the obligation to develop the high-quality, fuel-efficient vehicles their market would want. "The auto industry," says Donald W. Mitchell, managing director of Mitchell & Co., consultants in Cambridge, Massachusetts, "is the perfect example of short-term strategic planning."

The unpleasant truth is that the American auto industry has ridden too high and too long on the once-successful precept that you can persuade consumers to buy what you want them to buy and then make a fortune supplying them with it. Detroit continued to try to produce and sell bigger, flashier cars, ignoring the need for smaller, fuel-efficient, environmentally sound vehicles. It devoted too much of its time to fighting the government on environmental and energy legislation instead of swallowing the expenses of switching its product lines to meet new rules at a time when it could still afford the cash drain. Result: The auto industry is in dire financial straits, and it looks as if it is dragging down the rubber industry, which had blithely continued to put its money into the expanded production of tires for American autos.

The rubber industry hewed to the simple road of increasing tire production along with the rise in U.S. vehicle population in the 1960s. Now the entire industry is in its eighth consecutive year of financial difficulty because of its heavy dependence on tire sales at a time when the domestic auto market is declining and the use of long-lasting radial tires has been spreading. The top five rubber companies, at their historic profit-to-sales margins of 4 to 5 percent, should have earned about $1 billion in 1979. Actual profits were $268 million, and in 1980 they fell to $170 million.

Maximizing Near-Term Profits

Equally dramatic is the consistently worsening failure of the U.S. steel industry. In what is becoming a familiar refrain from many executives, steel management has complained bitterly about (1) governmental policies that allow foreign steel to be dumped in this country at artificially low prices, (2) environmental and occupational safety and health legislation that adds huge sums to the cost of running a steel mill without adding anything to its production capacity, and (3) "unrealistic" investment tax credit and depreciation rules that do not provide the cash flow needed for modernization. In truth, there is some justification to all these complaints. But the factor that few steel executives admit—at least in public—is that they remain locked in to the idea that investors must be pleased at all costs. They have continued to pay out large dividends and write optimistic reports for stockholders instead of plowing the money back into their businesses. The result is that the industry is saddled with obsolete plants that have little chance of competing with the newer, better-maintained plants that Germany, Japan, and other countries are working with.

In 1979 U.S. Steel decided to close part or all of fifteen of its facilities, claiming that they had become "noncompetitive." Four years ago, Bethlehem Steel shuttered major portions of its plants at Johnstown, Pennsylvania, and Lackawanna, New York. "As we looked at the situation in 1977, we concluded that the decline in our profit margins had permanently undermined the economic viability of certain of our marginal facilities, and that additional capital investment to modernize and add pollution controls to these facilities could no longer be justified," explained former chairman Lewis W. Foy.

The closing of these major steel complexes, as well as similar plant closings in the automobile, tire, and other manufacturing industries, is a dramatic concession from today's chief executives that management has not been keeping its plants up to date in order to meet foreign competition. Such a concession represents decades of maximizing profits to look good for the short term while ignoring the long-term consequences. Now those short-term decisions are coming home to roost. Just when the world economy is sagging and profits are sinking, U.S. industry must rebuild its plant if it is to compete at all in basic industries.

Overall, the estimated cost in 1978 to replace all technologically outmoded facilities at manufacturing companies was about $126 billion, of which steel represented 25 percent. Even today, steel companies are modernizing only at a $2 billion annual rate, less than half of the $4.4 billion annually needed to keep plants up to date on a 25-year cycle.

Indeed, the failure of industry to modernize is nowhere more egregious than in steel. For the most part, business experts, even including one chief executive of a steel company, blame poor management, parochialism, and accounting methods and financial decisions that have made steel companies appear to perform better than they actually did. "All those steel chiefs knew about was tonnage," claims one executive. "They just kept those mills rolling. They didn't look at where markets were located, capacity, or what anyone else in the world was doing."

That situation may have changed, but decisions to look good despite the bad news have not. For example, even though the two major U.S. steel companies have taken huge write-offs in the past 4 years and have built up debt in the past decade by nearly 100 percent, they are unwilling to let the impact hit investors too hard. In the last 5 years dividend payouts have averaged 72 percent of U.S. Steel's earnings and 83 percent of Bethlehem's earnings. That leaves little for modernization. U.S. Steel still operates rail mills that are powered by steam engines at its Fairfield Works in Alabama.

Ironically, the United States has been the leader in technological breakthroughs for making steel. In the 1950s, it developed continuous casting, a process that circumvents time-consuming, costly steps in converting molten steel to slabs and bars for final shaping. But only 16 percent of molten steel produced in the United States is cast directly into shapes, compared with 50 percent in Japan and 38 percent in Germany. Now domestic research and development in steelmaking is dwindling. Says one R&D chief: "The percent of our effort going into steel is constantly declining, because steel has not been very profitable." That, too, will dampen any further efficiencies to be realized in steel.

Of course, there are companies that have engaged in long-run thinking.

Corporations such as General Electric, Procter & Gamble, and Standard Oil (Ohio) have made huge investments in products and resources with no promise of quick returns in order to position themselves effectively for the future. Sohio is now flooded with profit (it earned $1.8 billion on sales of $11 billion in 1980) because of Alaskan oil investments that, at the time they were undertaken, created threatening debts for the company.

But short-term plans seem more prevalent, and not only in steel. In consumer products alone, recent efforts by Colgate-Palmolive and Genesco to divest themselves of companies they acquired only a few years ago bespeak the lack of foresight that has been the rule rather than the exception in the 1970s. In some cases—for example, the machine-tool producers who in 1980 were enjoying somewhat of a boom but have not expanded capacity sufficiently—the pain is yet to be felt.

Even in industries that have not fallen on hard times, the major distinction between successful companies and lackluster ones often has been the ability of the winners to keep one step ahead of changing tastes in their markets. It is no coincidence that McDonald's has captured increasingly greater shares of the fast-food market, while companies like Sambo's and Wendy's—both growth leaders once in the industry—are seeing their earnings plummet. McDonald's recognized the need to expand its menu—for example, by introducing a breakfast business—at a time when its basic hamburger business was still doing well. The other two companies figured they would leave well enough alone, with the result that the saturation of their markets caught them short, without new products and services to lure new customers and retain old ones. Again, the ghost of short-term thinking is haunting the companies.

While most corporate executives have been blind to the need for focusing on the future, many of their gadflies have not. Consultants and academics have been sounding a red alert for some time.

"The economic cost of just the auto collapse is incalculable," says Richard Morgan, vice president of the Princeton Strategy Group, a division of the big consulting outfit, Kepner-Tregoe. "It is extraordinarily dangerous [for short-term planning] to continue." Even some politicians have been sending out strongly worded condemnations. "The measure of achievement and the goals to be reached [in U.S. companies] are as short-term as a politician's next election," Lloyd Bentsen (D-Tex.) told participants at a Harvard conference on U.S. competitiveness in April 1980. "When you want to make this year's annual report look as good as possible, why engage in market entry pricing in East Asia? Why accept losses for 2 to 3 years to build volume and brand recognition?" he asked.

Why indeed?

When pressed, most corporate chiefs will admit that Bentsen's rhetorically scathing questioning was fair. Even Koppers' Byrom wistfully admits that he does not know "how many potentially good investments never got to the point where my managers presented them to me because they didn't show a 25 percent return." Yet he is not changing that pay-back requirement.

Catering to Wall Street

But at least Byrom admits that the financial myopia may be scuttling good projects. In most cases, buck-passing for shortsightedness is rampant. Most corporate leaders say that pressure from Wall Street and from their own boards of directors has effectively tied their hands. "Stock analysts don't begin to spend the time researching key management structure and ability in the same manner they research the financial aspect and the numbers," complains Peter G. Scotese, vice chairman and CEO of Spring Mills. Edson W. Spencer, chairman of Honeywell, echoes that complaint: "No matter how much I say about building the company longer-term, short-term performance is the issue that seems to take on most importance."

Some corporate heads even claim to desire mergers just to be relieved of the need for making public their short-term performance. B. Charles Ames, president of Reliance Electric Corp. at the time of Exxon's takeover bid, said that he would welcome a reprieve from showing visible quarterly earnings growth. "If I had the license to stop worrying about short-term earnings, I could grow this business through the roof," he said. Microdata Corp. fell into a merger—albeit reluctantly—with McDonnell Douglas in 1979 for similar reasons. According to Donald W. Fuller, CEO of Micro-data, the only way he could raise capital for his company's minicomputer business was to make sure that his stock soared. And Wall Street, he says, would push the stock only if the company showed phenomenal growth. Thus Fuller admits he kept postponing the establishment of a much-needed direct sales force and announced new products before they were commercially ready, all with the goal of showing good earnings and impressing analysts and investors. The upshot was that Microdata's stock fell anyway, it had no cushion to fall back on, its credit dried up, and it was forced into the merger. Fuller is bitter about the whole episode but blames it directly on Wall Street's policies rather than his own short-sighted attempts to meet all of Wall Street's criteria. "When you are down, you can't sell future performance worth a damn on Wall Street," he grouses. "Chief executives of medium-sized companies too often get trapped into a bunch of short-term strategies."

To be sure, such complaints have some validity. But it is fair to say that Wall Street analysts, more often than not, are responding to CEOs who, for whatever reason, continue to stress short-term performance in their presentations, press releases, letters to shareholders in annual reports, and the like.

While complaints by business executives about Wall Street myopia are widespread, they are by no means universal. Thomas V. Jones, chairman and CEO of Northrop, insists that "Wall Street can understand investment in the future. Investors who are interested only in the short term shouldn't be our stockholders, and analysts' reports on our company reflect this." In fact, the fat profits that Northrop is today booking on its 747 business with Boeing stem from a $62 million investment the company started making in 1966. Although it was a drain on profits for a number of years, Jones states, "If we hadn't dared to make the investment, we wouldn't have the profits today."

Similarly, James E. Burke, chairman and CEO of Johnson & Johnson (J&J), insists that "one of J&J's tenets is not to be too fearful of failure." In the 1950s, he recalls, J&J took a $9 million loss on an abortive attempt to use collagen to replace catgut as a suture material. Yet that research led to a lucrative business which uses the same collagen for sausage casings. Currently the company is suffering heavy losses on its acquisition of Technicare, a maker of high-technology diagnostic imaging devices, but Burke is not fearful. "Diagnostic imaging is going to be important," he states simply.

Why are so few business leaders willing to chance bucking Wall Street by taking similar risks? The reasons are multifold. Some stem from a society that has stressed immediate gratification to a fault. Many stem from the structure of the typical company. But most stem from the people who are running the corporations.

Apparently, there is a great overlap among psychological, cultural, and structural reasons for the tunnel vision pervading executive suites. While corporate chiefs may rant about their board members and shareholders pressing for immediate rewards, the chiefs grew up in the same culture as the shortsighted people they decry. And they, in turn, have shaped the cultures of their companies.

Managers Who Won't Take Risks

Not surprisingly, the people who work for companies that have remained entrepreneurial and long term in their focus tend to agree with this view of the corporate malaise. "A certain culture of people attracts a certain class of people. Thus the nonentrepreneurial background of top managers attracts similarly minded people whose outlook is to make the fast buck and not plan for the future," says Friedrich W. Schroeder, director of corporate development at Hewlett Packard, which is known for fairly innovative management. Peter R. Sugges, a professor of management at Temple University, adds that the occasional maverick who bucks the system rarely makes it to the top of the company. "You can only become a manager if you adopt the mores and strictures of managers," he says. "The only way to change any company is to change the way people at the top think about the way business should be operated."

Ironically, the change that is needed probably would involve turning the clock back about 30 years. Before the merger craze of the 1960s, corporate leaders were, for the most part, autocratic entrepreneurial types who were ready to take risks for ideas they felt in their gut would pan out. David Sarnoff took RCA into space-age technology. Thomas Watson Sr. and Thomas Watson Jr. plunged into computers when they were still in the realm of science fiction. Edwin H. Land would have grimaced at the idea of doing a discounted cash flow on research for the Polaroid camera.

Of course, Land and a few others are still around. But for the most part today's corporate leaders are "professional managers"—business mercenaries who ply their skills for a salary and bonus and only rarely for a vision. And the skills themselves are generally narrow and specialized. Just as the general practitioner who made house calls is a dim memory, so is the hands-on corporate leader who rose through the ranks, learning every aspect of the business before managing it. Today's managers are known as great marketers, savvy lawyers, or hard-nosed financial experts.

Too often, the companies they manage are polyglots of products, all serving different markets and requiring their own brand of expertise. Perhaps Harold S. Geneen's legendary ability to understand every aspect of ITT's business was a fluke. But in general, can any manager be expected to fully understand the intricacies of making and selling both white bread and telecommunications equipment? Can a Charles Bluhdorn, head of Gulf & Western, have the same degree of expertise in the company's mining operations and in its Paramount Pictures subsidiary? Does it take the same talents to successfully publish a magazine like *Playboy* and to manage a chain of hotels and gambling casinos?

The human mind is simply not capable of absorbing all the subtleties of all the businesses that the modern-day corporation is involved in. So, lacking a gut feeling for the gestalt of their businesses, today's corporate chiefs delegate responsibility and then keep control by scrutinizing the numbers as their only recourse. At the extreme, many of them do not even insist that those numbers be generated through internal growth. All too often they see themselves as managers of a portfolio of companies, much like a portfolio of stocks. They become more concerned with buying and selling companies than with selling improved products to customers.

According to Robert H. Hayes, a professor at the Harvard Business School, American corporations spent more than $40 billion in 1979, not to create or improve their products or processes but simply to gobble up other American corporations. They spent more on purchasing companies that year than they spent on research and development, Hayes notes. James Farley, chairman of Booz Allen & Hamilton, observes that as often as not the acquisitions not only added nothing to the country's economic health but did little good for the buyer. "People used to talk about synergy, but they no longer do," he says. "There really is no synergy in most acquisitions." How can there be, when antitrust legislation prevents many companies from purchasing companies in their own or related industries and leads them instead to buy firms that are totally dissimilar from their own?

But while that may be a valid argument for lack of synergy in acquisitions, it does little to excuse the lack of synergy between departments and divisions at most companies. The blame for that lack can again be laid at the top manager's doorstep. Theodore Barry & Associates, a West Coast consulting firm, recently studied fifty companies and, according to James B. Ayres, a company principal, concluded that "most executives have never participated in the line management process, and so there is no sensitivity to the problems in this area." Ayers warns that we will "have to see a shift in the background of top executives to technical and operating skills because now their attention never goes beyond financial reports."

Measurement Mania

It does not look like that switch will happen soon. Korn/Ferry International, an executive search firm, recently queried more than 1700 corporate vice presidents—the group from which future top managers are most likely to be drawn. About 47 percent began their careers in either marketing or finance, and nearly 64 percent say that those two areas are the fastest track to the top. "Senior-level executives are geared to getting product out the door as opposed to being creative about it," says John A. Sussman, Korn/Ferry's vice president for research.

That type of bias filters down to all levels in the organization. Too often chief executives send mixed signals to their staffs. On the one hand they demand creativity, and on the other they reward the numbers. Anthony J. Marolda, vice president of corporate development services at Arthur D. Little, tells about a former client, a U.S. television manufacturer, that lost "bundles of money" by sticking with tube technology while its competitors switched to solid state. "The president, who had a financial background, told his engineering staff, 'If you want the new technology, you can have it—but keep in mind that your bonus is based on profits next year,'" Marolda recalls. "He told me later that he wasn't comfortable with the technology, and so he passed along the technical decisions to others."

Not surprisingly, the easiest way for executives to feel comfortable with alien technological or marketing concepts is to devise a technique for measuring them. Not only has internal rate of return and discounted cash flow replaced educated instincts for deciding on new projects, but quantitative approaches—or, at best, formularized ones—have even pervaded human resource management. The old days of motivating employees by example and by general day-to-day closeness to the field have given way to consultants' techniques such as behavior modification, climate and attitude surveys, and the like. It is little wonder that top management has become isolated from its employees.

The disservice that managers do to their companies and their employees when they insist on convenient measurements for things that may not in truth be easily quantified is dramatically pinpointed in the productivity improvement arena. Consultants have had a field day selling corporations on such productivity improvement schemes as participatory management, job enrichment, time-motion studies, and salary incentives. Client companies have eagerly embraced these ideas only to find that most dramatic productivity improvements are temporary and fail as the novelty of the change wears off. One of the basic reasons for the consistent failures of these programs is that management, with its penchant for measurement, fails to distinguish between productivity as it relates to the overall GNP and productivity as it relates to individual workers. It is easy enough to measure the country's basic output divided by basic labor input and come up with a productivity number. But when managers try to do the same thing on the corporate level, they fall into a trap. Productivity on a countrywide scale is dramatically affected by such factors as capital investment and obsolete vs. modern plants. Of course, these factors are important to corporations—but the individual worker's productivity takes on a great importance as well.

The problem is that as we move increasingly toward a service economy, worker productivity gets harder and harder to measure. Assembly-line workers and typists can still be clearly rated in terms of tangible output. But in the no man's land of "knowledge workers," those educated white-collar employees who fill the bulk of managerial and professional ranks, the distinction between productivity and performance is muddied. Are sales representatives more "productive" when they service existing accounts, thus bringing in orders, or when they spend a good deal of time cultivating clients in an industry that normally does not use the company's products? Today, sales commissions are based entirely on current sales, and the disincentive to cultivating future markets is obvious. If, on the other hand, managers rewarded their sales people on the basis of effort and initiative—or, stated another way, redefined sales productivity as something that must be described and evaluated in terms of subtleties as well as numbers—the signal to the sales force would be to go out and ensure the company's future by expanding its markets.

Sales commissions are not the only part of remuneration that is being meted out by mathematical formula. Salary administration as a whole has become almost totally depersonalized. Although the term "merit increase" still hangs on in business parlance, most salary programs have degenerated into automatic percentage allocations.

Because the link between payroll and performance has become so fuzzy, corporations have tried to develop incentive compensation systems. But these, too, have been formularized into a percentage of salary and a percentage of profit so that a manager's bonus is as much tied to the general economy or windfall sales as it is to individual performance. Managers are well aware that the people making the bonus compilations often have had little chance to know them personally or to see them work, and that numbers will be their criteria.

For many corporations, the answer seems to be management by objectives (MBO)—a system in which employees set their own goals and, after management has approved them, are rewarded on the basis of whether they have met those goals. In fact, many companies have started using performance appraisal systems that are based on goal setting and review. And, to be fair, a few companies—Allied Corporation is one example—have made a point of encouraging employees to include nonfinancial criteria in their MBO goals; at least part of the annual bonuses is based on reaching those goals. But at most companies, the goals are still couched in terms of increasing sales, profits, or productivity. Even the manager's personal goals are generally stated in terms of specific objectives, for example, returning to school to get an MBA degree. If there is a company that actively encourages managers to set a goal of, say, doing basic research that may or may not lead to product breakthrough in the foreseeable future, it has yet to make its presence felt.

It is a frustrating situation for managers who believe that spending on such intangibles as basic research and development is essential to the viability of the corporation. Walter L. Abel, vice president of research and development at Emhart, notes that he had a very difficult time getting management to accept development costs for Emhart's microprocessor-controlled shoe-stitching machine, now one of the company's hottest sellers. Yet now management pesters him to come up with a similar success. "I say, 'Damn you, you won't put up money for 3 years of building up research knowledge, yet the stitching machine took 7 years, and that was a fast one.'"

The problem lies as much in executive mobility as in executive myopia. The contrast between a successful person's career path in the United States and that of his or her Japanese counterpart is striking. In Japan it is considered normal for employees to retire from the same company they joined for their first job.

The feelings of loyalty between the Japanese employee and employer are analogous to feelings within a family. It rarely occurs to the Japanese to make decisions based on how they will affect personal advancement or personal bonus—one's career is linked to the corporation's, one feels a duty and responsibility to the corporation, and the corporation's future is inextricably linked with the employee. Employees know that unless they do something inexcusably stupid or unethical, their careers are assured, and the seniority system will guarantee advancement. The clear-cut signal to employees is to take the long view and not give much thought to short-term numbers.

That sort of description could not be less applicable to the system of relationships and expectations between the American employer and employee. American workers have seen their colleagues laid off when sales got bad, or kicked aside for much younger whiz kids, and generally treated as expendable cogs in corporate machinery. Because they feel that the corporation does not have loyalty to them, they do not have loyalty to the corporation. And they feel the best way to "fast-track" themselves is to skip from company to company, commanding an impressive raise or title with each change.

Robert Hayes, a professor at the Harvard Business School, notes that job tenure is less than 5 years nowadays, half of what it was in the 1950s. Although a CEO is less likely than a middle manager to leave a company unless pushed, habits built up over a lifetime career are hard to break. "Their careers have been determined in a competitive job market that reacts to 1- to 5-year results, not 20 to 25 years," notes J. Clayburne La Force, dean of the Graduate School of Management at the University of California at Los Angeles. Not surprisingly, it is psychologically difficult for the typical CEO, who is nearly 60, to make decisions that may depress current earnings but will prove lucrative for the person who follows in the job.

And even if the CEO wanted to, chances are excellent that it would prove difficult within the organizational structure of the typical large corporation. Our major corporations have blossomed into multiproduct, multidivisional, multilocational hydras. Not only do they have too wide a range of products for any one corporate leader to absorb, their sheer size has become too much for any one person to embrace. So, one after the other, formerly monolithic companies have decentralized into such things as profit centers, strategic business units, and the like. Every profit center has to have a general manager or a divisional president. Corporate headquarters have to have new staff people to whom the divisional people will report. Layer upon layer of management jobs have been added to the structure. This layering of management creates numerous operating-level jobs, making executive job hopping not only feasible but fashionable, according to Hayes.

And the would-be job hoppers quickly learn that the best way to get fast-tracked in their own companies—or raided by another company—is to turn out good quarterly numbers. That view has become reinforced by bonus systems that reward executives for those same good numbers. The worst-case example would be the recent scandal at H. J. Heinz, where management at three subsidiaries allegedly tinkered with accounts payable and receivable in order to smooth out earnings pictures and have an easy crack at meeting each year's financial goals.

Resisting the Winds of Change

No one is saying that the moves toward decentralization, incentive compensation or even scientific management techniques were not good ideas at the time. Even the merger movement made sense in that many companies had grown to the point where they needed the benefit of both professional management support and the kind of cash cushion that only a larger conglomerate could provide.

But trends and decisions that may have worked excellently in the past can have mediocre or even counterproductive results today. And resistance to change remains endemic in corporate America. "The greatest danger in turbulent times like ours is not the turbulence but the fact that you act rationally in terms of yesterday," says Peter Drucker in his book *Managing in Turbulent Times*. Theodore F. Brophy, chairman of General Telephone & Electronics, strongly agrees. "If your raw materials were cheap in the past, you may have been able to increase machine speed, even if that meant increased rejected product," he hypothesizes. "But if the price of raw materials goes up, you may find that strategy is no longer economical." Too many companies, he warns, switch strategies too slowly. "It's possible for people to become captives of their own good decisions," he concludes.

An excellent example of such psychological captivity exists in the American corporation's unwillingness to think in terms of becoming an exporter of goods abroad. For most of the last quarter century, U.S. companies have taken their overvalued dollars and invested them in foreign operations, to the tune of some $200 billion. Labor seemed cheaper, land seemed cheaper, and all of the economics pointed to the wisdom of hitting the huge overseas markets with products made off American shores.

Times have changed, of course. The American dollar declined in value during the 1970s, and real worker compensation in the United States in the 1970s increased by only 11 percent compared with 48 percent in Japan and 62 percent in Germany. But while most corporate executives recognize these changes, few see the enormous opportunities that they represent. Indeed, European and Japanese firms are increasingly opening operations here. Bringing manufacturing operations back to home base may seem like a radical idea. But if U.S. executives don't move quickly, they will find themselves far behind the foreign competition.

Corporate managers, with a few exceptions, have been caught short by social change as well. The beleaguered auto industry did not confine its errors of judgment to continuing to produce cars that were too big, too wasteful of gas, and too polluting. The auto makers also paid dearly for failing to recognize early enough that Ralph Nader's objection to the Corvair was a forerunner of a broad-based consumer movement for safer products and tougher liability standards. Similarly, by ignoring early protests and warnings from environmentalists—never believing that the government would wind up squarely on the side of the "environmental kooks"—hundreds of manufacturers were forced to retrofit plants with pollution-control gear that could have been incorporated more cheaply in the original plant design. Nestlè had to endure a worldwide boycott of its products after it seemingly ignored the public outcry against its marketing of infant formula in underdeveloped countries because it was a far too expensive substitute for mother's milk.

To be fair, many companies are trying to remedy their social isolation. They are banding together in groups like the Diebold Corporate Issues Program, a management consultant-sponsored group that brings together heads of such corporations as AT&T, IBM, and Sperry—all fierce competitors in the marketplace—to share ideas on social change and developments. Others have employed "environmental scanners"—people whose job is to read diverse publications with an eye toward spotting social and political trends that may have an impact on the business environment.

But such companies are still few and far between. And worse, even in those firms where there is heightened awareness of the need for social predictions, often the gap between that awareness and implementation of new policies is cavernous. One corporate chairman, whose company has had an environmental scanner for a couple of years, was heard to complain recently, "My executives are reading the scanner's reports religiously, but they are reading them for entertainment value. They are not doing a damn thing with them in terms of setting policy."

This consistent myopia—to social change, to long-term goals, to employee development—has resulted in European executives losing respect for the American management system. Until as recently as 5 (or even fewer) years ago, the United States was still considered the most sophisticated country in terms of management education and management systems. Our consultants were hired overseas in ever-increasing numbers. Our business schools were emulated. In general, our methods were revered.

This is no longer the case. Roland Berger, a German consultant, notes that German companies now laugh at American management systems. "We just feel you have 'systematized' everything," he notes. Much of the problem, in Berger's view, is the specialized education we insist on in this country. "It is not unusual in Germany for someone with a background in the social sciences to wind up heading a consumer products company, because we know he will understand the mentality of the consumer market," Berger points out. The fact that in the United States we are likely to insist on an MBA for that job is incredible to Germans.

Indeed, American managers are captives of their own education. Warns Marolda of Arthur D. Little, "Large corporations have been virtually overrun by a proliferation of profit-zealous MBAs who are turning every nut another half turn to get a payoff." Class after class of MBAs is graduated prepared to apply specific skills to entry-level jobs in specific specialties. The unabashedly quantitative schools such as Carnegie-Mellon University are at least honest about what they are doing—teaching students the mathematical and technique-oriented skills of management. But the qualitative schools do not encourage risk taking or original thinking any more than the quantitative schools do. The case histories coming out of Harvard rarely channel thinking along the lines of taking a potentially profitable plunge in a chancy market.

Some deans admit to the problem, but they claim that their hands are as tied by corporate demands as the CEOs say theirs are by stockholders. "Business schools are an effective reflection of what's happening in the larger corporate community," admits David H. Blake, associate dean of the University of Pittsburgh's Graduate School of Business. "We find that most of the corporations who come to campus to interview our graduates are looking for students with specific skills and characteristics that will be applicable to an initial job. My fear is that we've allowed our clientele to determine what it is we do to a great extent."

That clientele, of course, includes the students themselves, and many academics complain that today's youth is oriented to the quick buck in a way that would make the flower children of the 1960s cringe. Robert W. Lear, Columbia University's executive in residence, has a set speech that he gives to most graduating classes at the school. "None of you want to be horses," he tells them. "You want to be jockeys, bookies, have the hay concession for the stables, be the jockey's agent, or best of all, the management consultant to the racetrack. That's why none of you will ever be CEO of a major corporation in the United States."

The danger, of course, is that Lear is wrong, and that it is exactly these dollar-oriented specialists who will be the leaders of tomorrow.

5
WHERE LABOR AND MANAGEMENT WENT WRONG

For a quarter of a century after World War II, the adversary relationship between labor and management worked reasonably well. Fast economic growth meant that the economic pie that was to be divided between unions and companies was continuously expanding. But in today's world of slow growth, slumping productivity, and fierce international competition, that relationship has become destructive. On Capitol Hill and at the bargaining table, shortsighted animosity has led organized labor and management—like milk-wagon horses with blinders—up and down the same old streets, ignoring the competition from abroad. In the workplace, unions often limit management's flexibility; and companies—in both union and nonunion plants—continue to impose a nineteenth-century authoritarian style of management on what is increasingly a better-educated and more independent labor force. As a result, the industrial relations system has responded much too sluggishly to the need for change.

This has been one of the reasons—although not the primary one—for the competitive decline of such basic industries as steel, autos, and rubber. Collective bargaining in the United States has worked reasonably well in distributing economic gains; and despite bursts of harmful strike activity, work stoppages have not created significant economic or social turmoil in the last thirty years. Moreover, the system has produced some highly successful mechanisms—grievance and arbitration procedures, for example—to regulate industrial life.

But the evidence of a too-rigid adherence to old ways is mounting now, especially in industries that are losing out to international competition. The results of collective bargaining by powerful unions in large industries have a pervasive influence on wage movements throughout the economy. From 1975 through 1979, as inflation rates rose, annual wage adjustments under major contracts exceeded national productivity growth by an average of 7 percent. This made it more difficult to mount an effective fight against inflation and made many industries even more vulnerable to low-cost imports. "We're saying to wage earners, 'We appreciate the fact that you didn't start inflation, but wage increases of this magnitude contribute to it,'" says Lloyd Ulman, a labor economist and former member of President Carter's Pay Advisory Committee. "By the steel industry's standards," Ulman adds, "the steel settlement [in April 1980] was a restrained bargaining performance, but from the point of view of the economy, it was still costly." The steel settlement will increase wage and benefit costs by 34 percent over 3 years, assuming an annual inflation rate of 10 percent.

Increased Conflict

At the national level, the animosity between top leaders of the AFL-CIO and business associations prevents cooperation between two of the most powerful interest groups in the United States on vital economic policy issues. Irving S. Shapiro, former chairman of Du Pont and former head of the Business Roundtable, observes that in Japan and West Germany "labor, industry, and government work together as a team. Every time I've seen Chancellor [Helmut] Schmidt, he's had industry and labor leaders with him. I think there is simply a necessity for getting rid of adversarial relationships."

In contrast, labor and management in the United States are moving even further apart in some important respects. Trade unions are not accepted as a fixture of corporate life, as in Japan and Germany. The labor forces in those countries are highly organized, and bruising battles to determine whether a union should represent workers at an individual plant are practically unheard of. But United States companies usually exercise their right to oppose union representation, and the election fights are often fierce. In a few notorious cases, companies have knowingly violated federal labor law by firing or otherwise intimidating workers for union activity, and yet they have escaped penalties for many years by engaging in legal stalling maneuvers. A few unions, meanwhile, still threaten or use violence against nonunion employers. The system that was set up under the National Labor Relations Board to regulate union-management affairs is awash in litigation representing the animus between labor and management.

Indeed, unfair labor practice complaints, most stemming from company or union activities in organizing campaigns, have more than doubled over the last 10 years; 44,057 were filed in the fiscal year ending September 30, 1980. And this conflict between labor and management has been exacerbated, in organized labor's view, by the growing trend of some companies to hire consultants who devise programs, sometimes with illegal tactics, to keep unions out or drive them out. A climax in this constant warfare occurred in 1978, when business groups—including even many corporations that get along well with unions—marshaled forces to defeat amendments to the labor law that would have speeded up the legal processes and imposed heavier penalties on corporate violators.

In this combative climate, union membership as a percentage of the U.S. labor force has slowly dropped from its peak in the 1950s. Only 24 percent of the private, nonagricultural labor force belonged to unions in 1978, down from 33.2 percent in 1955. This decline, which is partly a result of management opposition to unions, has had some unfortunate consequences. Some unions, fearful of their inability to organize workers in new industrial areas of the country such as the South and Southwest, have erected barriers to change so as to preserve union jobs. Many companies, on the other hand, try to exploit the unions' vulnerability. Instead of working with unions to solve problems that might prevent plant closings in the Northeast and Midwest, companies are increasingly attempting to create a "bona fide open shop movement," as economist Arnold R. Weber calls it, by shifting production overseas or to the Sunbelt.

Management's fight against unionism also makes it difficult for labor leaders to cooperate openly with business leaders on national policy matters. Militant unionists take the view of William Wimpisinger, president of the International Association of Machinists. "Why should we cooperate with people who are clearly out to bury us?" Wimpisinger asks. Some business leaders complain that this attitude merely reflects labor's hang-up about the defeat of labor law reform legislation. But in fact, a top-level labor-management committee collapsed in 1978 when union leaders resigned from it, charging that business was waging "class warfare" against unions.

Nevertheless, American labor, by and large, has no desire to alter the capitalist system. This is because the system, up until now, has provided very fertile ground for collective bargaining. As long as the unions could obtain a share of industry's profits to improve the welfare of their members, they demonstrated almost no interest in attempting to control the means of production through European-style codetermination (labor membership on corporate boards). This is beginning to change, though slowly, and American unions are now debating the merits of issues they had ignored in the past—board representation, employee stock ownership, and union control of pension funds, for example.

A Creaky System of Collective Bargaining

The methods and patterns of collective bargaining in the United States are also beginning to show signs of old age. The adversary relationship worked reasonably well at the bargaining table when the economy and productivity were growing at a smart pace. Not only is the adversary principle endemic in American society, it is particularly suited to collective bargaining, in which two sides with somewhat differing interests must strike a bargain.

However, industrial relations theorists such as Jack Barbash are beginning to reevaluate the adversary principle in labor relations. Barbash, a former union staff man, is an economics professor at the University of Wisconsin, where John R. Commons developed the first theory of industrial relations in the 1920s. "The founding fathers of modern industrial relations thought that once we overcame the historic class struggle, the adversary relationship would remain as a hard kernel," Barbash says. "But they saw it also developing into a collaborative relationship. Instead, we've continued to play the game in sheer adversary terms." For example, bargaining does not yield realistic results—and, in fact, can be harmful to the parties—when labor and management negotiators indulge in a "macho, games-playing process," as Barbash puts it. "The American economy in its present state cannot now afford the costs of out-and-out adversarialism," he adds.

Most business leaders want to avoid unions not out of ideological opposition but merely because it is easier to manage without them. Management seldom accepts a union willingly, and when a union is established at a concern, it immediately sets about negotiating a complex system of rules governing shop-floor behavior that sharply restricts management. These rules are meant to protect workers and their union in what is perceived to be a hostile climate. "It was almost inevitable that unions would want to restrict management's flexibility, because otherwise the wage rate would have been meaningless," says Audrey Freedman, chief labor economist at the Conference Board.

Unions negotiated rules preventing managers from assigning workers multiple work tasks. They often won provisions prohibiting management from reducing work crews or scheduling mandatory overtime or speeding up an assembly line beyond a certain rate. Seniority rules, which were established to prevent favoritism in employment practices, sometimes are so strict that management cannot consider ability as a factor in promoting workers. These provisions were not especially debilitating so long as profits and productivity were high. Jerome E. Mark, Assistant Commissioner for Productivity and Technology of the Bureau of Labor Statistics, feels that such rules forced companies to manage more efficiently and innovatively. But, Freedman adds, "they have also narrowed management's ability to do anything," including the ability to adapt to changing economic conditions.

Some unions have also refused to recognize that markets and competition have changed markedly since the lush days of the immediate postwar era. One result is that the bargaining structure is "no longer coextensive with the market," as Arnold Weber says. Unions such as the United Auto Workers (UAW), the United Steelworkers (USW), and the United Rubber Workers (URW) led the labor movement in establishing industrywide wage patterns. They also managed to extend these patterns, with very high compensation levels, to related industries such as auto parts manufacturing, steel fabrication, and miscellaneous rubber and plastic product manufacturing, areas in which low-cost competition is increasing. Managements accepted these industrywide patterns both to eliminate wage competition and "to insulate themselves against whipsawing" in negotiations, Weber says. A labor expert in the Nixon administration and now president of the University of Colorado, Weber believes that unions now must either decentralize this bargaining structure or see a shrinkage of large segments of the industries in which they once were strong.

Bargaining has also come to encompass increasing numbers of compensation issues over the past two decades, and this has led to automatic—and in some cases uncontrollable—increases in labor costs. For example, the cost of simply maintaining health care and pension benefits has risen at a double-digit rate each year since the mid-1970s. In some industries, companies and unions have negotiated increased levels of benefits without considering the cost to society as a whole. In the health care area, for example, the ever more comprehensive levels of medical treatment provided by union contracts have tended to increase the use of health care services out of proportion to the real need. This is one reason why health care costs have been soaring for several years.

Surging inflation has also prompted unions to seek and improve cost-of-living adjustment (COLA) clauses. Some 9 million workers are covered by COLAs, and the effect on companies in a period of both high inflation and recession can be devastating. For instance, the UAW's COLA helped boost General Motors' labor costs per hourly employee by 20 percent in the 12 months ended September 30, 1980. At the same time, GM's production and profits plummeted.

Aside from these structural factors, the bargaining system has also suffered from occasional abuse and a lack of expertise on both sides. Perhaps the best example of irresponsible bargaining occurred a decade ago, when the building trades, seizing an opportunity created partly by a shortage of skilled workers and a fragmented industry, negotiated first-year wage increases of 12.6 to 17.6 percent between 1969 and 1971. This sharply raised the cost of building new plants, induced skilled workers in manufacturing to seek—and win—similar gains, and started a round of cost-push inflation that affected the entire country. "Why did it take so long for the building trades to discover they were pricing themselves out of the market?" Barbash asks. Nonunion contractors have increased their share of commercial and industrial construction to about 40 percent.

Other notable examples of union intransigence involved resistance to technological change by the printing trades and railroad unions. The long battle over locomotive crew sizes on diesel engines played a major role in reducing the profitability of railroads and raising freight rates. Manufacturing unions such as the UAW and the USW have not fought technological advances in their industries, but these and other unions have paid much less attention to the impact of their bargaining on national economic trends than do unions in Germany.

On the other side, most companies fail to use long-range planning in bargaining. "In many industries practically no planning goes into an agreement until a few weeks before the deadline," says William P. Hobgood, an Assistant Labor Secretary in the Carter administration and a former federal mediator. "Many, many times, management waits until the heat of bargaining to make its case, and this being an adversary business, no one believes them," says W. J. Usery Jr., former Secretary of Labor and now a labor-relations consultant.

Companies too often install sweeping changes in the production process without warning or consulting workers. In their reluctance to give up unilateral control of the workplace, many employers create deep antagonisms, both in union and nonunion shops. A company that fails to inform its employees about the health hazards connected with work materials, for example, poisons the labor-management relationship. If workers do not trust their boss, they are not likely to put much credence in a plea for understanding when the company runs into financial trouble. Most nonunion companies still do not provide a procedure under which a discharged employee can appeal to an impartial tribunal. Jack Stieber, a labor-relations expert at Michigan State University, estimates that about 1 million private-industry workers with at least 6 months' service were fired in 1977 without the right to a fair hearing.

Many nonunion companies devote a great deal of time and effort in developing a modern industrial relations system, both to be fair to their employees and to keep the unions at bay. But most employers, union and nonunion, still operate with an authoritarian style of management, despite increasing evidence that today's workers are more independent and better educated and live by considerably different values than those of even one or two generations ago. Management, by and large, has failed to restructure jobs and train supervisors to take this into account. "One of our major problems is a lack of leadership at the first-line level," Usery says. "We still have a lot of people who think 'I'm paying you, and you come to work and do what I say.' But people are tired of being regimented. They can quit or move or get food stamps."

Adversity and economic necessity have forced some changes in labor-management relationships. Longshoremen on the East and West Coasts agreed to automation that may have halved the size of their unions. Both the Amalgamated Clothing and Textile Workers Union and the International Ladies' Garment Workers Union have provided leadership in their fragmented apparel industries for wage restraint and technological advances. The USW agreed to rule out industrywide strikes in basic steel, and unions in the tobacco and utility industries followed suit. In 1980 the UAW accepted major contract concessions to help keep Chrysler afloat. (Critics argued that the concessions should have been greater.)

These are a beginning. But many more changes must be made in the bargaining process, in the way management treats workers, and in the way business and labor view each other philosophically if the U.S. system of industrial relations is to be counted on to help revitalize the country.

Expectations that Can No Longer Be Met

American unions and corporations have developed a system of compensation with built-in wage and benefit increases that has been partly responsible for creating ever-rising expectations about the standard of living. Flowing from this has been a change in what Americans expect from the unions they belong to, from the companies they work for, and from the government they pay taxes to. These new attitudes challenge older beliefs about the need to save and invest for the future as well as the notion that rewards should be based solely on effort and achievement. In the workplace, this has led to increased tension between younger workers and older workers and supervisors, who still venerate work as a goal in itself.

Of course, these new attitudes were shaped by history. In the immediate decades after World War II, memories of the Depression began to fade. The high rate of increase in the nation's standard of living in the 1950s, coupled with significantly higher educational levels, expanded leisure time, and exposure to new social and political ideas during the upheavals of the 1960s produced a striking counterpoint to the Depression psychology. What took hold was the idea that the U.S. economy was virtually limitless and its industries invulnerable. By the 1970s, says public opinion expert Daniel Yankelovich, a psychology of affluence began to replace the psychology of scarcity inherited from the Depression. Unfortunately, this happened just about the time that the enormous production capacity of the American economy began to falter. Yankelovich, who is chairman of Yankelovich, Skelly & White, says that the psychology of affluence contains two major assumptions about life in the United States. "One was, you didn't have to settle for either a good living or quality of life, but you could have both," he says. "You could have clean air, leisure, and high living standards at the same time. Second, not only could you reasonably ask for these things, you were entitled to them."

In short, the American people came to believe that the U.S. economy could support an ever-rising standard of living; create endless jobs; provide education, medical care, and housing for everyone; abolish poverty; rebuild the cities; restore the environment; and satisfy the demands of blacks, Hispanics, women, and other minority groups. Unbroken growth was taken for granted, and the assumption of U.S. omnipotence, long a factor in American thinking, obscured the reality of economic decline.

Social betterment in the United States has always depended on constantly expanding growth, following the principle that a rising tide floats all ships. But the underlying conviction that the American system could do everything engendered subsidiary attitudes that helped undermine growth. One of these was the concept of "entitlement." Throughout the late 1960s and early 1970s, groups struggling for more jobs, more federal assistance, and a cleaner environment began to feel that these were rights to which they were entitled. When young people went to work at giant corporations, they found high wages and a panoply of welfare benefits— noncontributory pension and health care plans, vacations and holidays with pay, unemployment benefits—waiting for them. These were not things that had to be earned or fought for in a long strike; they were entitlements in the eyes of the workers. Similar entitlements were accepted as their due by employees in managerial jobs. Furthermore, people began to feel that they were entitled to everything; trade-offs and compromises were out. The system, in this view, can satisfy all desires—and it should.

A second attitude supported the entitlement concept. Equality of opportunity was no longer viewed as sufficient. Since people are manifestly unequal in ability and condition, those who espoused this view argued that it was the obligation of government to make them equal. Society, Harvard philosopher John Rawls argued, should follow a "principle of redress" in dealing with disadvantaged citizens. This principle, together with the notion of entitlement, helped spawn an enormous expansion in government programs aimed at correcting inequities. The thrust is made clear by the fact that many are called "entitlement" programs.

There also emerged at this time in the public psychology a fierce adversary attitude toward societal institutions. Government was incompetent, and its leaders were not to be trusted. Business, it was felt, had put profits ahead of public safety and health. The failure of government and business to meet every demand, despite the widespread perception of American omnipotence, led to the belief that both must be acting in bad faith, Yankelovich says. And aggrieved citizens were justified in forcing them to comply. Nonnegotiable demands, demonstrations, boycotts, takeovers of buildings, and trashing or destruction of property became commonplace tactics. Business and government contributed no small amount to this mistrustful attitude by reacting arrogantly or failing to perceive that people were no longer willing to accept unquestioningly the dictates of authority.

The belief in permanent affluence, coupled with new values that arose as Depression scarcity retreated into the past, produced changed attitudes toward work. Some business leaders and even union leaders believe that this has destroyed the work ethic. But the work ethic is a facet of personality, a willingness to expend energy doing productive work. A decline in the ethic, then, would mean a change in human behavior to such a degree that society could no longer depend on human labor and would have to carry on by robotizing the business of the nation, suggests psychologist Raymond A. Katzell. But Katzell, a professor at New York University who has studied worker attitudes, thinks that the socioeconomic environment, rather than personality, is responsible for the changing values toward work. "The affluent society hasn't made people lazy, but it takes something different to turn them on than it does impoverished people," Katzell says.

People want something more than material rewards for work. They may want more time off to pursue a hobby, for example. Or they may want more challenge in the job itself. Labor economist Clark Kerr explains: "The work ethic has not disappeared. People today are willing to work hard on 'good' jobs, provided that they have the freedom to influence the nature of their jobs and to pursue their own life-styles."

Many people do not accept Kerr's argument, but viewing the new attitudes with dismay will not inculcate the older values in people who have never lived by them. Yankelovich has theorized that the "baby boom" generation that was born and raised in the first 25 years after World War II brought the new values to the workplace: a desire for self-fulfillment and challenge on the job and an unwillingness to make work the center of life. This generation now dominates the labor force, and Yankelovich thinks that only slightly more than half the force still responds to the old incentives, focusing on material success and status. For the younger group, the incentives have changed, but the incentive system has not. Furthermore, the United States lacks an all-embracing consensus on the goals of society. "To be motivated," Katzell says, "people have to feel that what they're doing is worthwhile. If we're uncertain what our goals are as a society and how individuals fit in, then people will be less motivated to work hard."

It is possible to build a social consensus, Yankelovich says, because the feeling is still widespread that economic well-being is a good thing. But there must be leadership to give purpose to that consensus. "If it were a choice between saving and spending, wasting or not wasting, people would prefer to save and not waste, if they got any real reinforcement," Yankelovich says. "But you can't do it solely by enriching the rich, and you can't do it in a climate where people feel it doesn't make sense to act in the public interest because nobody else is." On the other hand, to the extent that the new attitudes, especially in their extreme manifestations, focus attention and resources solely on how the economic pie is divided, they divert attention and resources away from how to make the pie bigger. Says Reginald H. Jones, former chairman of GE: "We have become so concerned with problems of redistributing wealth that we've forgotten all about creation of wealth."

Shifting the emphasis back to making the U.S. economy more productive and competitive, even while realizing that the clock cannot be turned back on values that have changed, will require a major national effort. It must involve a recognition of new realities, one of which is that limitless growth can no longer be taken for granted: it must be worked for both by labor and by management.

PART TWO

CREATING THE CLIMATE FOR GROWTH

6
FORGING A NEW
SOCIAL CONSENSUS

The most urgent piece of business facing the nation is to reverse the economic and social attitudes that have contributed to its industrial decline. It is a task that must involve all elements of society: business, labor, government, minorities, and public-interest groups. It requires a new social consensus, a remodeling of what the eighteenth-century philosopher Jean Jacques Rousseau termed the "social contract" that brings individuals together to form a society. All citizens, wrote Rousseau, contract to bind themselves under the "general will" for the common good. It is the nature of that general will that must be altered.

The modern use of the term "social contract" can be traced to a Fabian tract written by British economist Thomas Balogh in 1970. Balogh, a Labor Party theorist, said that the power of labor unions in Britain was a primary cause of rising inflation in the 1960s, and he urged the labor movement and the Labor Party to formulate an incomes policy to control wages and prices. "The achievement of full employment necessitates a complete reconsideration of our attitude to economic and social policy, a rethinking of social institutions and obligations and responsibilities, both for individuals and groups. We need a new *contrat social,* a deliberate agreement on economic and social policy," Balogh wrote. A social contract in the British sense is not suited to the decentralized economic and social structure of the United States. But a social consensus is.

What a Social Consensus Requires

For the United States today, all social groups must come to understand that their common interest in returning the country to a path of strong economic growth overrides other conflicting interests. The adversary relationships of the past were tolerable because they centered mostly on how to distribute an expanding output of goods and services. Taking growth for granted is no longer possible.

If the country tries to pretend otherwise, further economic decline and social disruption are inevitable as various groups struggle for more and more of less and less. Continuing economic decline means that no group in society will achieve its aspirations.

At the center of the new consensus must stand the recognition that each social group will be measured by how it contributes to economic revitalization. Each group's income must be related firmly to its economic achievement. But the distribution of income must be fair. As a first step, Americans are being asked to consume less and invest more. This means sacrifice. Sacrifice, however, must not be exacted from the groups—the poor, for example—that can least bear it.

For management this means renewed emphasis on production and productivity, long-term goals, and risk taking instead of short-term profits, financial juggling, and risk avoidance. In short, management must be judged by how well it manages growth.

For industrial relations this means that wage bargaining must truly reflect economic circumstances and that today's workers must be offered the new incentives needed to motivate them to higher levels of productivity.

For government this means that all policies must be scrutinized ruthlessly and changed, where necessary, in ways that promote rather than impede economic growth.

Finally, it means that business, labor, and government—the dominant leadership groups—must find ways to bring excluded groups into the system, especially alienated black and Hispanic youth. This does not mean reviving the storefront training programs of the past, which were aimed at nonexistent jobs. New thinking is needed, and some of it is already emerging. Robert L. Woodson, a former Urban League official who is now a resident fellow at the American Enterprise Institute for Public Policy Research, talks about using "transfer payments as a source of investment capital" and is studying ways of redirecting some of the "millions and millions of dollars" now spent on welfare programs into funds for creating new enterprises and jobs.

Such thinking suggests that, with will and imagination, forging the new consensus lies within our grasp. Many minority members want to substitute work for welfare dependency. Labor leaders and workers are finding ways to cooperate for greater productivity and job satisfaction. And signs suggest that the broader public not only would support a new industrial plan but also would welcome one that made sense, even with sacrifices, provided that the sacrifices were seen as fair.

There are dangers. One is that business leaders, fully absorbed in the problems of the economy, will push social problems to the background. The riots and killings in Miami in 1980 show forcefully that the racial powder keg can still ignite. Daniel Yankelovich feels that reaching out to minorities is the price that will have to be paid to achieve any new social consensus.

With that condition, Yankelovich, who regularly takes the public pulse, is optimistic about the chances for new agreements. He finds that anxiety over the economy and the country is moderating conflicts and making people more ready to compromise. "At leadership levels," Yankelovich concludes, "you have a climate that is increasingly propitious."

This extends to the broader public. While many people distrust business (they distrust government even more), principally on health and safety issues, "they are not especially punitive," the pollster adds. And they rate business high on ability to get things done, whereas government is rated low. What they really want is for business and government to get together and solve problems." People are confused about what society is all about, says Raymond A. Katzell, an expert on worker attitudes, and so there is no consensus about what is worthwhile. By contrast, Japan and Germany have a national consensus, one which has existed since the end of World War II: rebuilding from the rubble heap. "They have the same kind of consensus today that America had in the nineteenth century, when we were going to build a brave new world. We can diddle through for a long time with a lack of consensus." But the longer that goes on, Katzell adds, the less likely it will be that American culture will dominate the world—and *some* culture has always dominated the world. So where does the consensus start? "Whoever starts it will be a leader, and wherever it starts, that institution will be the leader," Katzell says. Just as the Germans and Japanese managed to build a new social consensus from amid their bombed-out cities and industrial plants, the United States now must act with the same sense of urgency.

Government Must Take the Lead

Devising a successful government policy for reindustrializing the United States requires a markedly changed attitude in Washington, both by the elected representatives and by the career bureaucrats who staff government agencies. To bring that about, the government first has to assign a high priority to the development and implementation of such a policy. During the past 20 years, U.S. policy has emphasized improving the quality of life, particularly through attempts to redistribute income to low-income groups and minorities and to create an egalitarian society. Now it is clear that the government cannot achieve such goals, no matter how admirable, without economic growth. And the United States cannot have economic growth in the future unless its industrial base is modernized.

To start the government process, however, a consensus has to exist among labor, management, and other major interest groups. The climate is right for a consensus approach. "If America is to be successful in meeting the challenges posed by our competitors in international and domestic markets, there is a great need to build a consensus on economic and trade policy," was the conclusion of a seminar of government-business relationships at a 1980 Harvard University conference on competitiveness. The chairman of that seminar, Representative Richard Bolling (D-Mo.), who is also chairman of the powerful House Rules Committee, believes that the great growth the United States enjoyed after World War II resulted from a national consensus that led to the Marshall Plan, the Employment Act of 1946, and the civil rights laws of the mid-1960s.

The war in Vietnam ended that consensus, according to Bolling, who now talks of putting together a new coalition that could pass a fundamental piece of legislation—analogous to the Employment Act—to encourage industrialization of the United States. With this act as a centerpiece, additional legislation would be passed to achieve such a goal.

Representative Henry S. Reuss (D-Wis.), chairman of the congressional Joint Economic Committee, proposes a slightly different approach. He suggests that government, business, and labor "adopt the cooperative approach that has been tried and proven by several of our major allies and rivals, notably Germany and Japan."

"Ideally," Reuss argues, "independent teams from government, business, and labor should be constituted to look into the problems of each of our major sectors. The teams' objective should be to devise sectoral policies and develop plans covering corporate restructuring, new investment and its location, remedial regulatory legislation, and public financial assistance where required."

In a similar vein, financier Felix G. Rohatyn calls for the creation of a temporary national economic commission with representatives from government, business, labor, and academia. Among other things, the commission would recommend to the President and Congress an "industrial strategy which, coupled with tax policy, would have as its objective to reverse the decline of the manufacturing sector."

Arnold H. Packer, former Assistant Labor Secretary for Policy, Evaluation, and Research, sees the need for a continuing forum in which interest groups would examine industrial problems and make recommendations to the President and Congress.

Certainly there are doubters who question whether any type of social consensus can work successfully in the context of the U.S. system, in which labor and management seldom view each other as partners and battle for economic power, while the government ostensibly acts only as a public-interest referee. George C. Eads, who was a member of President Carter's Council of Economic Advisers, for example, feels there is probably too much pluralism in the U.S. system for a "social contract" to work well.

The challenge, of course, is to develop a consensus-forming framework in which government, business, labor, and other major interest groups—without compromising their traditional roles—can agree on trade-offs that would both strengthen the economy and, in the end, prove beneficial to all. John D. Ong, chairman of B. F. Goodrich, is optimistic that labor and management can find grounds for agreement. "If you look at taxation, foreign trade, and the whole area of capital formation, [we have] a lot more in common than what is standing between us," he says.

For its part, labor agrees—in principle, at least—that the nation's manufacturing base must be rebuilt. At the suggestion of Lane Kirkland, president of the AFL-CIO, the federation and the Carter administration formed a task force to discuss reindustrialization.

In theory, the congressional hearing process should be the forum for consensus making. In practice, however, congressional hearings are often unstructured, interrupted, and dominated by short-term thinking and political considerations. Moreover, because interest groups use them for special pleading, the hearings often become adversary.

But Congress welcomes those rare occasions when it is presented with an already achieved consensus. "If it were possible for business and labor and one or two other groups to join together [before going to Washington], it would have a much larger impact on political leaders," says Ruben F. Mettler, chairman of TRW.

Amitai W. Etzioni, a former Columbia University sociologist and specialist in developmental economics who served as an adviser to former President Carter, foresees "10 years of belt tightening" as a result of reindustrialization because "we have to rewire the country and reinvest heavily in all the elements that make up the capital infrastructure, including human capital."

As part of the new social contract, unions will come under pressure to limit wage gains in the first phase of reindustrialization. In return, both government and business will have to present convincing evidence that such a sacrifice will pay off in the long run by steering the economy toward high employment at decent wages. Government and business also must make sure that reindustrialization creates new jobs—particularly for blacks and other minorities—and that adequate provisions are included for helping workers in dying industries.

Since the more than $6.5 billion per year the government now spends on job training often amounts to little more than income maintenance, reindustrialization should involve a major overhaul of this program to make it more productive. In addition, the administration and Congress should unscramble the complexities they have written into the employment tax credit to encourage small businesses to make more use of it. Moreover, an effective industrial policy implies a plan and a process for determining which industries are to be encouraged and which discouraged.

The idea of industrial planning under government auspices stirs legitimate concern because of the danger that government, since it is sovereign, would in the end resort to coercion. Etzioni, for example, feels that reindustrialization should not involve "a high degree" of government planning. He thinks the government should essentially limit its role to providing long-term, investment-oriented tax and regulatory incentives and to funding a quasi-governmental agency that could make limited loan guarantees to sick industries until the investment climate improves.

A plan acceptable to all interest groups, however, would be far preferable to the current practice of having the government keep its hands off until it becomes necessary to rush in at the last moment with an ad hoc rescue program for a financially failing industry or major company. The Reagan administration has moved quickly to bolster the auto and steel industries, by easing regulatory burdens, but is avoiding specific reindustrialization efforts.

Aside from working cooperatively with business and labor in formulating reindustrialization goals, government must start removing—or easing—policy impediments of its own making. Reindustrializing clearly cannot succeed without farsighted tax, trade, and regulatory policies. Government must face up to the fact that the explosion of federal regulations placed on business to achieve social goals—a cleaner environment, equal employment, and a safer workplace, for example—has diverted vast amounts of capital from production and research and development.

Deregulation

The move toward deregulation of the airline and trucking industries in the last few years has created the illusion that government regulation of business was declining. The facts indicate the opposite. Murray L. Weidenbaum, chairman of President Reagan's Council of Economic Advisers, pointed out before the Reagan election victory that in the areas of environmental controls, job safety, equal opportunity enforcement, and consumer safety, "the number of agencies, regulatory programs, and authorizing statutes—and the budgets to carry them out—are continuing to grow." Although the Reagan administration is trying to reverse that trend, the going in Congress and the federal bureaucracy is difficult. The reason is that the historical growth of regulation dating back to the Sherman Antitrust Act of 1890 reflects a deep-seated distrust of corporations in the United States by the public and perhaps even more so by government itself. An increasing number of voters have viewed the corporations as uncaring, impersonal machines that will respond primarily to only two things—money and force.

Public concern with social problems, such as protection of the environment, has intensified the distrust of business. The problem, however, is that companies take their signals from the market, where the demand for products—in terms of what the public will pay for them—and the supply of products—in terms of what it costs business to produce them—are balanced and the market determines the price and quantity of each product sold. But that works only for what economists call "private goods," such as dog food and pencils, where the recipients of the benefits from the goods are those who purchase them. When it comes to "social goods," such as clean air and clean water, where the public as a whole benefits, the market system is unable to factor the public's demand into the calculation. In a system in which profit is the measure of performance, business is unable to really respond to the demand for values that cannot be easily quantified and incorporated into the market mechanism. And so when problems of air and water pollution or product safety are involved, the public has turned to government for action. In effect, it uses the political mechanism to make the economy respond to demands it would have ordinarily ignored.

But government has gone about its task to regulate business with a vengeance, it seems. Instead of trying to balance the costs of regulation against the benefits to society, it has, more often than not, imposed standards that cost business—and eventually the public—much more than they return in benefits. For example, the coke-oven emission standard promulgated in 1976 by the Occupational Safety and Health Administration and estimated to save twenty-seven lives a year would end up costing industry as much as $1.3 billion, or some $48 million a life, according to an analysis by John F. Morral (who was with the Council on Wage and Price Stability). Clearly such expenditures appear unjustified in a society whose limited resources should be directed to situations in which lives could be saved at a fraction of those costs.

The standard setting by the Consumer Product Safety Commission (CPSC) also appears to be directed toward areas that promise few benefits and away from those where the benefits are huge. The basis for government intervention here rests on the free market's failure to provide information that would enable consumers to make rational decisions. Standards should thus be reserved for sophisticated products, such as microwave ovens, where hazards are not clearly defined and where it is difficult to get and interpret technical information. The CPSC, however, spends most of its time investigating the possibility of setting safety standards for such mundane products as matches and kitchen knives.

Without a doubt the regulation of business has resulted in benefits to the public, but the costs of such regulation have placed a huge burden on American business. (According to Weidenbaum, the administrative costs to government alone amounted in 1980 to $6 billion, and the compliance costs to business came to a staggering $120 billion.) Because regulatory goals are, in general, broadly accepted and beneficial to society at large, they are not likely to be abandoned. But business rightly argues that regulatory programs must be managed more efficiently and effectively and in a less adversary and litigious fashion. The government should consider the following regulatory reforms, which economists from across the political spectrum have long advocated:

- Set an overall regulatory goal and leave business free to find the most efficient way to meet it, rather than specifying detailed methods of compliance.

- Forgo direct regulation of products, where possible, and instead let agencies provide relevant information that will enable consumers to choose whether to buy.

- Use economic rewards or penalties to achieve regulatory goals in place of rigidly enforced standards.

Changing Its View toward Antitrust

Antitrust policy is another area in which the government's adversary attitude toward business has been most evident and where it must undergo dramatic change if the social contract between government, labor, and business is to work. Indeed, there is a growing consensus among economists—including some leading liberals—that the decline in U.S. competitiveness at home and abroad is in part the result of outdated antitrust enforcement. Economists since Adam Smith have decried the evils of monopoly, arguing that it results in higher prices and less output for the economy. Yet they are now saying that the government's view about what constitutes market power is far too restrictive, and they are calling for major revisions in policy to give business a freer hand.

Their proposals range from softening the Clayton Antitrust Act to substantially reducing the antitrust enforcement powers of the Federal Trade Commission (FTC). Such harsh critics as liberal economist Lester C. Thurow of the Massachusetts Institute of Technology are even urging that the government abandon almost its entire system of antitrust laws and enforcement mechanisms.

To be sure, government should be as vigilant as ever when it comes to overt monopolistic practices, such as price-fixing. But it is wrong simply to look at the structure of an industry and conclude that a small number of companies automatically means less competition and higher prices.

Although the tendency in concentrated industries is to avoid price cutting to maintain high profit margins, it does not necessarily follow that prices would be lower if the industry were more fragmented. Because of the economies of scale possible in a concentrated industry, unit production costs and therefore prices are often lower than if there were more companies competing. For instance, prices of such appliances as refrigerators and stoves have been declining in real terms, even though these industries are highly concentrated. And as David Schwartzman of New York's New School for Social Research says, there is growing evidence that many oligopolies, particularly in such high-technology industries as computers, are efficient, well-managed, and innovative, and are constantly lowering rather than raising prices.

Antitrust policies have done more harm than good, economists now believe, because they have:

- *Prevented companies from making horizontal mergers with smaller ailing companies.* "Horizontal mergers in some industries, such as steel, would have been good for the economy because they would have improved efficiency by generating greater economies of scale," says Schwartzman. Instead, companies with cash and a desire to expand have diverted resources into less efficient conglomerate mergers. "This is mostly nonsensical and inefficient, because companies have been putting their resources into areas where management lacks expertise," adds Schwartzman.

- *Contributed to the noncompetitive behavior they were designed to combat.* Strong companies, particularly in some declining basic industries, have protected ailing, highly inefficient competitors for fear that antitrust enforcers would try to dismantle the efficient companies if they became too big. "There is a tacit understanding that no one will rock the boat—not out of defiance for the antitrust policies but because of them," explains Hendrik S. Houthakker of Harvard University.

- *Made companies waste hundreds of millions of dollars waging lengthy court battles and maintaining extensive legal departments.* Those familiar with the American Telephone & Telegraph antitrust case estimate that $350 million to $500 million has been spent in its 6-year battle against the Justice Department's efforts to break it up into smaller companies. A good part of these costs went to analyze and process the millions of documents that were subpoenaed in the litigation. And Thurow says that IBM may spend as much as $1 billion to fight the Justice Department's attempts to break it up. "Such costs vastly exceed the benefits," argues Thurow. "Those dollars ought to be invested in production, not court cases."

- *Curtailed the ability of U.S. companies to compete in international markets.* A major problem is the enormous confusion about when domestic antitrust laws can be used against the foreign dealings of U.S. companies. The Webb-Pomerene Act of 1918 lets manufacturers bid collectively on certain foreign projects, something they cannot do in the United States. But there are numerous interpretations of what kinds of projects are, in fact, exempt. "As a result, there is a tendency for U.S. companies to play it safe, and they end up operating in Jakarta in the same way that they do in the United States," says Paul Mac-Avoy of Yale University. This helps make U.S. companies less able to compete with foreign companies that have no such restrictions.

The antitrust policies are also helping make U.S. companies less competitive with foreigners in the United States. Traditionally, antitrust enforcers have measured market dominance by computing U.S. companies' shares of the domestically produced market. This overlooks the realities of international competition. For example, although General Motors' major domestic competitors, Ford and Chrysler, are in deep trouble, GM is not substantially increasing its market share because of competition from imports. GM accounted for 64 percent of U.S. auto production in 1980, but it made only about 45 percent of total sales. U.S. companies should be allowed to be as strong as necessary to keep up with international competition. "U.S. companies should be free to compete on equal terms with a German oligopoly, a French oligopoly, and a Japanese, whether at home or abroad," says Thurow.

Such drastically changing views of the effect of antitrust enforcement are not confined to economists. The Democrat-controlled Ninety-sixth Congress attempted to rein in the fiercely independent FTC in 1980 by making its trade regulation rules subject to congressional veto. Indeed, the FTC appears to have softened its position somewhat. For example, it gave its okay to Du Pont to expand its share of the titanium dioxide market. FTC staffers had argued that Du Pont's aggressive use of a cheap production process amounted to unlawful monopolization. But the commissioners held that it was just good business strategy.

The courts are also responding to the shift in economic thinking, in part because they rely on economists as expert witnesses. In particular, the idea that big companies or concentrated industries can achieve economies of scale is helping to limit the judges' definition of what constitutes noncompetitive practice. But economists argue that further significant changes are needed. In the year ended June 30, 1980, 97 percent of all civil antitrust cases brought in federal courts were started by private plaintiffs, most of them companies. "Most private cases were unwarranted and are clearly designed to protect certain business interests from efficiency rather than to preserve competition," says H. Michael Mann of Boston College.

Mann, who headed the economic division of the FTC during the Nixon administration, recommends doing away with laws that allow companies to collect triple damages from corporations if the courts decide they have been the victims of predatory pricing. This would reduce sharply the number of suits and the costs of defending and settling them. In general, politicians across a broad spectrum seem to share economists' views that antitrust policies are not working well. In testimony before the Joint Economic Committee, former Democratic Representative Barbara Jordan said that she believes that the economic problems confronting the country might require substantially changing the antitrust laws. "The Sherman Antitrust Act," she told her former colleagues, "may at this point be an anachronism."

7
BUILDING A NEW PARTNERSHIP
IN THE WORKPLACE

Our will is always for our own good, but we do not always see what that is; the people is never corrupted, but it is often deceived. . . .

—Jean Jacques Rousseau

Rousseau's point in this passage from *The Social Contract* is that people often fail to perceive what is in their own best interest. In the case of labor and management, where the goal of both is to remain in business, the two sides have too often behaved as if there were an unbridgeable gulf between worker and boss. It is almost as if they were trying to perpetuate a class-struggle notion in one of the least class-conscious of nations. But a social contract in the United States can work only if labor and management see where their interests coincide and put the energy they employ as adversaries to work solving mutual problems.

These problems arise at three levels: in national policy-setting forums, at the bargaining table, and in the workplace. An inertia that defies easy change exists at each of these levels, but increasing numbers of labor and business leaders and workers—especially in declining industries such as steel, autos, rubber, and electrical equipment—are beginning to recognize that the survival of their institutions and jobs is threatened. "The work force today is better educated, and there is a deep understanding that we are in economic difficulty," says Frank P. Doyle, vice president for employee relations at General Electric. Adds Douglas A. Fraser, president of the United Auto Workers, "Things have to get sufficiently bad before we address the problem, and maybe we're reaching that point."

Signs of Progress

The best signs of progress toward establishing a "collaborative relationship," as Jack Barbash, a labor theorist at the University of Wisconsin, calls it, are occurring in the shops and factories. Increasingly, unions are cooperating with management in installing new work relationships—some fairly radical in nature—that seek to give workers a voice in workplace decisions, eliminate the old authoritarianism of supervisors, and improve product quality and output. Perhaps more than anything else, these programs try to reduce the conflict between workers and bosses and to substitute "problem-solving skills for adversary skills," says Delmar L. Landen Jr., director of organizational research and development at General Motors. "There's no question that the organizations capable of doing this more effectively will be the ones best able to cope with a rapidly changing social, political, and economic environment," he says.

The terms "worker participation" and "management participation" are often construed to refer to worker membership on the board of directors, as in the European system of codetermination. In the United States, however, the economic and political structures are not easily adaptable to codetermination; Fraser's election to the Chrysler board in early 1980 was a singular quid pro quo for UAW wage concessions and is not likely to be emulated in many other companies in the near future. Instead, the movement toward greater worker participation in decision making—with its twin goals of making work more satisfying and more productive—is occurring at the shop-floor level, where workers can have a voice in establishing production and quality standards and rules governing their relations with supervisors.

By implementing worker participation, or quality-of-work-life (QWL) programs, as they are often known, a company and a union move away from a relationship that is dominated by adversary procedures. The adoption of this approach at the plant level could play a vital part in establishing an overall social consensus. But there can be no such pact in this country unless top business and labor leaders cooperate in determining—along with government and other interest groups—broad economic goals for the country.

The adversary principle in labor-management relations must be reassessed at this high level as well as in the factories. And many labor and management leaders have called for increased cooperation. Lane Kirkland, president of the AFL-CIO, has strongly campaigned for a reindustrialization policy in the United States, and at his suggestion former President Carter included an economic revitalization board in his proposed reindustrialization program. Kirkland's idea is that representatives of labor, management, government, and other interest groups would recommend investment and other policies for modernizing industry. The Reagan administration is apparently opposed philosophically to such an approach, but Kirkland's proposal is a strong indication of labor's interest in a social contract concept. Corporate executives such as John D. Ong, chairman of B. F. Goodrich, would also like to see a reduction in hostilities. Managers and labor leaders "grew up tending to think of each other as adversaries," Ong says. "I think that's a negative when we get into areas of public policy where we have a lot in common." Ong opposes centralized planning, but he adds that "if you had labor and management taking a combined point of view on key pieces of legislation, that would begin to form a national consensus on what might lead to some intelligent long-range coordination of the economy."

But relations at the top have been decidedly cool ever since the bitter battle in 1978 over legislation to reform federal labor law. The unions perceive that management is sparing little effort to do without them. Many companies are "ambivalent about whether they should work with unions to improve collective bargaining or keep unions on the defensive and move into the nonunion area," says Thomas A. Kochan, an industrial relations expert at the Massachusetts Institute of Technology.

Labor leaders take the position that top-level cooperation is possible only if management recognizes that "organized labor has a role to play in American society," as one union staff man puts it. Management, for example, could adopt a neutral stance toward union organizing activities, as some auto, steel, and rubber companies have pledged in their labor contracts. This would mean standing aside when union organizers approach workers at a company's nonunion plants and refraining from mounting any opposition to the election of a union as bargaining representative—a demand that many employers, particularly those in traditional nonunion industries, would consider unacceptable. Short of pledges of neutrality, however, management could consider supporting—or at least not opposing—moderate changes in the National Labor Relations Act to speed up procedures for elections and make it more difficult for companies and unions to thwart due process by engaging in stalling tactics.

The difficulties in winning such a commitment should not be minimized. Although manufacturing is one of the most heavily unionized sectors of private industry, large segments—the textile industry, for example—are nonunion. Employers in these industries have an antiunion attitude that is almost religious in its intensity, and they would resist any attempt to interpose a "third party," as they term unions, between them and their employees. And there is evidence that many workers reject unionization without undue management pressure. Nor is the Reagan administration likely to lead business in this direction. The prospect, then, is for some degree of cooperation between labor and business leaders. As pragmatists, union officials will not jeopardize their unions or their members by rejecting all calls for common action when jobs are threatened. But a full partnership will not be possible as long as "management is trying to knock us out of the box at every opportunity," as one unionist puts it. American labor believes that its acceptance of capitalism and its rejection, so far, of socialist politics must be balanced by management's acceptance of unions.

MIT's Kochan, in a 1980 book that assesses important trends in industrial relations, points out that efforts to "develop a dialogue and consensus at the national level" have occurred periodically through most of this century. The most successful attempts came during the two world wars, when important reforms in industrial relations were made. In each case, after the war ended, the "absence of an external threat to society led the parties to return to their previous power struggles and conflicts," Kochan writes. But he believes that the economic stimuli "to start the change process" are once again present, particularly in the heavy manufacturing industries. "The link we're missing," he adds, "is an organizational mechanism at the national level that can turn stimulus into real action. It requires direct leadership by the federal government."

One mechanism is the presidential labor-management committee, with high-level labor and business members, which has been used to varying degrees by every president since Kennedy. Another approach, at the industry level, is the tripartite committee, such as the labor-management-government group formed in 1979 to address problems in the steel industry. Similar committees could be formed in many industries to discuss prices, wages, productivity, environmental regulations, investment needs, and technology. The goal is to identify problems that impede growth and to reach a consensus on how to deal with them. Ray Marshall, Labor Secretary in the Carter administration and long an advocate of the tripartite concept, says that it requires an effective exchange of information, which is credible to all sides. Furthermore, Marshall says, "it must be clear that all benefit [from the discussions] and that no one is threatened."

Labor-management cooperation at the national level, however, cannot be expected to have a great impact on collective bargaining at the industry or company level. It can create a climate for easing tensions and for recognizing the need for trade-offs between wage restraint and job security. But a top committee cannot impose change on bargaining practices in specific industries; the U.S. bargaining structure is much too decentralized for that. Obtaining changes at this level may be the most difficult structural problem facing management and labor.

For the most part, contract bargaining has performed reasonably well in the United States, and many practitioners see little need for change. "You have the risk of glossing over the adversary system, which embodies both conflict and cooperation and which has done a lot of good," says Frank Doyle of GE. "An accord doesn't allow you to confront day-to-day conflict. The high level of discussion is not terribly useful down where the real accommodation must take place." GE, however, has managed to maintain more than a parity of bargaining power with its unions, partly because they are fragmented and represent only slightly more than half the corporation's employees.

This is not the case in the steel, auto, rubber, and trucking industries, where individual unions hold close to monopoly power and negotiate nearly uniform terms throughout the industry. Until recently, high unemployment in these industries had little restraining effect on wage bargains, and in other ways, too, the negotiating did not conform to economic reality. Arnold R. Weber, president of the University of Colorado and a noted labor economist, urges a "new configuration of bargaining structures" in these industries. He also believes that these unions must reassess their high wage and benefit levels. "Those were fine when they were operating in a protected market environment and a low rate of inflation, but now the unions have got to choose between unemployment and wage increases," Weber says.

Nobody is seriously suggesting that collective bargaining be shorn of its adversary nature; it would then no longer be bargaining. A certain amount of tension and brandishing of power is necessary if labor and management are to divide the gains that they jointly produce. However, the University of Wisconsin's Jack Barbash says that the United States no longer has the resources to permit the two sides to indulge in constant warfare. "There is a good deal of macho which has nothing to do with bargaining," says Barbash, who was a union official at one time. "What we need is for two guys who don't call each other names to sit down and bargain a contract. Union democracy makes it difficult to get away from the pageantry, but there's nothing left these days for game playing."

Unions, however, are political organizations, and the necessity of getting elected gives union leaders a vested interest in playing the adversary role to the hilt. Management negotiators must often make a demonstration of taking a hard line with the union to impress top management and the shareholders. In this politically charged atmosphere, the dangers of making mistakes that produce costly strikes or unrealistic wage settlements are greatly enhanced. In both cases, the negotiators tend to engage in adversary theatrics for the benefit of their constituents. The question is how to ameliorate the resulting conflict in a way that does not expunge, at the risk of even more turmoil, democratic procedures such as contract ratification by the rank and file.

This is where the third level of the labor-management relationship— on the factory floor—assumes large importance. If rank-and-file workers can be given more responsibility and be drawn more deeply into the relationship (though not in a paternalistic way), a better understanding of the real constraints on bargaining may spread through the system. At the same time, redesigning jobs to allow greater worker participation in decision making can reduce alienation and give workers a sense of control over their work. In work-improvement projects, labor and management representatives try to solve problems instead of carrying on bureaucratic warfare. In the traditional adversary relationship, GM's Landen says, "the union tries to make economic and distributive-type demands, and management opposes them. That's legitimate, because there will always be differences of opinion about those things." Landen adds: "But you need to be able to shift from an adversary to a problem-solving relationship sometimes, and the skills acquired in those relationships will eventually spill over into the adversary area."

Reforming Work Practices

Work-reform efforts are directed essentially at breaking down the rigid hierarchies that exist in most workplaces, particularly in heavy manufacturing. The means of doing this are practically unlimited, ranging from highly informal ad hoc efforts by supervisors and their crews to the establishment of more formalized labor-management committees, teams, and quality control circles. These programs go by many names, but "quality of work life" (QWL) is coming into wide use as a generalized term referring to the entire process of reforming work practices. A few companies were engaged in work-improvement programs in the 1960s, but the QWL movement generally has been under way for about 10 years, mostly in nonunion plants and increasingly now in unionized ones with union cooperation. Nobody knows how many companies have these programs, although the number must be in the hundreds. GM, the acknowledged leader in this country, had QWL programs in place at ninety-five plants by the middle of 1981.

Many unions have opposed QWL because they fear that newly created mechanisms, such as semiautonomous work teams, will undermine their position as the representative of the workers, or they worry about being co-opted by the company. But a growing number of unions are now participating in QWL experiments, perhaps largely because they see no other alternative to declining market power and the loss of jobs in slumping industries. The UAW, long an advocate of labor-relations innovations, has been a leader in the QWL movement since 1973, when it agreed to cooperate with GM in a corporatewide program. The UAW's cooperation is based on several conditions: that jobs will not be lost, production standards increased, or collective bargaining agreements changed as a result of a QWL program. Irving Bluestone, a senior vice president of the UAW before his retirement in 1980, championed the QWL cause for many years. QWL programs he concluded, bring improvements in discipline, product quality, absenteeism, and labor turnover. Most important, he said, they lead to "one of the most fundamental objectives of unionism: the enhancement of human dignity and self-fulfillment at work."

Other unions have now embraced the QWL philosophy. The United Steelworkers and nine major steel companies agreed in 1980 negotiations to set up "labor-management participation teams" in selected plants. The Communications Workers of America and American Telephone & Telegraph are cooperating in QWL programs. Work-reform projects have been endorsed at one or more companies by unions as diverse as the International Union of Electrical Workers, the Newspaper Guild, the American Federation of State, County & Municipal Employees, and the Bakery, Confectionery & Tobacco Workers. Despite labor's growing receptivity, the QWL movement could wither away in the 1980s unless more unions and more companies recognize the value of workplace cooperation.

In a union situation, setting up informal contacts between the boss and the worker can help to "unfreeze" the antagonistic climate that has been produced by a "them vs. us" attitude on both sides. By implementing a QWL program, management acknowledges that the old authoritarian concept of managing workers no longer applies. This means seeking the workers' ideas on everything from improving the production process to scheduling work hours. "Management is getting away from the old 'I'm the boss, you're the hoss' attitude," says Raymond Calore, president of UAW Local 664 at Tarrytown, New York, where the union and General Motors have a successful QWL program.

The Tarrytown Experiment

The Tarrytown program is only one of many now under way in U.S. companies, but it has significance beyond GM because it illustrates one of the most significant trade-offs that management can offer to induce worker cooperation in QWL. "When you're making a radical shift that is very threatening to the whole organization, you need good job protection," says Jerome M. Rosow, president of Work in America. Workers understand, he says, that by improving quality and productivity "they'll be more competitive, they'll increase their company's share of the market, and, in the final analysis, they'll keep their jobs."

By 1971, after a decade of fairly rapid changes in the makeup of the work force, the Tarrytown assembly plant was in trouble. Absenteeism was high, product quality was poor, and union-management relations were so bad that as many as a thousand complaints clogged the grievance mechanism at a time. Ideally, an effective grievance procedure is an indispensable method of adjudicating workers' complaints about unfair treatment on the job. Where constant labor-management warfare exists, however, the grievance procedure is often used as a weapon. The union files grievance upon grievance without discriminating between frivolous and justified complaints, and management refuses to resolve the grievances early in the procedure, instead forcing the union into time-consuming and expensive appeals and arbitration. This kind of adversarialism does not solve human problems, at least not very well.

"Everybody was mad at one another," says the UAW's Ray Calore. "The foremen felt you had to have severe discipline, push and shove. The generations had changed, but they hadn't changed. The workers had no authority, no identity. It was dehumanizing." It became apparent to him, Calore says, that GM management might not invest more money in Tarrytown.

Calore and local management began to meet informally to solve the labor problem, and the program became a formal one when the UAW and GM agreed in 1973 to embark on a QWL program throughout the corporation. The core of the program at Tarrytown involved 3-day orientation sessions for all workers in the plant and those who have been hired since. In these meetings, company and union goals were explained, workers were shown the interrelation of one assembly-line job to another, and they were given a chance to meet workers from other departments. "They ended up knowing more about the plant than the supervisors," Calore says.

GM management welcomed suggestions from rank-and-file workers on improving assembly-line procedures and product quality. At the same time, the UAW local leadership and plant management met frequently to solve problems as they arose rather than waiting for the next round of local negotiations or the filing of grievances. Supervisors stopped applying discipline in a heavy-handed way, absenteeism dropped, and product quality improved. The grievance backlog now seldom exceeds twenty or thirty complaints at a time. In 1979 Local 664 and the Tarrytown management reached agreement in local negotiations long before the strike deadline, largely because of the improved climate in the plant (the same was true in most other GM plants that had QWL programs). "We're no longer involved in the adversary rat race," Calore says. "What we're trying to do is create an atmosphere in the workplace so that a person has the same freedom of expression and dress [on the job] as at home."

A job on the Tarrytown assembly line still has elements of monotony that alienate many workers, and the line still turns out a car a minute. But bosses no longer intimidate workers, and an easygoing atmosphere permits socializing on the job. Partly because of the improved labor climate, Tarrytown was retooled a few years ago and is now one of only three GM plants that produce the popular Chevrolet Citation, Pontiac Phoenix, and Buick Skylark. While 89,000 other GM workers were on indefinite layoff at the end of 1980, Tarrytown's full force of about 4800 hourly employees was working a 40-hour week. GM, aware that company boasting about productivity gains often inhibits labor-management cooperation, has made no public declarations about an improvement in output per worker at Tarrytown. But its production volume of 278,195 units in 1980 was the highest since 1955. And, as Rosow says, "GM is smart enough to know that if you improve the quality of work life, you improve efficiency. It isn't that you make the people happier. You make them more effective, and that produces satisfaction."

Quality Control Circles

Another trend that could have a major impact on the American workplace is the increasing use of quality control circles. This originated as an American concept that was largely ignored by U.S. companies and embraced by the Japanese. A circle is a committee of workers and supervisors (or sometimes workers alone) who meet to discuss product quality improvement. The circles proliferated in Japanese industry during the 1970s. Robert E. Cole, an expert on Japanese labor relations and a University of Michigan professor, says that by early 1978 one out of every eight Japanese employees was involved in a quality control circle. Thomas J. Murrin, president of Westinghouse Electric's Public Systems Company, believes that the use of the circles is the "single most significant explanation for the truly outstanding quality of goods and services" produced in Japan.

U.S. companies are now rediscovering the circle concept, although only 400 companies had active programs by the end of 1980. Westinghouse, for example, has established 150 "quality circles," as it calls them, at fifty locations. At its Baltimore defense complex there were sixty-three circles at the end of 1980, in departments employing 4500 blue-collar workers. The circles, with a membership of six to ten workers, meet weekly during working hours. Supervisors who run the meetings make no secret of the fact that their purpose is to find better ways of producing quality goods rather than to serve as a sounding board for worker complaints on a broad range of issues.

"You have a better relationship with your supervisor, the communication is better, and you really feel part of it," says Cardell Jones, a circle member who assembles microcircuitry for components of weapons and radar systems. Ronald Shenton, an inspector, says he often tells management "things that make them mad," but he is a zealot about quality and believes that "if you don't come up with better quality, you lose."

So far, the three unions that represent Westinghouse workers at Baltimore have not objected to the circles, although some union officials worry that the company is using the circles to circumvent the unions on labor matters. A Westinghouse labor-relations official says, however, that the company simply wants the unions to "stand aside and let the circles meet." He adds: "We're not trying to jeopardize the unions in any way." And several Baltimore workers who were involved in circle activity told a reporter that their concern for their own jobs was more important than whether the union approved of the circles.

In mid-1980 Westinghouse said the circles had made changes resulting in more than $1 million in savings in the 2 years of their existence. The company's defense business was booming then, and Murrin said that "we can virtually assure our current employees in Baltimore that they will not be put out of work by robots or quality circles."

All these workplace changes represent the beginnings of new industrial relations in the United States. By the end of 1980 QWL programs of one sort or another were under way probably in only a minority of workplaces, but the movement appears to be growing, if slowly. "I'm absolutely convinced this is where the future is in collective bargaining," says Irving Bluestone, former UAW vice president. One barrier to a faster spread of the concept is the lack of practical experience in making the reforms work. What is involved, after all, is no less than the creation of new forms of organization and the acceptance of radically different ways of managing people. The difficulties inherent in these processes deter many companies and unions. Moreover, there is a danger that naïve publicity about QWL will turn it into a fad of no lasting value; authorities say that throwing a QWL program into place without careful planning and with foolish expectations of what it will accomplish will usually kill the program.

Yet there can be no social contract without a new partnership in the workplace, and reforms are urgently needed if only because of the demographic profile of the American labor force. It is now dominated in numbers by the baby boom generation, which stresses values such as self-actualization and challenge on the job that are typically unattainable in the authoritarian workplace.

But many unionists remain skeptical of the benefits that flow to workers. "If QWL only makes workers feel subjectively better and doesn't get them any new rights, then management is simply trading us something that doesn't cost them anything," says a radical unionist in the auto industry. QWL enthusiasts argue that some programs have resulted in higher compensation and improved job security. But the movement is so new that there have been few comprehensive assessments of the costs and benefits for labor and management.

One QWL expert, Paul S. Goodman, of Carnegie-Mellon University, published his assessment of the QWL movement in August 1980. He reported: "(1) Most QWL projects seem to result in increases in job satisfaction, feelings of personal growth, job involvement, and organizational commitment. (2) Absenteeism, turnover, and tardiness are strongly and positively affected in most QWL projects. This finding agrees with the increased worker satisfaction. (3) Mixed results exist with respect to productivity. Productivity increases in about half of the QWL experiments, while it remains the same in the other half. (4) Most projects create more skilled and flexible work forces."

Most experts agree that increased job satisfaction does not necessarily lead to a rise in productivity, although absenteeism and turnover are usually reduced. While they applaud the humane considerations involved in a QWL program that has the general goal of improving the quality of work life, Goodman and others urge management and labor to set more specific goals for themselves. The economic benefits to be derived from a program should be very much in the planners' minds, says Richard E. Walton, a Harvard University professor who has designed QWL programs. "When changes in the work structure do not improve the work environment from a human perspective," he said in a 1979 article, "they will not increase employees' contribution to the business; likewise, changes in work structure that require managers to relate differently to workers but do not also benefit the business are not as likely to be sustained by those managers over time."

The record in the 1970s shows that many QWL experiments have lasted 5 years or less. A change of management is one cause of program collapse, but even with stability of leadership, it is difficult to maintain a permanent revolution. After a period of time, the psychic and economic rewards begin to fade as a motivation for both labor and management to continue the program. Many experts also say that programs fail if they were intended originally for the sole purpose of avoiding a union. Furthermore, workers withdraw their cooperation if they perceive that management is using the program to exploit workers.

Shuttering Plants

Workers feel particularly exploited when management suddenly, without adequate warning, shuts down a plant and puts all the employees out of a job. The problem of plant shutdowns has become so widespread since the mid-1970s, particularly in the Northeast and Great Lakes regions, that enormous pressure is developing in those areas for legislation to reduce corporate mobility. State laws that require corporations to give advance notification of closedowns and that call for penalty payments to the workers and communities involved are probably unwise. Such laws would probably keep new businesses from moving into that state.

But a social contract cannot exist without some provision for dealing with workers idled by shutdowns. According to a 1980 study by Barry Bluestone and Bennett Harrison, an estimated 2.5 million workers are affected each year by failing businesses, shifts of operations, and plant shutdowns and phaseouts. American businesses have always opened and shut at a relatively high rate, but because of technological change, foreign competition, and corporate mergers, the pace of these industrial shifts appears to have picked up. It probably will continue accelerating.

Many idled workers find new jobs fairly readily, but increasingly large numbers are being left behind in the old industrial cities of the North, where new jobs—especially for elderly workers and those with only narrow skills—are very scarce. Studies have shown increased rates of divorce, suicide, and alcoholism among workers idled by these shutdowns. In the new competitive environment, workers are under pressure to be more mobile than ever, even though there is conflicting pressure from society to settle permanently and create stable communities. Most important, it makes little sense to workers to cooperate with management if they have no confidence that the company is interested in their job security. Bluestone points out that one of the many reasons for a much closer collaboration between labor and management in Japan is that workers there retain their jobs for life. "When a guy has absolute job security for life, he has an entirely different view of his job and the company," Bluestone says. "In this country, a worker is more likely to feel, 'They want me to cooperate with them, but when they don't need me, they'll throw me into the street.'"

Unions and other liberal groups, recognizing the futility of having individual state laws on plant shutdowns, are clamoring for federal legislation that would restrict a corporation's ability to pick up and move. The chances of obtaining such a law receded considerably with the election of a Republican-dominated Senate and a Republican President in November 1980. But the clamor for legislation at some level will continue, especially in the Northern states, unless management recognizes and deals with the problem.

Plant closings can be treated in labor-management agreements, particularly with provisions that provide for several months' advance notification of a planned closing. Studies have shown that advance notification permits the planning and implementing of programs to soften the impact on workers and communities. A number of unions, including the United Steelworkers and the United Rubber Workers, already have advance notification provisions in their major contracts. Many contracts also enable a union to negotiate with management over the shutdown terms, which might include severance pay, early pensions for workers in their fifties, continuation of health care insurance, job-retraining programs, and transfer rights and relocation pay for workers who want to move to another plant in the same corporation.

These provisions may be costly, but the social costs of plant shutdowns for society are even more costly in many cases. Some corporations, although not yet enough, are beginning to accept the idea that they have an obligation to consider the impact of their decisions on workers and communities. The federal and state governments also must become involved in programs involving retraining, job search, and relocation, as well as efforts to direct new businesses into impacted areas. Plant shutdowns are inevitable in the American economy, and capital mobility should not be restricted. But a social contract cannot ignore the social costs of maintaining a mobile economy.

8
PUTTING THE FUTURE
INTO BUSINESS DECISIONS

Despite all the doom and gloom about the state of corporate America, and despite corporate America's protests to the contrary, many—maybe most—of the typical company's problems which have contributed to the loss of U.S. competitiveness have been internally generated. And thus they can be internally solved.

Companies can change the signals—and some are already doing so—in order to push their own people away from short-term myopia into long-term vision. They can reaffirm the need for basic research, for taking risks, for planning over the long haul. And they can create a climate in which educated risk takers not only feel that their jobs are secure but also feel that their willingness to take risks is both appreciated and rewarded.

Clearly, the message has to come from the very top of the organization. "You've got to preach commitment to long-range concepts constantly," says Thomas V. Jones, chairman and CEO of Northrop, a company with a good long-term track record. "We tell our guys they're supposed to take care of short-term profits with their left hand and long-term performance with their right."

Similarly, Ruben F. Mettler, chairman of TRW, making the management-meeting rounds at his company in mid-1980, stressed that there should be no cuts in research and development funding. He told his managers, "While we are in a recession and short-term actions are necessary, we don't want to take our eye off the long-term goal." And at Westinghouse Electric, not known for its visionary strategies in the past, chairman Robert E. Kirby chose "Decade of Determination" as the theme for the 1980 annual meeting of 225 key operational managers.

Although clearly defined messages on the importance of the long term are essential, they are far from sufficient. They must be backed up with new policies, plans, and procedures that continually drive home to staff members that they must be more than caretakers of the bottom line.

Rewarding Long-Range Risk Taking

Perhaps the easiest yet most critical fix needed in most corporations is an improvement in incentive compensation programs. Because the best long-range plans are, in effect, worthless if there is no money to carry them out, it would be foolish to completely eliminate bonuses based on short-term performance. Yet bonuses based solely on short-term profits must be abolished. There must be flexibility in bonus allocations in order to reward savvy decisions that do not result in immediate profits but help the company over the long run.

One possible way, suggests Donald G. Carlson, a vice president at Booz Allen & Hamilton, is to "leverage" bonuses. If under the conventional percentage-of-salary system a top executive would get $100,000, then in Carlson's plan the company would pay $50,000, promise another $50,000 for meeting short-range goals, and dangle an additional $30,000 if the executive takes a risk that pans out. "That way the executive loses nothing and has a lot to gain," Carlson says.

A few companies have already implemented their own variations on that theme. Honeywell and Spring Mills are rewriting their compensation schedules to reward managers for tapping new markets and developing new products. Johnson & Johnson awards executives making $70,000 and up shares of "phantom stock"—credits whose value are based on an internal formula that is tied to book value and profits. The executives get annual "dividends" on the shares for short-term performance, but they can cash them in only on leaving the company. Thus they can collect later on long-term decisions made now.

For lower-level executives, Johnson & Johnson and Du Pont have discretionary bonus systems that use no allocation formulas but allow bosses to allocate money on the basis of what they subjectively see as outstanding contributions, presumably including smart risks. Du Pont also has a second set of bonuses for "achievements above and beyond the call of duty," awarded by a special compensation committee headed by the company's president. One R&D manager was rewarded for suggesting a more expensive but safer manufacturing process. "It cost a bundle to put in, but he got a bundle," recalls senior vice president William G. Simeral. And the division manager who persuaded Du Pont to close down its entire nitrocellulose operation a few years ago also got "a very good bonus" that year, although his division showed a loss, Simeral says.

Some companies even try to reward attitude. International Harvester provides bonuses for employees who join professional societies or publish scientific papers. It has changed the minuscule $10 award the company had been granting for scientists who received patents to a sliding scale of cash bonuses that increase if the product winds up profitable.

All these compensation systems signal staffers that immediate bottom-line results are not the end-all and be-all. The message can be reinforced by the types of reports and oral presentations that managers are expected to make and by the criteria used for promotion. "The key is to tie the profile for promotion as well as for compensation to the long range," notes management consultant John Diebold, head of The Diebold Group. "Maybe we should have division managers do the equivalent of an environmental impact statement twice a year on long-term impact."

Few companies go that far. But several are making changes in their reporting requirements. Westinghouse, which recently reorganized 130 separate units into thirty-eight divisions, has switched from what used to be a voluminous financial reporting requirement to asking the thirty-eight divisional presidents for a single page of numbers projecting cash flow rather than profit and loss. But the presidents must submit plans every 2 years projecting 5 years out, and they must submit them orally as well as in written form so that they can be questioned. "What we want is a summary of what each business unit is really about—who the competition is, how we are positioned, how we can gain share or remain number one," explains a Westinghouse vice president of corporate planning, who was one of the architects of the new system. Johnson & Johnson is starting to ask for similar reports, and it purposely asks for them before annual operating and budget planning sessions to prevent managers from using their strategic plan to justify their budgets.

Significantly, neither J&J nor TRW nor 3M—all regarded as forward-thinking corporations—has anyone on board with the title of corporate planner. Which is as it should be, maintains Frederick W. Gluck, head of McKinsey & Co.'s strategic practice section. "I don't believe in strategic planning as being different from management in any way," he says, adding that planning must be an expected part of every manager's job.

Encouraging Employee Differences

But the glaring reality is that not everyone is good at all aspects of planning. And it is time that corporations recognized that different people have different skills and must be placed in the organization accordingly. All too often corporate executives ignore the fact that the entrepreneurial type of manager, who brought a product line from, say, a 2 percent share of market to 20 percent in 3 years, is probably the worst person to continue managing that line when it becomes a mature product with little growth potential. Very likely the entrepreneurial type's forte is risk taking and innovating, while cost-cutting and pushing productivity—the essence of operating a mature cash-generating business—may well be anathema. "Too often it's like trying to put your best guard into the quarterback's slot—it just can't work," says consulting psychologist Harry Levinson, head of the Levinson Institute in Belmont, Massachusetts.

There are signs that corporate America can change its ways. General Electric, Chase Manhattan Bank, Corning Glass Works, and a handful of others are already screening their staffs for such things as entrepreneurial flair, cost-cutting ability, and the like, in a real attempt to match their employee's strengths with the appropriate aspects of the company's strategic plans.

But unfortunately, most companies are still following rigidly structured lines of promotion. They are letting the controller, for example, automatically move up into the divisional manager's slot, or turning sales representatives and researchers into managers.

What is needed is a dual ladder, a method by which skilled people who do not want to move into management will not find their careers stymied. Analog Devices has one; so does 3M. Titles such as "senior fellow" garner prestige and money at Analog; 3M has an elaborate system of honor societies to convey status for scientific achievement in the laboratory.

But too few companies have extended the dual ladder up to the rarefied atmosphere of the executive suite. Robert W. Lear, Columbia University's executive in residence, speaks only half in jest when he says that companies should appoint a "vice president in charge of hope." James B. Farley, chairman of Booz Allen & Hamilton, says we must "separate those people who have strong financial accountability from those—call them futurists, planners, whatever—who say where we should be heading." He envisions high-level corporate types whose main role is to think. "If they're considered by critics to be a third elbow, then the courageous CEO has to say, 'Okay, we're a company with three elbows.'"

But to work, the think tank that Farley and Lear envision must have corporate clout. Some form of matrix management—a system in which most employees have two bosses—is probably needed. Employees would wind up accountable to a conventional manager for financial results, day-to-day operations, and the like; they would report to the thought leaders with their concepts, ideas, and research results. General Electric and Union Carbide have had luck with matrixes. Hewlett-Packard recently put in one in which many managers have dotted-line reporting arrangements to their own peers. "While a manager may have a given job and title, he may be asked to report to quite a few others to share information and increase communications," explains Frederich W. Schroeder, director of corporate development.

The setup at TRW Electronics, a division of TRW Inc., is more common. The groups developing new products report to the head of the new ventures operations during the "incubation phase" of development. Later, when the product is ready for commercialization, its management reverts to a product manager. A few other companies have moved at least somewhat in this direction, hiring high-level people to spot ways to apply high technology to conventional products. International Harvester recently appointed Robert J. Potter, a former Xerox executive, to the new post of senior vice president and chief technical officer and gave him a mandate to scout out technological improvements for the company's mainstay agricultural machinery business. General Electric has a new corporate production and operating services unit under a senior vice president whose charter is to "look at opportunities to infuse our manufacturing organizations with all the latest technical developments," says Reginald H. Jones, former chairman and CEO. Two years ago TRW expanded the responsibility of its vice president of manufacturing and technology, changing the title to vice president of science and technology to emphasize responsibility for new developments.

Keeping the Research Funds Flowing

Such people and their departments must be protected from the budgetary ax even in a rough economy. The best way to achieve this is to have research budgets that cannot be touched by operating people. At Control Data, William C. Norris, chairman and CEO, has a "chairman's budget" of several million dollars that is used entirely for following up new ideas. "If that were in the operating budget, it would have been cut," he says.

Similarly, Texas Instruments (TI) maintains separate operating and strategic budgets—a setup that enabled it to continue research into minicomputers during the 1974-75 recession. Today TI is the fourth largest minicomputer manufacturer in the country. "To try to get managers to cut more heavily into operating areas while holding together the strategic area is kind of counterintuitive, but that's what we attempt to do," says Charles H. Phipps, TI's manager of strategic planning.

Within the strategic research budget itself, it's not a bad idea to keep specific funds for "pure" research. Joseph W. Davison, vice president for research and development at Phillips Petroleum, sets aside 3 to 5 percent of his annual budget for "blue-sky" ideas. "There are a great many short-range opportunities that are very high priority now, but the long-range and blue-sky categories are the areas from which our future business is built," he insists.

Separate funding for basic research also prevents operating departments from cannibalizing research budgets. That is a problem that irks

Walter L. Abel, vice president of R&D at Emhart. Abel cites a study that shows that about 75 percent of what companies define as R&D costs actually went for efforts that were just product improvements or line extensions and as such should have been charged to marketing, manufacturing, or the like. "If marketing goes to R&D for customer help, it should be charged to marketing, and if manufacturing needs a little help with a process, R&D's time should be charged to them," he says.

The best answer, however, is to move basic R&D away from the pesterings of operating departments. "We must have outposts of basic research with real channels of application," insists Nobel laureate Herbert Simon of Carnegie-Mellon University. "Bell Labs and GE are good at this, but few other companies are. You need small clusters of basic scientists working within industrial corporations, but without pressure for immediate commercial applications."

Realistically, not many companies can afford to maintain staffed and equipped scientific think tanks. But they can certainly make better use of universities. David Packard, chairman of Hewlett-Packard, observes, "It is essential for the electronics industry to make a larger commitment to more basic research—if not in its own laboratories, then in university laboratories." And Emhart's Abel says he is trying to persuade his management to establish a manufacturing and engineering applications center at a nearby university.

Universities can also provide a neutral ground for competitors to jointly sponsor and use research. The fruits of such cooperation were exemplified in 1977, when Georgia Institute of Technology, the National Science Foundation, the University of Missouri, the Illinois Research Institute, and various companies from Georgia's granite industry joined forces to see whether the noise from plasma jets used to cut granite could be reduced to a level acceptable to the Occupational Safety and Health Administration. The NSF made funds available to the local granite trade association, which in turn contracted with researchers at the universities. The result was a process using high-pressure water jets to cut granite. The granite companies are now forming a consortium to manufacture and distribute the new OSHA-acceptable cutting tool.

At least one CEO agrees that cooperation between companies is essential. "I believe executives should be looking around to see what other companies they can work with on R&D," says Control Data's Norris, who has spearheaded joint ventures with Honeywell, NCR, and others to produce computer tape drives, disks, and tapes. Norris has also set up small-business resource centers across the country to help incubate new small ventures. "We have technologies we can't use, and we encourage small companies to use them," he says. "Working with small companies can be beneficial. You have to stoop, and that's good exercise for executives."

Norris is not the typical CEO either in attitude or in background. He not only heads Control Data but also founded it. Under Norris the company has invested $150 million in Plato, a computer-based education system that has still not broken even. Yet he insists on continuing full funding. He knows his business inside and out and has a clout with the board of directors that most professional managers never get. Yet Norris's attitudes—his willingness to back money-losing projects because he believes in them, his fearlessness of Wall Street, his willingness to cooperate with other companies and other researchers—are exactly what is needed in the next generation of managers to run corporate America.

Promoting the Young Tigers

That raises a question that is frightening to most people who are concerned with the future of American industry: What is to prevent the next generation of managers from falling prey to the same stockholder pressures, specialized orientation, and tunnel vision that characterize the majority of today's managers? The current crop of executive vice presidents and divisional presidents—the people who seem targeted for tomorrow's top jobs—are cut from the same cloth as their CEOs. If they were not, they probably would not have attained the positions they now hold.

The problem may simply be one of age. The few companies that have young managements are simply more willing to take risks. Gary E. MacDougal, who in his early forties has already attained the chairmanship of Mark Controls Corp., a manufacturer of $233 million worth of industrial valves per year, did not particularly care when Mark's earnings were recently penalized 50 cents a share because the company had pumped money into a new valve that will not be profitable for several years. "Maybe it's because our management is in its forties that we can look at this longer-term," he surmises.

Booz Allen's Farley suggests that companies skip a couple of generations and reach for the "32-year-old tiger" as the next potential head. This would bring a fresh approach to the executive suite and would give the top manager impetus to take risks, since he or she might still be around when they paid off.

But fresh blood is not enough. Attitudes and forward thinking are not linked to age alone. Armand Hammer, at 82, still supplies the imagination and vision for Occidental Petroleum in a way that none of his younger executives can match. Thus corporations must also make sure that the younger managers are not allowed to specialize too quickly and too extremely. Both the internal and external educational systems must change. Job rotations—not uncommon years ago but not used as frequently today—must be reinstated so that managers get a feel for several disciplines and for the entire business. James E. Burke, chairman at J&J, says that top management plays a "chess game" with people to broaden them. Most inside members of the company's board have worked in at least two of J&J's four market segments, and the president, David R. Clare, has manufacturing and marketing experience from several of J&J's operating companies. This sort of broadening should spread to other companies.

Although nothing replaces good hands-on job experience, new types of educational seminars would certainly not hurt. But they should not be technique-oriented—teaching specific behavioral ways to manipulate employees or financial formulas to judge potential projects. They should teach ethics and global thinking—maybe even philosophy and English literature—if for no other reason than to teach managers how to think and ask questions. Money spent on such mind-broadening experiences as the Aspen Institute or the Dartmouth Institute is rarely wasted.

It is a promising sign that more and more companies are setting up in-house education programs for executives, and more and more executives are returning to the campus to get advanced degrees. If nothing else, it is an admission on the part of business that the world changes too rapidly for the educational process to have a finite end. Westinghouse, for example, puts about 8000 professional employees through in-house courses on engineering and manufacturing, marketing and sales, and problem solving and general management each year. General Electric's financial training program is often enviously referred to by other corporations as one of the best "MBA" programs around. Columbia Broadcasting Systems has been running its own school for both top and middle-level managers for a few years now, and every one of the student-managers contacted felt that the 1-week course was of immeasurable benefit.

Overhauling the Business Schools

But the fact that corporations are assuming more and more of the educational burden does not exempt the business schools from doing their part in getting the thought processes of the next generation of managers back on a progressive track. Before anything else, the schools themselves have to refocus their goals and priorities. For example, the American Assembly of Collegiate Schools of Business still decides whether to grant accreditation to a school on the basis of the number of degrees its professors hold or the size of its libraries. Whether the schools are giving students an adequate education does not enter the picture. Similarly, the "publish or perish" rule thrives as much in the business schools as it does in liberal arts colleges, where a case could be made that the erudition of professors has a direct link to their value as teachers. Business schools still favor the business Ph.D., who may well never have spent a moment in a genuine business environment, over the experienced business executive who wants to give teaching a shot. For example, there are numerous retired General Electric executives living in the Cape Cod area who claim they would love to spend some of their new free time teaching business courses at the local community college. Yet despite their years of experience at a company that is known for being in the vanguard of modern management techniques, their services are not welcome at the college because their educational background does not fit the proper mold.

There are a few encouraging signs that the schools are recognizing some of these problems. At business schools across the country, guest lecturers and adjunct professors from the business community are being invited in to bring a "real world" perspective to the classroom. Students are encouraged to participate in work-study projects with local businesses. One genuinely new type of program is being offered at Rensselaer Polytechnic Institute, where promising engineering students who have been pinpointed as having management capabilities are offered special sessions in which both faculty members and local corporate executives lecture. A talk by a marketing professor is followed, for example, by a lecture by a director of marketing from a local corporation. "The faculty member sees his role as laying the groundwork, while the business executive relates it to real life," explains Lyle F. Schoenfeldt, the program's director.

But there are still some fundamental educational problems that the schools must begin to address before they become a truly effective part of the solution to the reindustrialization crisis. Bringing more business managers and real world expertise into the classroom may turn out students better equipped to deal with the current world of business. But it is the world of business itself that needs changing, and management philosophers say that the business colleges are still turning out legions of MBAs who make decisions by the calculator rather than by informed instinct, who are naïve in dealing in the international marketplace, and who are oriented to short-term performance at the expense of innovation and long-term investment.

A large part of the problem stems from the fact that consulting firms have traditionally been the primary "customers" at the top-tier business schools. They pay the highest starting salaries and often offer the most prestigious starting titles. But many business gadflies insist that the same qualities that make for a good consultant—someone who can analyze a problem, come up with a solution, and move on to the next issue—are qualities that militate against becoming a good business leader. Charles D. Baker, chairman of Harbridge House, a Boston consulting firm, puts it this way: "The analogy would be medical schools that turn out people to go into medical research and academia rather than to practice medicine."

A similar criticism can be leveled at the manner in which business schools teach international business. American society as a whole is chauvinistic. It still believes that "smart" foreigners know how to speak English, but it does not expect its own citizens to speak a foreign language. It fully expects Europeans or Asians to understand and adapt to American culture when they are in the United States or are dealing with U.S. firms, yet it rarely offers the same courtesy overseas.

There is a telling anecdote making the rounds that pinpoints the ignorance of international matters prevalent in the United States. An international business consultant reportedly asked twenty-five high-level executives at a major U.S. company with considerable business interests in the Middle East to write the name of Saudi Arabia's king on slips of paper. He gathered up the answers and began to read them aloud. Sadat, Hussein, and Faisal were the most popular choices. In fact, almost every major Arab leader was mentioned, with the notable exception of King Khalid, Saudi Arabia's actual monarch.

Such ignorance is frightening in the sense that the executives did not feel there was any need for them to know anything about foreign competitors or foreign customers. This is an attitude that the business schools must try to change. It does not help to isolate international subjects in a few special international courses, as most of the schools do. International awareness must become an integral part of every course. Marketing courses should include sections on how to market overseas. Corporate finance courses should dwell heavily on currency exchanges. Business law courses should focus as much on international law as on American law. And foreign students should be encouraged to express their views in American classrooms, even if it means castigating both their fellow students and their professors.

Perhaps most important of all, business graduates should be bilingual. Granted, the 2-year MBA program does not provide enough time for an in-depth language course. But there is no reason why proficiency in at least one foreign language should not be a requirement for admission to a business school. If the American educational system accepts the idea of pre-med courses and prelaw courses, why not a prebusiness course that requires social anthropology, languages, and maybe even philosophy to help get the corporate leaders of tomorrow comfortable with thinking in the abstract?

Despite their protests, schools can provide an environment in which business students are convinced of the merits of taking risks and thinking without numbers. In the traditional "management game," an exercise in which students make a series of management decisions about a hypothetical company and a computer reveals the results of these decisions in terms of the company's profitability, there is no reason why the criterion for determining the winner need be stock prices. Why not let students choose their own goals and then let the computer evaluate their decisions in terms of those goals? Dartmouth tried it, and at least one graduate MBA says it was a great experience. "My team opted to go for market share, and at the end of the game we had only just turned a profit. Yet we won," he recalls. The message was that you can win in business without showing a short-term profit.

Perhaps the hardest task facing the schools is getting students to think about the impact of world events on business and the impact of business on the world. One way to do it is to tap into the resources of nonbusiness professors. Carnegie-Mellon, for one, is offering an ethics course taught by a philosophy professor. The Sloan School of Management at MIT has brought in an historian to teach a course on the links between the private and public sector. William F. May, former head of American Can and currently dean of New York University's Graduate School of Business, notes that the student body is growing more diverse. "Many people with Ph.D.s in the humanities are coming back for their MBAs," he points out, "and they are bringing a quality of reflective thinking and an ability to communicate that is sorely needed."

Corporate America has got to keep the pressure on the business schools to continue their slow but steady trend toward broader education. Perhaps it is time for a resurgence of the old liberal arts major as an acceptable entry into business by itself, without being supplemented by an MBA later on. The sudden competition from the undergraduate schools for the top jobs might force the business schools to accelerate any moves they are making toward change. The fact is that for the long pull, business schools will not really stress long-range thinking and global orientation until companies stop recruiting MBAs with calculators permanently attached to their right arms.

Again, what is required is a willingness to bury the past and look to the future. The mathematical techniques of management—so well taught by the business schools in the last decades—have made an important contribution to the growth of American corporations. But it is time for the pendulum to swing back to visionary, insightful managers who place emphasis on gut feelings and on an understanding of the total business picture. Of course, they must understand the profit motive—but they must also understand the difference between maximized short-term profits and optimized long-term profits. As the itinerant philosopher in Koppers' annual report put it: "For those of you who may not understand the difference between optimum and maximum, let me put it this way: Optimum body temperature runs about 98.6°F. Maximum body temperature is likely to kill you."

PART THREE

A BLUEPRINT FOR REINDUSTRIALIZATION

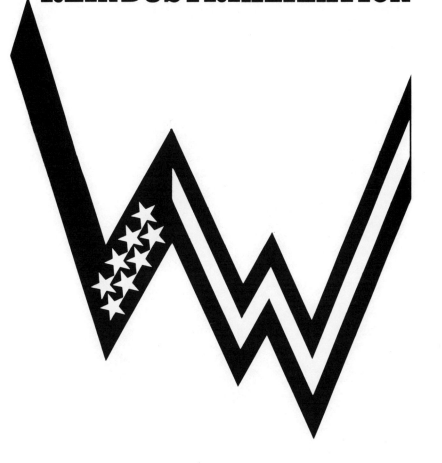

9

LAYING FOUR CORNERSTONES
OF NATIONAL POLICY

Reviving Savings

An increase in capital formation is essential to the restoration of the competitiveness of U.S. industry. But to jolt Americans out of their low-saving habits so that the nation has the wherewithal to finance its required investment growth, the first essential is to substantially change the tax system. For openers, the incentive for Americans to save could be revived by a slowing of inflation and a reduction in the government's punitively high marginal tax rates. But ultimately the job will require a major overhaul of the federal income tax to eliminate its inherent bias against savings.

Such change will not come easily. The vast majority of economists argue that savings in the United States has historically been insensitive to the rate of return, and so there may not be much payoff to increasing tax incentives for savers. Furthermore, economists note that the biggest savers are taxpayers with the highest incomes, and any changes in the tax code favoring this group would make the system less progressive, lowering the tax burden of the rich relative to that of other income classes. Thus tax law changes along these lines have been exceedingly difficult to get through the Congress.

However, in the last few years, several economists have mounted a serious challenge to the conventional wisdom on savings. Michael J. Boskin of Stanford University, for example, has estimated that a 1 percent increase in the real after-tax rate of return on savings produces a 0.4 percent rise in the savings rate. "Surveys showing that people won't increase saving simply assume they won't change behavior if the incentive is changed," says Boskin. "How can people answer the question when many don't even know their exact tax rates at the time they are surveyed?"

115

Other economists complain that they have not been able to confirm Boskin's research, but his findings already are helping to break down the walls of political resistance to new savings incentives. Says F. Thomas Juster of the University of Michigan: "Boskin says there's a lever, and people in Washington are grabbing it."

Taxing Expenditures

The most sweeping approach to eliminating the tax system's bias against savings would be to tax consumption instead of income. Taxpayers would be assessed each year only on what they spend. To calculate this expenditure-tax base, they would add up their income from all sources, including sales of stocks, bonds, and other assets and money withdrawn from thrift accounts, and subtract all their new investments, savings, and debt repayments. The remainder would show what was spent for consumption during the year. That amount would be adjusted for exemptions and exclusions and would then be subject to taxation.

In a widely acclaimed Treasury Department publication called *Blueprints for Basic Tax Reform,* Princeton University economist David F. Bradford suggested in January 1977 that individuals might have registered accounts with banks or other concerns that would keep track of all their savings and dissavings during a year and provide a single net figure to subtract from income at tax time. This way, an individual with, say, $50,000 of salary income in a year and new savings and investments netting $15,000 would presumably have spent $35,000 and that would be the tax base. The more that people save, the lower their tax base and in turn their tax bill in any given year. The Bradford study even outlined ways to make the transition from the present tax system to an expenditure base without disruption of the economy and—if desired by the public—without a loss of progressivity.

"The expenditure tax could be fashioned to maintain the progressivity of the current system and even raise the same amount of revenue," says Victor Thuronyi of the prestigious Washington law firm of Miller & Chevalier. "But within each bracket, those who consume would make up the tax revenue which is lost to those who save."

Gerard M. Brannon, former director of the Treasury Department's Office of Tax Analysis, concedes that "the one-time effects of the transition to an expenditure tax would be pretty rough, but the payoff for saving would be great." One way to cushion the shock would be to leave the income tax system in place and levy a new tax on consumption itself. Brannon would start by cutting income tax rates 20 percent and replacing the revenue with a value-added tax (VAT)—a form of national sales tax levied on goods and services at each stage of production and distribution. "This would take a fifth of the burden off saving with one shot," he says. Thuronyi prefers the direct expenditure-tax approach but would apply it only to taxpayers in the highest brackets after cutting their top marginal rate from 70 percent to 49 percent.

Even some experts who are skeptical about the prospects for improving the savings rate through tax changes look with favor on the expenditure-tax idea. Says Thomas F. Field, executive director of Taxation with Representation, a tax reform lobbying group in Arlington, Virginia: "There is considerable logic to the basic idea of the consumption tax, which goes back to Irving Fisher in the United States and John Stuart Mill in Britain. The income tax is based on the early-1900s populists' grand social objective of using the tax system to redistribute income and wealth, but the system has failed to do that. The income tax essentially is a tax on wages, since most income from capital escapes taxation. The result is that small savers, who do not have the tax shelters of the rich, bear a very heavy tax burden on their small stores of capital."

Thus Field believes that on equity grounds alone, the income tax should be scrapped in favor of an expenditure tax, even though he is doubtful about the impact on savings. "The consumption tax is essentially an income tax with a full deduction for savings," he says. "The increase in the deduction for interest on thrift accounts to $200 a person from $100 in 1980 was just another step in that direction." As for progressivity, Field argues, as do many other tax experts, that a proportional tax system would be far more efficient and that "the needs of the poor and investment in education and human capital could be handled much better through the spending side of the budget."

Adjusting for Inflation

While efforts to push the United States toward an expenditure tax will continue through the 1980s, Washington has turned to less radical approaches to increasing the incentives for savings and investment. The tax program long favored by President Reagan—based on the Kemp-Roth bill—will attempt to improve those incentives by cutting tax rates for individuals by 25 percent over 33 months. Starting in 1985, the new law will index the tax system so that rates and exemptions will automatically be adjusted each year to correct for inflation and only real gains in income will be taxed. Without indexation, the increases in income that taxpayers receive keep pushing them into ever-higher tax brackets. Because of the higher marginal tax rates, this extra income usually fails to keep up with the rate of inflation.

Indexation of the personal income tax through bracket widening and other devices has been a favorite approach of U.S. economists for years, but until recently the idea lacked any significant political support. For one thing, the cost is forbidding; for another, it would deprive Congress of the chance to gain favor with the public through cutting taxes periodically. In the waning days of the last Congress, the powerful Senate Finance Committee passed a major tax-reduction bill containing a one-time 7 percent adjustment in bracket widths, and with the support of the new chairman, Senator Robert Dole (R-Kans.), this measure has become a basis for congressional tax action in combination with the multiyear personal rate cuts proposed by President Reagan.

In addition, explicit indexation of parts of the tax base, such as capital gains, stands a better than 50-50 chance during this decade. While many Washington lawmakers favored increasing the present 60 percent exclusion of capital gains from taxable income to 70 percent, thereby cutting the top tax on such income from 28 percent to 21 percent, an even deeper cut to 20 percent has been achieved by reducing the maximum tax rate on investment income to 50 percent from 70 percent.

Indexation proposals also abound for interest on thrift accounts, and possibly for interest on corporate bonds and other financial instruments. In effect, such proposals would tax only the real interest income on savings and exempt the inflation premium, thereby protecting the original capital. A simple way to do this would be to exempt the first 5 or 6 percent of the return on savings. Part of the economic appeal of such proposals is that they would increase the saving incentive for high-income savers, who already squirrel away far more money than was affected by the old tax exclusion for dividends and interest.

Other Spurs to Savings

However, unless indexation for lenders and savers is matched by some method of taxing the inflation gain attained by debtors, "there is a possibility for all sorts of arbitrage games," says Thuronyi. Thus complexity as well as cost makes financial indexation less than a 50-50 bet.

The most feasible political approach may be to expand or extend incentives already in the tax code for savings and capital gains. Existing law, for example, defers taxes on income from pension, profit-sharing, and stock bonus plans. Thus employees are not taxed on their employers' contributions to qualified pension plans—and the investment income of those plans is not taxed until the benefits are paid out. Similar laws aid individuals not covered by qualified pension plans by deferring taxes on income they set aside in individual retirement accounts (IRAs), and self-employed persons can get the same benefit through Keogh plans. The 1981 Senate Finance Committee bill raised the deduction for both IRA and Keogh plans and allows participants in employer-sponsored plans to set up IRAs. And Senator Dole has introduced separate legislation to allow IRA-type plans for savings to finance home buying and education.

One top congressional aide describes such proposals as "incredibly expensive." But Representative Barber B. Conable Jr. (R-N.Y.) of the House Ways and Means Committee says: "We'll get there by establishing special funds. We'll do a lot of IRAs and eventually turn them into one system." Of course, that would come close to converting the U.S. tax system to an expenditure base piece by piece. "As more and more saving and capital income is exempted from taxation, you approach a consumption tax," says Tom Field. "That's just a matter of arithmetic."

Triggering Investment and Innovation

The push for sweeping changes in the U.S. tax code to stimulate investment and to encourage the revitalization of U.S. industry is gaining momentum. Tax cuts that primarily benefit business and investors are still tough to sell politically, especially when they are weighed against ever-growing pressures to balance the budget. But the American public now seems far more receptive to the idea than it did over the last two decades, when most people thought that tax reform meant closing tax loopholes for the rich and redistributing income to the poor.

Until recently, the driving force in U.S. taxation could be summed up in a neat aphorism authored by MIT economist Lester C. Thurow: "Equality is a superior good. The richer we become, the more of it we can afford." Now, after several years of seeing the United States lose its momentum in the growth of productivity and the improvement of its standard of living, Americans may be modifying their goals, realizing they are not quite so rich after all. Instead, says Charls E. Walker, former Deputy Secretary of the Treasury and Reagan's top adviser on tax issues during the 1980 campaign: "Attention has shifted from the question of how income should be distributed to how best it can be produced." And that question points to a new emphasis on increasing and upgrading productive capacity in the United States.

The turn in mood was sharply signaled in 1978, when Congress stood President Carter's tax reform program on its ear. Instead of stiffening the taxation of capital gains, as Carter originally proposed, Congress increased the tax exclusion for long-term capital gains from 50 percent to 60 percent, reduced the corporate income tax rate from 48 to 46 percent, and extended the investment tax credit to certain structures. In 1979 Capitol Hill completed the rout of traditional tax reformers by repealing a 1976 estate tax provision that would, in effect, have taxed capital gains at death by making an heir liable for taxes on the entire gain in an inherited asset's value since the time the decedent acquired it.

But before the new mood can be translated into further and more extensive pro-capital tax changes in the 1980s, the United States will have to come to grips with some critical choices. The budget restraint required to fight inflation will not allow room for every appealing tax-reduction scheme. Says tax expert Walker: "The fundamental fact of inflation is a federal budget that has run deficits in 21 of the past 23 years." Fear of exacerbating the budget problem caused Congress to delay action for 2 years on the 3-year 30 percent tax cut first proposed by Representative Jack Kemp and Senator William Roth in 1978 and finally to scale the cut down to 25 percent. It also forced the authors to rewrite their bill to include an explicit requirement that federal spending be reduced.

The Supply-Side Panacea

In theory, the large across-the-board personal tax cut provided by Kemp-Roth would eventually bring back much of the revenue initially given up by the Treasury, its proponents contend, by unleashing a flood of extra work effort, saving, and investment that would greatly expand national income. And since it is hoped that the response to this measure would be an increase in supply rather than the surge in consumption caused by conventional Keynesian tax cuts, Kemp-Roth—or Conable-Hance, as it is now known—would also improve productivity and lower inflation. This scenario is the centerpiece of what has become known as supply-side economics and is the heart of Reagan's economic program.

But many economists—including some of the President's top advisers—have been extremely skeptical about this approach, fearing that it might simply stimulate demand, exacerbate inflation, and deepen the deficit in the short run. If supply-side tax cuts are to be effective, the Reagan administration will have to effect a rapid change in the public's deeply ingrained expectation that severe inflation is here to stay. Otherwise, consumers will simply rush out and spend the extra income freed by Kemp-Roth rather than put it into savings and investment that would face continued erosion by inflation. And business executives, workers, and consumers—acting on their inflationary expectations—would continue to push up wages and prices to protect profits and maintain their standard of living, thereby undermining the economy's real growth.

To reverse these inflationary expectations as quickly as possible, Reagan and his top economic advisers hope to make government policy

How tax cuts have spurred capital investment

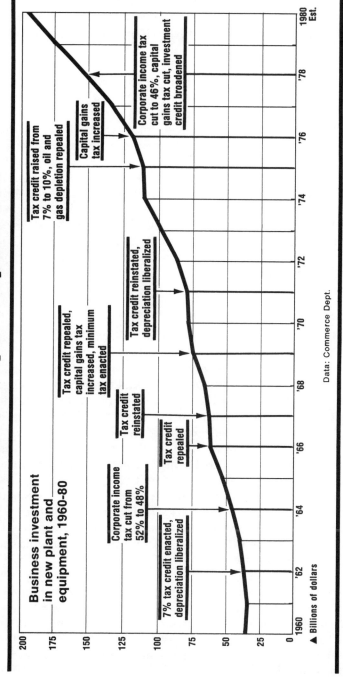

Business investment in new plant and equipment, 1960-80

7% tax credit enacted, depreciation liberalized

Corporate income tax cut from 52% to 48%

Tax credit repealed

Tax credit reinstated

Tax credit repealed, capital gains tax increased, minimum tax enacted

Tax credit reinstated, depreciation liberalized

Tax credit raised from 7% to 10%, oil and gas depletion repealed

Capital gains tax increased

Corporate income tax cut to 46%, capital gains tax cut, investment credit broadened

▲ Billions of dollars

200 175 150 125 100 75 50 25 0

1960 '62 '64 '66 '68 '70 '72 '74 '76 '78 1980 Est.

Data: Commerce Dept.

predictable from the beginning to the end of his term. And to do this, they are trying to lock fiscal policy onto a consistent track for the next 4 years with their version of the multiyear Kemp-Roth tax cut, lock monetary policy onto a similar track by pressuring the Federal Reserve Board to concentrate on controlling the growth of the money supply instead of interest rates, slash government regulations where they are not economically justified to help business take maximum advantage of tax incentives, and perhaps most important for credibility, slash nondefense spending to reduce the role of government and shift resources to the private sector.

Drafting the pro-capital tax package and steering it through Congress was the most challenging part of this program. In addition to dealing with congressional resistance to multiyear tax cuts, the Reagan administration had to overcome the fear of some lawmakers that capital-formation tax incentives might pull investment toward capital-intensive industries at the expense of labor-intensive industries. And broad-scale tax changes of the supply-side type must compete for funds with industrial policy measures targeted to help specific industries. The final bill represented a variety of compromises.

A Rich Array of Options

But the bright side of this coin is that policymakers do have a rich array of pro-capital tax options from which to choose, and several have already proved to have a major investment bang for the revenue buck. For example, a combination of accelerated depreciation and the introduction of the investment tax credit in 1962 "resulted in a dramatic stimulus to capital formation," according to Harvard economists Alan J. Auerbach and Dale W. Jorgenson, helping to raise business fixed investment by 40 percent over the following 4 years. High on almost anyone's list of broad-brush tax options for the 1980s are further liberalization of the investment credit and revision of a depreciation system that shortchanges business on the recovery of capital costs because of entrenched inflation. Such measures, along with a few that raise revenues but reduce the tax system's bias against savings and investment, include: liberalizing depreciation, broadening the investment tax credit, cutting the corporate income tax, and finding a new revenue source.

Liberalizing Depreciation. Basing annual capital recovery allowances on the historical cost of an asset instead of its generally much higher replacement cost is hypothetically justifiable as necessary to measure business income accurately. However, raging inflation raises the profile of asset prices so fast that even accelerated depreciation methods fail to offset the distortion.

Several major proposals to correct this problem have been under study by Congress for the past year, and one of them, the Conable-Jones bill, or the 10-5-3 proposal, became a rallying point for business and a prototype for the 1981 bill. Sponsored by Representatives Barber B. Conable Jr. (R-N.Y.) and James R. Jones (D-Okla.), the bill abandons the current practice of depreciating assets in line with their estimated useful lives, as set forth in complicated Treasury Department schedules. Instead, it permits write-off periods of 10 years for factories, 5 years for equipment, and 3 years for autos and light trucks. As proposed by President Reagan, the bill shortens write-off periods for real estate investments to 15 years.

But there was one problem with Conable-Jones that made it difficult to pass in its original form. Treasury's potential revenue loss, not counting "feedbacks" of taxes from increased economic activity, has been estimated at $4 billion in the first year of implementation, $50 billion a year after 5 years, and a peak of $86 billion after 8 years. Yet Congress passed a similar plan in 1981 after 10-5-3 backers signaled that they would accept a less generous version of their proposal as long as it broke the historical cost connection. As Irving S. Shapiro, former chairman of Du Pont, puts it: "Any system that helps recover your capital before it is eaten up by inflation is going to help."

In 1980 Congress was presented with two such plans, either of which was certain to influence legislation in 1981. Al Ullman (D-Ore.), chairman of the House Ways and Means Committee, who was defeated in the 1980 Republican landslide but whose party still retains control of the House, proposed a "simplified cost recovery system" that would place all depreciable property in one of four classifications, with recovery periods of 3, 6, 9, or 12 years. The amount of depreciation allowable in a year would be determined by the unrecovered cost left in such an open-ended account, and the choice of depreciation method (which could be changed each year) would be among the conventional 200 percent of balance, 150 percent, and straight-line rates. The other plan, based on a proposal by Senator Lloyd M. Bentsen, was part of the $39 billion Senate Finance Committee tax-reduction bill. Under the Bentsen plan, most depreciable assets would be placed in one of four open-ended recovery accounts corresponding to depreciation terms of 2, 4, 7, and 10 years. In general, this means that new assets would be depreciated over a period at least 40 percent shorter than under current law. Depending on their use, most structures could be depreciated over 15 or 20 years—far shorter than today but far less generous and costly than under 10-5-3. President Reagan endorsed the Bentsen plan during the 1980 campaign but later switched back to Conable-Jones, which is the basis for the Administration's 1981 proposal—the Accelerated Cost Recovery System (ACRS).

Despite the much faster write-offs permitted by these plans, many business managers would prefer simply to expense capital outlays to beat inflation entirely. Economists Auerbach and Jorgenson suggest a start toward that goal through a first-year capital recovery system. This plan would allow the whole deduction for an asset to be taken in the year it is acquired rather than be spread out over the lifetime of the asset. But since the money recovered almost immediately could be reinvested and earn interest, its "present value" would be greater than the value of the dollars that would normally be recovered over a period of years. To compensate for this windfall, Auerbach and Jorgenson would discount the deduction by the real rate of interest (the interest rate less the inflation rate) expected to prevail over the life of the asset. Thus the discounted present value of $1 invested in a long-lived manufacturing plant might come to 50 cents, while a short-lived pickup truck would be worth 75 cents on the dollar for tax-deduction purposes.

Although this plan is economically elegant, one Treasury Department economist gives it little chance of acceptance. "Imagine trying to convince a businessman that 50 cents today is good deal, even though the dollar he eventually recovers under the current system would be worth less." Furthermore, the choice of an appropriate discount rate would be extraordinarily controversial.

The Auerbach-Jorgenson plan does, however, include features that influenced depreciation plans that finally emerged from Congress. Today's tax code includes an asset depreciation range (ADR) system, which was established in 1971 to simplify the determination of useful lives and salvage values for virtually all types of new and used depreciable property. Under ADR, the Treasury Department assigns all assets to 129 classes—14 based on the type of property and 115 grouped by the activity in which the property is used—with a predetermined depreciation life listed for each class. Taxpayers can choose a depreciation life within 20 percent above or below the assigned figure. Auerbach-Jorgenson would scrap that highly complex system and replace it with about thirty categories—ten for structures and twenty for equipment. It also would virtually eliminate record keeping for past asset purchases through the use of open-ended accounts. These ideas were reflected in the first-year expensing plan offered in 1981 by the Democratic-controlled House Ways and Means Committee as an alternative to President Reagan's ACRS.

Thus the likely path for depreciation reform in the 1980s is toward vast simplification and much faster write-offs. A shorter-term fix for the inflation problem that would cost the Treasury less is to widen the fast write-off bands in the ADR system from 20 percent to 40 percent or so. Another approach favored by some members of Congress is simply to index the depreciation system to correct for inflation year by year.

Broadening the Investment Tax Credit.   The 10 percent investment tax credit (ITC) may be the most potent of the direct, broad-scale tax incentives for capital formation and is now worth close to $20 billion a year to business. While faster depreciation simply shifts the timing of a business's tax liability, the ITC lowers it, acting as a direct subsidy for investment.

Since the ITC's revival in 1970, Congress has raised it from 7 percent to 10 percent, made it permanent and therefore more predictable for business, and widened its applicability. The 1978 extension of the ITC to the rehabilitation of buildings in service for at least 20 years reduced the credit's bias toward equipment. And the 1978 Energy Tax Act created a kind of "super ITC" by granting extra credits of as much as 10 percent to investments that foster oil conservation.

On the macroeconomic front, the clear trend now is toward widening the investment credit's applicability and possibly increasing the basic rate to offset the effects of inflation. Other steps may include a reduction in the useful life an eligible asset must have to qualify for the full 10 percent credit. Since the ITC and rapid depreciation interact powerfully, the Senate Finance Committee bill does not increase the investment credit in general but would raise it to as much as 25 percent for the rehabilitation of industrial and commercial structures.

Cutting the Corporate Income Tax.   The long-term trend is clearly to keep slicing the corporate tax rate or to eliminate eventually the tax entirely. Such action would reduce or end the double taxation of dividends, curb the existing bias in the tax system against equity financing, and cut the effective cost of capital. Of the major tax policy options, this is the most neutral since it would benefit labor-intensive as well as capital-intensive concerns.

Under present law, the 46 percent corporate tax rate is really a surtax which does not kick on until taxable income exceeds $100,000. Up to that level, tax rates range from 17 percent up to 40 percent, which is especially important for small businesses. Under the 1980 Senate Finance Committee bill, the rate schedule would be reduced over a 2-year period to a range of 15 percent to 44 percent, with the top rate applying only to corporate income above $200,000. Under the 1981 House Ways and Means Committee plan, the basic 46 percent rate would be cut to 34 percent by 1987, aiding both large and small corporations.

However, some business executives argue against working on corporate rate cuts right now. Their reasoning during the 1981 debate was that rate reduction, worth about $2 billion a point, would diffuse business lobbying for the liberalization of depreciation, cut into whatever funds may be available for Kemp-Roth or other tax-reduction plans, have less impact on capital formation than depreciation or ITC actions, and dilute the value of corporations' current tax preferences.

Still, some of these arguments can cut two ways. If the U.S. economy requires a big tax cut for stimulative purposes as well as supply-side reasons, corporate rate reduction stands a chance as a way to broaden the appeal of the tax package, since it would spread the benefits to hundreds of thousands of small businesses.

Business leaders such as General Electric's former chairman Reginald Jones favor reducing the corporate income tax by a point or two in the short run whatever happens to the economy in 1981. However, Jones personally endorses the long-term goal of integrating personal and corporate income taxes to eliminate the double taxation of dividends.

Integration is the pet idea of many economists, but even the least expensive methods cost $5 billion to $15 billion in tax revenues. It would almost certainly require corporations to trade in some of their current tax incentives to foot the bill, and this likelihood, plus the probability that small stockholders would demand that management increase dividends and reduce retained earnings, gives many business managers the jitters.

A partial integration scheme may therefore be more palatable. One endorsed a few years ago by the Business Roundtable would allow a company to deduct its dividend payout as an expense, just as it deducts interest payments. This would clearly reduce the advantage of debt over equity financing, but it is not politically viable today because opponents of business could too easily portray it as a straight handout to corporations.

An alternative would be what tax experts call the "grossed-up dividend credit," which would give the tax benefits directly to stockholders rather than to companies. Under this plan, a stockholder would add to gross income both dividends and a prorated share of the tax paid by the corporation on the profit that generated those dividends. After computing taxable earnings, the stockholder would then subtract from the final tax bill a credit equal to the tax paid by the company. The corporate income tax would thus become simply a withholding device, and stockholders would gain a greater net rate of return.

Finding a New Revenue Source.   Any of the pro-capital tax cuts will eventually increase economic activity and thereby help pay for themselves by generating new revenues. But the extent of the feedbacks and the time they take are highly controversial. Their early cost will compound the major demands now facing Washington in the 1980s, such as further increases in the payroll tax to finance a social security system that is heading toward the red in mid-decade.

Former Ways and Means chairman Ullman and his Senate Finance

Committee counterpart, Russell Long (D-La.), who is still a power in Congress, have argued for moving to an entirely new revenue source to solve the financing problems of government in the 1980s, while at the same time shifting some of the burden from capital to consumption. In his tax restructuring bill in 1980, Ullman called for a value-added tax that would impose a 10 percent levy on goods and services other than food, housing, and medical care. By raising $115 billion in its first full year, VAT would permit the replacement of massive portions of the social security and individual income taxes and still cover the cost of large tax cuts for the capital income of business and investors.

Taxes Tailored to Industrial Goals.   Most of these proposals meet the economists' ideal of keeping tax reduction as general as possible and leaving to the marketplace the job of allocating capital. But the growing urgency of the nation's competitive position may also push the United States to an increasing reliance in the 1980s on tax measures targeted at single industries, groups of industries, or activities such as research and development.

"The markets will do anything after a while—if you can wait," says Jerry J. Jasinowski, a former Assistant Commerce Secretary who headed a Carter administration task force on industrial policy. "But there is room for a positive-adjustment approach to speed the market process. One way to go would be to take supply-side tax cuts down a step to a cross-industry level, where the impact is on several industries at a time." However, Jasinowski, who is now chief economist for the National Association of Manufacturers, has doubts about making tax incentives "too specific, too ad hoc."

Targeting Favored Industries.   In the business world, the view is more down to earth. "On strictly economic grounds, most businessmen prefer generalized tax approaches, and we clearly do not want to jeopardize the chances for depreciation liberalization," says John R. Mendenhall, general tax counsel for Union Pacific. "But that is not to say that we wouldn't like to go after other things as well if it were politically feasible. It does bother you a bit when you see super investment credits being given out for investment in energy conservation and production but realize they left out aid for the railroads, which will have to increase their coal-carrying capacity."

Mendenhall notes that the tax code is already loaded with provisions that favor specific industries and even specific companies. The railroads, for example, have been staving off a Treasury attempt in the last few years to end what amounts to a first-year expensing provision for track replacement—the "betterment method of track depreciation."

Thus Mendenhall and other business-oriented tax experts see no philosophical objection to adding new methods of targeting tax help to industry or rationalizing existing methods.

Refundable Tax Credits.　The clear preference of many tax analysts, including Charls Walker, is to widen the use of the investment credit by making it refundable. Under current law, the credit may be of little or no use to companies that may run up a string of years with low profits or outright losses, since the ITC is deducted from tax liabilities that are small relative to investment outlays.

Major losers under this limitation include a variety of companies that would benefit substantially with the right kind of investment stimulus: high-technology companies just starting in business, such as robotics and genetic engineering concerns, and industries that are vital to the economic infrastructure, such as railroads, airlines, and steelmakers that are still viable in the U.S. market. Congress has tried to solve the problem by granting generous carryforward and carryback provisions for the use of the ITC and increasing the amount of liability that may be offset in any year. But these changes still may not induce a company to make an investment if it fears it may not survive long enough to get the tax benefit.

"It is inherently sensible to include these people who are not getting the benefit of the ITC now," says Gerard M. Brannon, former director of Treasury's Office of Tax Analysis. However, Brannon would cut the overall ITC rate to make the wider use affordable. Indeed, cost is a formidable obstacle to general refundability. If it had been in effect in 1980, Treasury's revenue loss just for newly earned tax credits in that year would have come to about $4.5 billion. "With the carryover of unused credits, the bill might be double that," says one government economist.

A Boost for Innovation

The revenue damage could, of course, be limited by making refundability selective, targeting it to priority industries. Small high-technology companies leading the way to innovation and opening new fields of production could benefit heavily from this approach, since it would improve their profit-and-loss reports in periods when they are making their major outlays for research and development. In all, some seventy-five to eighty bills have been introduced in Congress in the past few years to spur industrial innovation, aid small growth companies, and provide new incentives for investment in venture capital enterprises.

In addition to refundability, there are schemes to grant the 10 percent ITC for wages and buildings as well as equipment and to make the credit

20 percent instead of 10 percent. The 20 percent plan, which could be applied to other priority areas, is basically the same as the "super ITC," or extra 10 percent credit granted under the 1978 Energy Tax Act to investments in solar and wind energy property, shale oil equipment, and several other energy assets.

Targeted tax credits can also be used to help industries modernize, if they are granted specifically for the replacement of antiquated plants or as an inducement to industries such as steel to dump excess capacity in some areas. And Reagan advisers, following up on a campaign pledge, have been looking into the use of tax credits or exemptions to encourage industrial development in the inner cities as a way to revitalize and bring jobs to such areas as New York City's South Bronx.

Some of the major innovation-oriented tax measures have been folded into the Senate Finance Committee's 1980 bill and similar proposals were introduced in 1981. They include:

- A 25 percent tax credit on the increase in a company's R&D outlays above the average for the prior 3-year base period. This would cover "all such costs incidental to the development of an experimental or pilot model, a plant process, a product, a formula, an invention or similar property, and the improvement of already existing property of the type mentioned"—as well as the cost of obtaining a patent.

- An increase in the capital gains exclusion from 60 percent to 70 percent, which would cut the top rate for capital gains taxes from 28 percent to 21 percent. Capital gains are especially important to investors in new high-technology companies that normally plow back all earnings into the company and therefore pay no dividends.

- Creation of an "incentive stock option" to treat profits on stock options as capital gains rather than ordinary income. This would make it easier for young high-tech companies to "hire top talent and attract employees with ideas by giving them an ownership stake in the business," says a congressional tax staffer.

- An increase from $150,000 to $250,000 in the earnings a company can retain to meet reasonable business costs without having to pay an "accumulated earnings tax."

None of these targeted approaches really satisfies economists who are interested in the overall efficiency of the U.S. economy and the fairness and neutrality of the tax code. But in one form or another, the United States has tried them all during periods of national emergency. In World War II and the Korean war, the government issued certificates of necessity to specific industries or categories of companies entitling them to specific tax benefits in return for making investments in capacity needed for the war effort. And necessity may once again be the rationale today—both for targeted tax incentives and for broad-based tax revision aimed at encouraging capital formation in general.

Channeling Credit to Business

In order for the United States to pursue policies designed to revitalize its industrial sector and to promote the international competitiveness of American exports, the government will have to play a major role in redirecting flows of capital in the economy. Washington must not only stop the massive drain on national savings caused by huge federal deficits, it must also reexamine and revise policies that allocate vast amounts of credit to politically favored interests, particularly housing and agriculture, at the expense of credit for industry.

Economists generally are loath to have the government intervene further in the allocation of credit within the private sector, noting that U.S. credit markets are the largest and most open in the world and that they generated more than $550 billion in business and consumer lending and corporate equity during 1980. They further contend that the brief experiment with credit controls run by the Federal Reserve Board in the spring of 1980 helped pitch the economy into a sharp downturn and led to record interest rates and a wrenching dislocation of financial markets later in the year.

But there is also widespread agreement that some vehicle, perhaps a revival of the Depression- and World War II-era Reconstruction Finance Corporation (RFC), is needed to channel capital toward ideas and processes that can increase U.S. productivity and competitiveness. "Even among those most enthusiastic about an industry-specific, activist government industrial policy, there is little enthusiasm for overt government credit allocation," says Curtis A Hessler, former Assistant Treasury Secretary for Economic Policy. "But what else can an industrial policy be? Capital is the scarce resource."

At the same time, the country must be on constant guard to avoid making credit allocation a jobs-preservation program, as it was in the Chrysler bailout, where the Band-Aid approach of loan guarantees was taken by Washington in place of a comprehensive recovery program. Furthermore, intervention in the credit markets would make far more sense as a way to promote winners and nourish potential winners rather than to allow losers to limp along.

With or without an RFC, government intervention in the form of loan guarantees or direct loans may be essential in some businesses in which new processes present opportunities to increase productivity. And they may be needed to maintain U.S. superiority in such areas as aerospace and microelectronics, where this nation is now clearly ahead.

All discussions of industrial policy ultimately deal, at least implicitly, with capital flows. Tax breaks for specific industries, for example, can work in the long run only by raising these industries' after-tax rates of return—whether by corporate rate reduction, liberalizing depreciation allowances, or increasing investment tax credits—thereby encouraging the market to direct financial capital their way.

But some advocates of industrial policy argue that a more direct approach is needed to foster the reindustrialization of America. Credit allocation, says Representative Parren J. Mitchell (D-Md.), "is a necessary component. You can't enforce priorities without it."

The government, of course, already is deeply involved in credit allocation. Traditionally, the major reason for federal borrowing has been to finance budget deficits. As a result, the share of total credit claimed by the government has been highly countercyclical, rising during and after recessions, when deficits are largest but private credit demand is usually weak. In recent years, however, the government has got itself much more deeply into lending in good times as well as bad, borrowing funds that it then relends to favored causes via agencies such as the Commodity Credit Corporation and the Government National Mortgage Association or steering them to such causes by guaranteeing repayment, as in the case of Chrysler.

The figures on the growth of the government's credit role are striking. Net new direct government lending, on and off budget, soared from $3 billion in 1970 to $22.7 billion in fiscal 1980. Net lending by government-sponsored enterprises, such as the Federal National Mortgage Association and the Student Loan Marketing Association, was $15.1 billion in 1980, up from $5.2 billion a decade earlier. And federally guaranteed loans—only $8 billion a decade ago—rocketed to $33 billion in 1980 and a scheduled $41 billion for 1981.

Being able to borrow from the government, whether directly or under a guarantee, provides the borrower not only with a sure source of funds but with a preferential interest rate substantially lower than what could be obtained in the market. The Office of Management and Budget estimates the value of these subsidies on direct and indirect loans outstanding at more than $27 billion.

Very little of this largesse has gone to industry. Industrial companies get a dribble of money from the Economic Development, Small Business, and Farmers Home Administrations, and they benefit from Export-Import Bank credits. But the major beneficiaries have been the long-favored housing industry and agriculture. Nor has this massive intervention in capital markets resulted from any conscious credit allocation strategy on the part of Congress or successive administrations. Congress has allowed loan guarantees to burgeon because it is a way of funding pet projects without committing any budget outlays. "We have to get these capital allocations onto the budget," says Representative Barber Conable. "We have to make sure that we aren't stifling discretionary capital."

Indeed, because of the growth of such off-budget activity, David A. Stockman, director of the Office of Management and Budget, argues that the unified budget deficit has become an increasingly poor measure of the federal government's impact on the economy and on financial markets. He would replace the current definition of the deficit with what he calls the "fiscal deficit"—the total of the on-budget red ink plus net lending by the federal government.

Stockman also favors an overhaul of federal lending programs, especially the mechanism by which the Treasury Department's Federal Financing Bank converts ostensibly private loans guaranteed by the government into direct Treasury debt. Although the bank was created by the Nixon administration to bring off-budget lending under control, Stockman and many other experts believe it has made matters worse.

Compared with its major trading partners and industrial competitors, however, the United States does less to allocate capital to industry than any other country except Germany. In Japan, government intervention in the credit market is pervasive, with obviously marked success. France, with its heavily nationalized financial system, has done extremely well in maintaining general economic growth, but years of government-induced flows of capital to the French computer industry have yet to make it an international competitor. And the failure of credit allocation to help solve Britain's severe economic problems proves that more than financial intervention is needed to revitalize a nation's industry.

To many U.S. observers, in fact, the British experience in credit allocation as well as nationalization of industry is a sharp warning. "The problem in the United States is that we do not have the structure to make extensive credit allocation work," says economic consultant Daniel H. Brill, former Assistant Secretary of the Treasury. "We'd end up putting our money into buggy whips and Chryslers." Senator Lloyd Bentsen adds: "The trouble is that we try to bolster our failing industries rather than pay attention to the ones that are growing. The Japanese are able to let companies that are losing market share go out of business and allocate credit to those which are growing."

A New Approach to Government Lending

But this country has had experience with large-scale credit allocation in the past—both for backing winners and salvaging losers. In the major experiment with this approach to industrial policy in the United States, the RFC lent out billions of dollars—and in special cases took equity positions. It reorganized failing companies and banks and later promoted new industries (such as synthetic rubber and aluminum) vital to the war effort. Although it ended in the 1950s mired in scandals, the RFC is regarded by many historians as a success.

With the country facing a clear need to steer capital toward businesses that can increase the nation's competitiveness, the idea of an RFC is once again gaining currency. Its most enthusiastic backer is Felix G. Rohatyn, general partner in Lazard Frères & Co.

Under Rohatyn's plan, the new RFC would be a quasi-private enterprise with an initial capitalization of about $2.5 billion—possibly with part of the equity sold through a public subscription—and with authority to issue $10 billion to $15 billion in loan guarantees. "It would also be allowed to buy common stock," says Rohatyn, "because that's the right way to go. The last thing many failing companies need is more debt." In a related move, corporate holders of a company's debt might be persuaded to convert their bonds to preferred stock, since intercorporate dividend payments are 85 percent tax-free.

A potential problem with the RFC approach is that it could become what a former Carter administration official calls "lemon socialism"; the government might end up rescuing losers, and nothing would be done to promote potential winners. "It's a serious criticism," Rohatyn admits. "But the RFC would not be required to make any given investment, and it would have to be allowed to put companies into bankruptcy if they can't make it or don't live up to conditions of the aid." Rohatyn argues that an independent RFC board would be able to set much tougher conditions on companies—including wage freezes—than Congress and the administration can manage in ad hoc cases.

Some supporters of the RFC approach say it would be better for the government to adopt a coherent policy toward financial bailouts rather than deal with each crisis as it arises. Others maintain that a vehicle of the RFC type is necessary to channel investment to industries that can make it pay off.

If the United States is to reindustrialize, the political system must come to grips with capital allocation. There are signs that it is ready to do so. "There's a lot of latent support for an RFC," says tax expert Charls Walker. Adds Washington economist Gar Alperovitz: "Some form of RFC is vital for a sectoral approach to rebuilding the nation's economic foundations."

Creating a New Trade Priority

The rebuilding of America's industrial base will require drastic changes in the trade policies of the nation. Until now most policy formulation in Washington has focused narrowly on domestic concerns, oblivious to the powerful forces in the world that are now shaping virtually every facet of the American economy and society. Successive administrations, Republican and Democratic, have paid lip service to promoting exports, but what has been lacking—and urgently needed—is an "export consciousness" in both the executive branch and Congress. "We need more groups in the government economic establishment that understand trade, technological development, and industry problems," says Lawrence Franko, professor of corporate-government relationships at the Center for Education in International Management in Geneva.

What this implies, first of all, is an understanding of the crucial importance of the global market for U.S. industrial expansion. To reverse the low priority that Washington has traditionally assigned to exports, policymakers and lawmakers must grasp the fundamental correlation between the nation's strength as a trader in an increasingly interdependent world economy, its domestic prosperity, and the augmented political influence that a competitive economy will enable the United States to exert around the world. Recognizing this, legislators and policy formulators must make a strong commitment to create a framework of laws and regulations that will encourage export industries, and beyond that must supply the direct government support that is indispensable if U.S. producers are to compete on equal terms against foreign rivals that are backed to the hilt by their governments.

No such commitment exists in Washington today, although the emergence of a Senate Export Caucus—a group of senators who are pushing legislation to help U.S. companies sell more abroad— is an encouraging sign. According to the Trade Agreements Act of 1979, all government agencies have been formally required to take into account the impact of major policy decisions on foreign trade. The requirement is honored mainly in the breach. The Justice Department, for example, continues to pursue antitrust policies aimed primarily at maintaining competition among U.S. producers, although the real competition, at home and abroad, is increasingly among U.S. and foreign rivals. And the Office of Management and Budget, abetted by Congress, continues to provide less money for export financing and promotion, relative to the size of the nation's foreign trade, than any other major industrial country.

In its early months, the Reagan administration has made it a major policy goal to get the federal budget under control. But perhaps ironically its chief targets include reductions in the lending authority of such business-oriented organizations as the Export-Import Bank. Clearly, this is shortsighted budget cutting that retards economic growth. Indeed, to provide new leadership on trade, the Reagan Administration will have to reorganize Washington's splintered trade bureaucracy by unifying in a strong Department of International Trade and Investment the functions that are now divided between the U.S. Trade Representative, who negotiates trade agreements and is the President's chief trade policy adviser, and the Secretary of Commerce, who administers trade programs. All other major industrial nations combine these functions in a single, powerful trade ministry that is able to mobilize support from a broad political constituency for exports and spearhead effective overseas sales drives. Congress will have to provide more money, too, for Commerce Department trade promotion programs that have been chronically underfinanced, even though they return many times their cost in the form of more jobs and increased production.

More important, the Export-Import Bank (Ex-Im)—the nation's principal financial weapon in the scramble for global markets—must be allotted far greater resources than the $5 billion in loans and guarantees that it was authorized to extend in 1980. Even though Ex-Im borrows its funds at commercial rates in the financial markets and regularly returns a profit to the Treasury, it is kept under stringent federal budget limitations. As a result, it was able to finance only 7 percent of U.S. exports in 1979; by contrast, 45 percent of Japan's exports, 33 percent of Britain's, and 31 percent of France's had official financial support. Stepped-up Ex-Im lending must be recognized for what it is—not a burden on the taxpayer, but an essential investment in the nation's long-term strength and security. "Frankly, we do not look at the funding of Ex-Im as an expenditure in the same sense as a transfer payment," says Reginald Jones, former chairman of General Electric and of the thirty-six-member Export Council that President Carter appointed in 1978 to recommend ways to boost U.S. sales abroad. Additional lending authority will enable Ex-Im to pursue aggressively its new policy of offering very long-term export credits, for up to 20 years, to counter the subsidized interest rates offered by competitors such as France and Japan.

Export or Die

In the tough global trade rivalry, the United States will also have to adapt other techniques from the array of sophisticated trade-promotion methods that have been developed by Europeans and Japanese schooled in the "export-or-die" tradition. Sales of hundreds of millions of dollars' worth of equipment for entire projects in developing countries, for example, are often influenced by the engineering firms that win the initial design contracts and tend to favor equipment from their own countries in drawing up procurement specifications. France gives its engineering firms an advantage in obtaining such design contracts by paying for preliminary feasibility studies of projects in developing countries as a form of foreign "aid."

For U.S. export expansion efforts to succeed, though, the United States must also ensure that global markets are not shut off by the new wave of creeping protectionism, in the form of proliferating "nontariff barriers," that is threatening world trade. The same thrust for reindustrialization that is occurring in the United States is also under way in Europe and Japan, and the attempt to launch or revamp entire industries is at the heart of the new protectionism. Besides breaking the rules of free trade by indirectly subsidizing and promoting exports, U.S. trade partners may build formal and informal protectionist walls around new industries in an effort to nurture them in a hothouse atmosphere. "The greatest long-term trade threat the United States faces is the possibility that governments will become increasingly involved in funding high-technology industries behind protective trade barriers and eventually squeeze the United States out," says Harvey Bale, Assistant U.S. Trade Representative for investment policy.

To open up the Japanese market for telecommunications equipment— a fast-growing, high-technology sector that Japan has jealously protected up to now—the United States won an agreement from Tokyo in December 1980 to allow foreign companies to bid on $3.5 billion worth of annual purchases by Nippon Telegraph & Telephone (NTT), an official monopoly. But to keep such international trade channels clear and open them even wider, the United States will have to push aggressively for enforcement of a half dozen international codes—designed to ease not only government purchasing discrimination but other nontariff barriers as well— that were agreed to in the "Geneva Round" of multinational trade negotiations.

Ironically, though, some of the biggest obstacles to exports are self-imposed. In recent years, exports have been discouraged by legislation and administrative decisions aimed at achieving a variety of foreign policy objectives: curbing trade with Communist countries and Iran, combatting the Arab boycott of Israel, protecting the environment, prohibiting corrupt practices by U.S. business managers abroad, easing bars to the emigration of Jews from the Soviet Union, and controlling exports of military-related technology. All these objectives are worthwhile, but in many cases the usefulness of trade sanctions in achieving them is limited. And taken together, such restrictions severely handicap U.S. exporters in their struggle for world markets against rivals in other countries for whom business is strictly business.

If this country is to regain its former competitive strength, these unilateral handicaps must be eased. Instead, the United States must find more suitable and cost-effective means, ranging from foreign aid to military power, for exerting its influence in specific situations abroad. "We have very few tools available to us—either positive or negative," says Michael A. Samuels, executive director of Georgetown University's Center for Strategic and International Studies. "Lacking a wide variety of alternatives, trade becomes an obvious target. More and better programs need to be devised."

Ironically, the same legislative branch that passed the laws that shackle U.S. exports is now leading the push for new ways to expand such sales. Congress should lose no time in reviving the Omnibus National Export Policy Act of 1980, a bill introduced in the last Senate session that would go a long way toward removing many of the export disincentives put on

How the U.S. Government Can Improve Its Aid to Exporters

Aids	How they work	How to improve them
Export-Import Bank	Finances machinery, aircraft, other big-ticket exports.	Current $5 billion annual lending must be increased to meet European and Japanese competition.
Domestic International Sales Corporations (DISC)	U.S. companies use 12,000 DISC tax shelters to aid exports.	Coverage should be broadened to benefit more small and medium-sized exporters.
Commerce Department export promotion	Provides market data, know-how, and other support for exporters.	Field staffs and trade development programs should be expanded.
Commerce Department grants for feasibility studies in third world	Studies lead to contracts for U.S. construction firms.	Program should be expanded to match big German and Japanese efforts.
Multilateral trade agreements	Six international codes aim to ease nontariff barriers and curb unfair trade.	The United States must aggressively pursue enforcement of codes.
Proposed export trading companies	Will provide expertise, marketing networks, and financing for small exporters.	Congress should enact pending bills to authorize such companies.

How the U.S. Government Can Reduce Obstacles to Exports

Obstacles	How they impede exports	How to ease them
Income tax disadvantages for Americans abroad	Deter Americans from taking export-related jobs overseas.	Congress should reduce taxes on Americans working abroad.
Strategic controls	Restrict exports with potential military uses to Communist countries.	Obsolete controls should be updated, licensing speeded up, and U.S. criteria aligned with allies'.
Embargoes and other foreign policy curbs on exports	Limit sales to Soviet Union and curb trade with countries such as Cuba and Iran.	Effectiveness should be weighed against market loss and creation of U.S. reputation as unreliable supplier.
Antitrust laws	Deter U.S. companies from cooperating to promote exports and bid on foreign projects.	Rules should be clarified and exemptions broadened.
Foreign Corrupt Practices Act	Imposes jail terms and fines for overseas payoffs by U.S. exporters.	Congress and the Justice Department should clarify uncertainties in the law's applications.
Nuclear export controls	Restrict sales and require guarantees to prevent spread of arms technology.	The United States should press competitors to apply equally strict export controls.
Anti-Arab boycott rules	Require U.S. exporters to forgo contracts that support boycott of Israel.	Commerce Department and Treasury Department should harmonize conflicting enforcement guidelines.
Human rights legislation	Restricts Ex-Im credits to Chile, South Africa, and most Communist countries.	Effectiveness should be balanced against loss of exports.
Environmental restrictions	Ex-Im is required to assess the impact of exports on foreign and global environments.	Assessment procedures should be streamlined to avoid delays in export sales.

the books in recent years. It would also clear the way, by relaxing antitrust rules, for the creation of U.S. trading companies along the lines of the great Japanese trading groups—and thus give thousands of small and medium-size U.S. companies access to the kind of far-flung sales organizations, financial support, and trade know-how that have carried Japanese products around the globe.

10
SETTING OUR
OWN DIRECTIONS

Learning from the Competition

The United States must look to other industrial countries for lessons in how and, more important, how not to revitalize its ecomony. This is a painful reversal of roles after decades in which Americans have become accustomed to thinking of their economy and society as a model for the rest of the world. But by the crucial measures of GNP growth and, equally important, rising GNP per capita, several major industrial nations and a number of smaller ones are doing better than the United States. Obviously, this country cannot simply imitate policies designed for very different societies, but it can and must learn from them.

"Many of our foreign competitors are developing their industrial policies in a much more systematic way" than does the United States, says Jerry J. Jasinowski, Assistant Secretary of Commerce for Policy in the Carter administration and now chief economist for the National Association of Manufacturers. "They have a theory, a vocabulary, and a history of industrial policy." He adds: "We have been slow to link domestic and international economic policies as effectively as the Germans and Japanese do. The U.S. government is quite deeply involved in industrial policy, but it is largely of a defensive nature, involving trade restrictions and succoring weak industries."

The experience of economically successful nations dramatically confirms that industrial prowess is achieved by adopting coherent strategies for channeling resources and labor power into activities with the potential for growth and expansion into world markets. Paradoxically, this can be done either by highly interventionist policies in which the government plays a leading role, as in Japan and France, or by relying primarily on free market forces and the ability of private business managers to find the most productive investment opportunities, as in Germany. By contrast, a sure path to industrial stagnation is to squander limited resources, as Britain and Italy have done, by attempting to underwrite the industrial status quo in a misguided effort to preserve jobs, or by pouring public funds into industrial development schemes that are shaped more by political pressures than by rigorous cost-benefit criteria.

What the pace-setting industrial nations have in common, despite profound differences among them, is broad support throughout their societies for basic national economic goals and for measures of industrial policy to achieve them. Even active U.S. government measures to promote industrial expansion would be likely to prove futile unless the United States also achieves such a broad national consensus among social groups on basic economic priorities.

The primary focus of the consensus that Japan, Germany, and other economic successes have—but Britain and Italy lack—is productivity. Productivity is perceived throughout their societies as the key to jobs, prosperity, and even national security. In Britain, by contrast, "we have never had the sense of urgency about productivity of the Germans or even the French," says Rupert N. Hambro, executive director of Hambros Bank Ltd.

The United States, too, if it is to succeed in reindustrializing, will have to create an understanding throughout its society that productivity is crucial to the achievement of other national goals. Whereas Japanese formerly flocked to this country to learn technology, Americans are now going to Japan to study productivity, notes Hiroshi Watanabe, managing director for research and development at Hitachi. "The problem in the United States is not one of technology but of economics and politics," he says.

Most of all, Americans must learn, from competitors who have long understood it well, the stark imperative for survival as a major industrial nation—the necessity of striving ceaselessly to win and keep shares in a fiercely competitive global market. Although the United States took the lead in promoting an open international trading and financial system after World War II, American industry is now facing, for the first time, the full rigor of this industrial "survival of the fittest." That is why the decision on whether, and how, to provide government help for the U.S. auto industry will be crucial in the nation's effort to reindustrialize. If Detroit, instead of being forced to compete, is given shelter behind barriers against imports of foreign autos, the United States will have taken a major step toward abandoning the world market irrevocably to more aggressive competitors, not only in autos but in other industries as well.

The debate on such issues must be seized as an opportunity to create a greater sense of urgency in the United States about the need to develop a national industrial strategy. Other countries' experience, although not entirely applicable to the United States, suggests policies that have proven effective in dealing with the critical problems that the United States now faces—and warns of policy pitfalls to avoid.

The Japanese MITI

Japan, the world's most successful industrial society, energizes its economy and steers business along fast-growth tracks by means of a pervasive national industrial plan. Its strategy is to identify and promote industries with the best prospects for developing new technologies and exploiting world market opportunities (see the chart on page 144) while shifting workers out of declining industries. The nation defines and works toward these objectives by means of a consensus that is developed through a many-tiered system of consultation that embraces practically the entire society.

A 357-page compilation of data, charts, and analysis, issued in April 1980 by the Ministry of International Trade and Industry (MITI), under the title "Industrial Policy Vision of the 1980s," is studied by Japanese business managers as an authoritative investment guide. By pinpointing industries that MITI considers to have the best growth potential, the report indicates the types of investments that are likely to be eligible for official financial assistance and incentives. "We expect top managers to agree with our views," says Yukiharu Kodama, director of MITI's Industrial Finance Bureau.

Kodama can make that statement with confidence because the report, although it carries MITI's imprimatur, is actually a product of Japan's broad policymaking consensus. The shaping of Japan's industrial strategy for the 1980s thus shows how consensus works to enlist virtually all sectors of Japanese society in a coordinated productive effort. The choice of favored industries was approved by an advisory board called the Industrial Structure Council, composed of more than fifty representatives from government, business, and academia. The document is the outcome of ten to fifteen industrial policy meetings at which consumers, labor unions, and other groups were represented, and of countless smaller sessions between MITI officials and these groups over endless cups of tea. Sessions of the council, according to Kiyohiko Fukushima, an economist at Tokyo's Nomura Research Institute, are like a "big meeting of relatives . . . they all know each other and can readily compromise their interests."

In the broad context of Japanese consensus, one such compromise was the settlement of 1980's spring "labor offensive" with wage increases well below the rise in the consumer price index. Because workers recognized

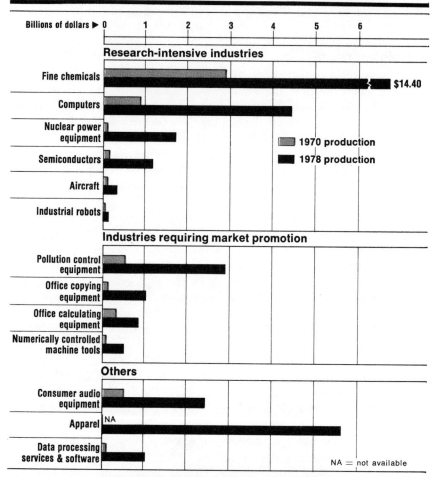

Japan's MITI picked these fast-growth industries as targets for government support in the 1970s...

Billions of dollars ▶ 0   1   2   3   4   5   6

Research-intensive industries

- Fine chemicals — $14.40
- Computers
- Nuclear power equipment
- Semiconductors
- Aircraft
- Industrial robots

1970 production
1978 production

Industries requiring market promotion

- Pollution control equipment
- Office copying equipment
- Office calculating equipment
- Numerically controlled machine tools

Others

- Consumer audio equipment
- Apparel NA
- Data processing services & software

NA = not available

...and it will back a new group to win the technological race of the 1980s

New products	Energy industries	Advanced high-technology industries
Optical fibers	Coal liquefaction	Ultra-high-speed computers
Ceramics	Coal gasification	
Amorphous materials	Nuclear power	Space development
High-efficiency resins	Solar energy	Ocean development
	Deep geothermal generation	Aircraft

Data: MITI

that they would ultimately suffer if their companies were hurt, Fukushima says that "it was easy to persuade the unions to take only small salary increases."

The development of advanced products and new techniques that MITI will promote in the 1980s is a continuation of the emphasis on "knowledge-intensive" industries that began in 1970, although the strategy for the 1970s also called for improvement of products and production methods in such industries as electronic consumer goods and apparel. Before that, MITI had successfully emphasized coal and steel production, from 1950 to 1955, and heavy industry—including shipbuilding, chemicals, and machinery as well as steel—between 1955 and 1970.

Financing for investments in favored industries will be provided by MITI in collaboration with the Ministry of Finance and the government's Japan Development Bank (JDB). In fiscal 1980, ending on March 31, 1981, JDB lent about $4.5 billion. But the government's lending also triggered a large volume of loans by commercial banks that take the JDB's actions as a signal of official support for the borrowers.

In research and development, the collective judgment of industrial managers largely determines how big government subsidies should be spent. "When MITI makes policy, it is not really their policy but is based on the consensus of Japanese industry," says Watanabe. Thus, when MITI began to stress the development of high-powered computers in the late 1960s, its policy was "based on the common understanding in the industry that something had to be done to defend ourselves against IBM," Watanabe says. MITI's final go-ahead was based on alternative super-computer technologies that were proposed by Hitachi, Fujitsu, and other firms and tested in the Ministry's laboratories.

Right now, MITI is wholly or partly funding nine "large projects" by Japanese companies working in teams to develop technologies ranging from steel production and jet engines to automated factories and "alternative" energy sources. A computerized pattern-recognition project ended last year after spending $100 million of MITI money since 1971. Participating companies, organized in an association headed by a Toshiba executive and a manager appointed by MITI, developed basic technology and devices and designed large pattern-recognition systems. The high-technology industries spawned by these R&D investments will create new, well-paid jobs for Japanese workers.

The counterpart to promotion of such vanguard industries—and equally crucial to the Japanese growth strategy—is Japan's policy of deliberately shrinking industries that face bleak long-term prospects because of "structural" changes in the world economy, such as the steep rise in energy costs. Japan's aim is to move workers and other resources out of activities in which labor productivity and the return on investment are low and into more productive and profitable enterprises. Thus, by continually pruning or abandoning laggard sectors, the Japanese also give an added thrust to their most dynamic industries. This approach contrasts sharply with that of the United States, which attempts to keep workers employed in declining industries by means of import curbs to protect makers of steel, textiles, and TV sets, and with European government efforts to prop up steel mills and other ailing industries with subsidies.

Japan's instrument for scaling down and weeding out industrial losers is a law on "structurally depressed industries" which provides for government "adjustment" aid to an entire industry if 50 percent or more of the companies in the industry join in petitioning for it. So far, thirty-nine industries, from shipbuilding to aluminum refining, have been designated for such aid, which enables companies to shut down or convert plants to other products and to trim their payrolls by means such as bonuses to workers for early retirement. In return for such benefits, companies must accept MITI guidance in reshaping their operations.

Japan's system differs in important ways from U.S. government "trade adjustment assistance," most of which is paid directly to laid-off workers, rather than to companies, in industries that are hurt by imports. Decisions by the Labor Department on whether to give the assistance are made on a company-by-company rather than an industrywide basis. Moreover, the intent of the law that authorizes such assistance is essentially defensive: to defuse protectionist pressures from labor unions and communities that oppose liberalization of U.S. trade. By contrast, Japan's adjustment aid, because it has the more fundamental aim of industrial restructuring, is also offered to industries that are in long-term trouble for reasons other than import competition, such as technological change or basic shifts in demand for products. Such an industrywide approach "should be considered as an alternative to U.S. trade adjustment assistance," says C. Michael Aho, an economist in the Labor Department's office of foreign economic research who has studied Japanese programs.

Although many elements of Japan's growth strategy would be difficult to graft onto U.S. society, some Japanese observers think that the cultural barriers to such adaptations have been exaggerated. "Japanese-style management can be done in the United States," says Nomura's Fukushima. "Successful firms like IBM and Texas Instruments don't have trade unions. The key to their success is how their system is suited to obtain their objectives, how they give their workers dignity and pride."

In fact, Sony, Matsushita, Sanyo, and other Japanese companies that have built or taken over plants to make TV sets and other products in the United States have already imported, and successfully applied, key elements of their management style. These include minute attention to details of manufacturing operations, systematic efforts to involve workers and employees in decision making, and the emphasis on quality that has gained the Japanese a worldwide reputation for making high-quality products. In Japan, workers and supervisors regularly form quality control circles (as noted in Chapter 7) to discuss ways of improving the quality of their products. There are an estimated 600,000 quality control circles throughout Japanese industry.

The German System

West Germany, Europe's industrial powerhouse and the world's biggest exporter of manufactured goods, pursues a strategy in sharp contrast with Japan's system of detailed "administrative guidance" to industry. It relies primarily on market forces and on decisions by individual companies to channel investments, labor, and management talent toward activities with the highest potential economic returns. To create a climate of confidence among investors, it applies steady, anti-inflationary "macroeconomic" policies. Germany harmonizes conflicting interests in its society by a system of "codetermination," involving labor participation on corporate boards of directors, and at times in recent years by "concerted action"—three-way consultations between government, business, and labor. The result has been a 5.2 percent average real increase in investment in the past five years, although the German economy started to slow down in 1980.

Bonn's industrial strategy is a corollary of the market-oriented philosophy that Germany has pursued since 1948, when Economics Minister (later Chancellor) Ludwig Erhard launched the country's "economic miracle" by sweeping away postwar controls. One major difference between Germany and the United States, which also relies primarily on the market to shape the pattern of industry, is that Washington has discouraged investment by failing to control the price spiral.

Moreover, German management and labor, unlike their U.S. counterparts, have achieved a tacit consensus to avoid inflationary wage outbursts. Since 1975 unions have settled for pay increases that are only slightly above the inflation rate. The resulting gradual increase in real wages gives German companies an incentive to keep investing in order to raise productivity and maintain their competitiveness in vital export markets. Even Fried. Krupp, in the troubled steel industry, has spent heavily on a complete revamping of production facilities. By contrast, in this country, where real wages have decreased, the amount of capital invested for each worker in industry has declined.

A key to Germany's high investment rate is the country's financial structure—a network of close, stable links between industrial companies and banks that encourages companies to invest with an eye to long-term growth. In the United States, where corporate financing is heavily dependent on public capital markets, managers are forced to emphasize short-term performance instead. As a result, although American corporate planning techniques are better than those of German companies, according to Herbert H. Jacobi, a partner at Frankfurt's BHF-Bank, "German planning decisions are better."

German bankers typically sit on the boards of companies that they regularly lend to and discuss future activities of those companies at a much earlier stage than their American counterparts. One benefit, for Volkswagenwerk, of such long-term relationships was the debt moratorium, never publicly admitted, that the auto maker's banks quietly allowed in 1975, at the depth of the auto industry recession, to enable it to finance new models to replace its aging Beetle.

The counterpart of German corporate managers' close ties with bankers is their regular consultation with labor unions—a major element in Germany's relatively tranquil worker-management relations. The system of codetermination, which puts union representatives on corporate supervisory boards, helps head off confrontations. More important, though, is the postwar shop rules law, which provides for elected worker representatives to serve on behalf of all employees and makes it illegal for them to work against the company's best interests. Managers, for their part, are required to keep workers' councils, roughly equivalent to union locals, constantly informed about company plans. "The essence of the German system," says an observer, "is that there are few surprises."

The French Lesson

France, the fastest-growing major industrial nation after Japan, uses a mix of "indicative" national economic planning to provide business and labor with a broad framework for decision making, and "strategic" planning to funnel resources, as Japan does, into high-technology, fast-growth industries. In indicative planning, the government indicates the thrust of policy and thus provides business executives with a coherent, though not compulsory, framework for relating their investment decisions to government policy. The development of these plans is guided by France's elite government bureaucracy, closely linked with leaders in business and the professions in what Thibaut de Saint Phalle, a former director of the U.S. Export-Import Bank, describes as a "mandarinate."

The systems of indicative plans that the French launched in 1947 are the nearest thing to central planning in the West since World War II. They are a far cry, of course, from the economic "command" system of Communist countries, because the French system relies on incentives and administrative nudging to achieve its objectives. But measured by

The French will channel support to strategic growth sectors

Strategic industry	Objectives	Actions planned
Electronic office equipment	To achieve a 20 to 25 percent world market share and avert an anticipated $2 billion trade deficit in such products by 1985, on present trends	In strategic sectors, the government will negotiate "development contracts" with individual companies, setting specific goals for sales, exports, and jobs. Companies that make such commitments will receive tax incentives, subsidized loans, and other official aid
Consumer electronics	To create a world-scale group including TV-set and tube makers that will each rank among the top three globally; to eliminate the $750 million annual trade deficit in such products	
Energy-saving equipment	To ensure that government grants to companies and households to install such equipment are spent primarily on French products	
Undersea activities	To recapture second place in the world (after the United States)	
Bioindustry	Objectives not yet defined	
Industrial robots	Objectives not yet defined	
	The six strategic industries are expected to add $10 billion in sales and double their work force to 135,000 by 1985	

Data: CODIS

France's real growth rate, which averaged an impressive 3.7 percent in the past 10 years, indicative planning has been successful.

The original purpose of the plans was to provide business managers and other decision makers with a "macromodel" that projects future economic activity as a guide for investments, wage bargaining, and other activities. Macromodeling highlights the possible trade-offs between complex policy goals rather than providing a "general market survey," according to Pierre Masse, a former plan commissioner.

But instead of trying to devise policies for entire sectors, such as steel, autos, or electronics—which may each contain both successful companies and failures—French thinking is now shifting to strategic planning. What this means is that the government will indicate industrial areas that it considers promising and listen to concrete investment proposals for ventures that may merit official support. (See the chart on page 149.)

Reflecting the fierce worldwide competition that French industry now faces, the plan drawn up by the previous government marked a return to the emphasis on building a competitive industrial base that characterized the first four plans from 1947 through 1965. The preceding three plans were more concerned with social policies designed to "share out the growth that resulted from the sizable economic progress made in the earlier plans," says a French official.

The new socialist government of President François Mitterrand promises to continue the planning process, launching an interim two-year plan mainly emphasizing job creation. That will be followed by a more traditional five-year plan for the 1984-88 period that will stress structural economic change, focusing on sectors of the economy that produce goods with high margins of added value. The planning process, as it has evolved in France, is based on a set of broad aims or "options" drawn up by the National Planning Commission, an agency with 250 employees that reports to the Prime Minister. The options are discussed by the Economic and Social Council, made up of representatives of business, labor, and other groups, and by a series of committees. The completed plan is submitted to Parliament and enacted into law, but the only binding obligations are on the government.

The political difficulties in indicative planning, however—in France and in the United States, if such an approach were tried in this country—were reflected in the previous government's decision not to include in the plan any formal targets for economic growth, inflation, or investment. A major reason is that such targets imply trade-offs among the interests of business, labor, and other groups that participants in the planning process are reluctant to face.

Nevertheless, the planning process itself is important in France because the French social consensus is still fragile, with labor-management relations that are embittered by antagonisms between politically motivated union leaders and backward-looking managers. Discussions of the plan provide one context in which business executives and labor leaders work closely together.

The British Austerity

Britain has failed to halt a long slide from being one of Europe's richest countries to being one of its poorest, despite nearly two decades of government-directed efforts to reshape the economy through a network of government-business-labor councils—and despite $130 billion of government grants, subsidies, and equity investments aimed at propping up a variety of industries. Now the industrial planning and promotion mechanisms created in Britain over the past two decades by both Conservative and Labor governments are being drastically cut back by Prime Minister Margaret Thatcher, a firm believer in the free market. Instead, she intends to rely basically on macroeconomic policies, including government spending restraints, monetary measures to reduce inflation, and a shift in taxes from income to consumption in order to stimulate investment.

Thus she is curbing the National Economic Development Council (NEDC) and the National Enterprise Board (NEB), both designed to operate on the strategic planning principle of picking industrial "winners" and channeling government support to them. Both had some success in this role, although not nearly enough to offset the debilitating effects on industry of fundamental British ills, ranging from the disastrous "stop-go" economic policies of previous governments to the near warfare between trade unions and employers.

The NEDC, set up in 1961, served at its peak as the umbrella for working parties, made up of representatives of the government, the Trades Union Congress, and the Confederation of British Industry, for each of thirty-eight industrial sectors. Their purpose was to identify viable investment prospects and recommend government support for them.

The NEB, set up in 1975, is specifically aimed at guaranteeing and financing investments, including share purchases, in internationally competitive, export-oriented industries. In fiscal 1980-81, NEB got only about $150 million for new investments and concentrated mostly on high-technology ventures in microelectronics, computer software, and office equipment.

Thatcher also is slashing the huge bailouts by previous Conservative and Labor governments of industrial "losers," ranging from the Clydebank shipyards to the British Steel Corporation. And she is slashing heavy "regional development" grants for financing of industries and infrastructure in depressed areas of Scotland, Wales, and northern England.

In Italy, aid to state-run companies has become a prop to inefficient money losers

Government holding company	Activities	Number of employees	1978 sales	1978 losses	Debt at yearend 1978
			—Billions of dollars—		
Istituto per la Ricostruzione Industriale (IRI)	Controls 559 banks, steel mills, airlines, electronics manufacturers, auto maker Alfa Romeo, and other companies	545,000	$18.8	$1.4	$24.8
Ente Nazionale Idrocarburi (ENI)	Controls 229 companies engaged in oil production, refining, engineering, fiber manufacturing, and other activities	120,000	15.9	0.2	9.0
Ente Partecipazioni e Finanziamento Industria Manifatturiera (EFIM)	Controls 41 companies engaged in mining, metallurgy, food processing, and other activities	31,000	2.7	0.1	1.7

Data: Ministry of State Participations

The Italian Losers

In Italy, government aid to industries has served mainly to bail out inefficient, money-losing companies and thus to avoid structural changes in Italian industry that are urgently needed. Italy's industrial strategy, based on a trio of state-controlled holding companies that funnel investment into industry (see the chart on this page), worked fairly well until 1973 in building up steel, shipbuilding, chemicals, and other heavy industries. Guido Carli, former governor of the Bank of Italy and now president of L'Union des Industries de la Communaute Europeene, a Western European manufacturers' association, argues that such an approach was an effective means of developing key sectors of the economy that private companies alone could not finance. But since the oil crisis plunged many Italian companies into heavy deficit, the holding companies have become channels for massive government bailouts of money-losing ventures and for political pork-barreling.

Spreading unemployment also shifted the main emphasis of Italy's state capitalism from strengthening key industrial sectors to creating jobs, especially in poor southern regions, and maintaining employment in other areas. But lush government financing and tax breaks for investors, together with a ruling that 80 percent of new outlays by state-run companies must go into the southern regions, backfired. "With all that money being offered, companies built capital-intensive, not labor-intensive, industries," says economist Luigi Spaventa, an independent leftist member of Parliament. Thus the southern regions are studded with giant petrochemical plants of ailing Montedison, ANIC (controlled by Ente Nazionale Idrocarburi, the government oil company), and the now-bankrupt Liquichimica and Societa Italiana Resine.

The expanding government role in industry also created other problems, including a pattern of careless lending by financial institutions to dubious ventures. "Any financing for an investment in the South had pretty much a government guarantee, and so the lending institutions did not do their homework," says Bruno Brovedani, chief economist of the Banca Nazionale del Lavoro. Moreover, business managers, as well as labor unions, lobby the government to take over failing companies.

Economist Romano Prodi, a former Minister of Industry, says American colleagues assure him that the United States could avoid the kind of political interference that has undermined Italy's industrial strategy. But his answer, he says, is always, "I have my doubts."

Pushing Some Industries and Pruning Others

In the ideal world of David Ricardo, who more than 150 years ago formulated the well-known Law of Comparative Advantage, there was no need for an industrial policy. Free trade ensured that all nations concentrated on what they were best at producing. But in the less than ideal world of the 1980s, the unfettered market has become obsolete. The industrial plans of other nations, enforced by a growing web of subsidies, tax incentives, and other arrangements, indicate that international competition is becoming increasingly influenced by government policy. And the United States has no real option but to develop its own industrial policy to avoid falling behind. The U.S. response so far—protectionism with apologies—has mainly been a way to avoid the serious issues.

To a great extent, industrial policy overseas is becoming a contest among countries in which each government attempts to pick the winners from potential export-oriented industries and push their development as hard as possible. Thus the lists of target industries that come out of government offices in Paris and Tokyo are solidly packed with high-technology enterprises. The United States, of course, must do the same. It is still the world's technological leader and should push that advantage.

But there are dangers in relying too much on sophisticated technology.

Indeed, one reason for the declining competitiveness of U.S. industry is an overconcentration on the state of the art and a failure to pursue the mundane improvements of industrial processes that increase productivity, improve quality, and lower costs. Then, too, the United States, unlike its major competitors, has a rapidly growing labor force, much of it unskilled, and U.S. wages will be declining relative to those abroad. The economy will therefore have the resources to staff mass-production industries, such as autos and textiles, that the other advanced countries will begin to de-emphasize because of incipient labor shortages and rising wages. But the United States will have to make these industries much more efficient, since it will be coming into increasing competition with the newly industrializing countries of Asia and Latin America, where labor costs will be much lower.

Since economic resources are limited, it is virtually impossible, in the context of an industrial policy, to push all industries. It becomes critical, therefore, to develop criteria—either objective or subjective—for choosing which industries to foster and which to prune. Beatrice N. Vaccara and Patrick MacAuley of the Bureau of Industrial Economics, in their study *Evaluating the Economic Performance of U.S. Manufacturing Industries,* correctly point out that U.S. competitors who need to pay for imports of food, fuel, and raw materials have used one overriding criterion—export performance—in determining which industries to encourage.

But in evaluating and deciding which U.S. industries to encourage, Vaccara and MacAuley say we need to consider the multiplicity of the nation's overall goals. These include achieving full employment, increasing productivity, promoting exports, providing for national defense, and achieving more balance in regional and economic growth.

Obviously, it is no simple task to incorporate all these factors and produce one overall measure for evaluating which industry will produce more bang for the buck and should therefore take priority over others. Vaccara and MacAuley evaluated the performance of twenty-two manufacturing industries, using just six measures which reflect output growth, price trends, returns to factors of production, and foreign competition. Coming out on top was the chemical industry, followed by tobacco, technical instruments, motor vehicles, and nonelectric and electric machinery. Poor performances were turned in by leather, steel, furniture, and apparel. Here is how some of the nation's bedrock industries fit within a much wider framework of national goals.

Aerospace

The federal government is already supporting the industry through U.S. military spending. The big U.S. lead continues, but the attempt of Europeans and Japanese to foster civilian aircraft production will doubtless mean a further erosion of the U.S. share of the market. To meet increased foreign competition in this fast-growing world market, the United States should consider an exemption from antitrust laws to allow U.S. plane manufacturers to collaborate on new design projects, since the costs and risks are enormous. This might mean that Boeing, which signed up with Italian and Japanese partners for its new 767 airliner, might develop a plane with Lockheed or McDonnell Douglas. The arrangement would have the further advantage of slowing the international transfer of technology, a process that in the aircraft field is disadvantageous to the United States.

Computers

Computers also represent a fast-growing high-technology market. The United States has a commanding lead, and its position appears to be unassailable for the foreseeable future. Computers, however, are a high-priority target for a Japanese export drive that has been disturbingly successful in its initial stages. The United States should therefore provide adequate financing for its exports, particularly to developing countries, which are expected to be an increasingly important market. Domestically, there is no problem of access to capital for large computer companies, but small concerns, in which many of the important innovations are made, probably need additional support. The personal computer sector should be particularly encouraged for its export potential.

The United States should also allow companies to do joint research in order to maintain its current lead in semiconductor technology. The key to future markets, however, may not be so much the development of new devices as the development of new products and processes from the current crop of discoveries.

Petrochemicals and Plastics

These are high-technology industries whose exports may actually have to be somewhat discouraged, despite past successes. To the extent that the U.S. comparative advantage has resulted from superior research and development, it is on firm ground, but at least part of the U.S. edge has been based on access to subsidized domestic oil and gas. The resulting subsidy of petrochemical exports has the effect of increasing U.S. oil imports. Since oil imports have both an economic and a political cost, it seems to make little sense to concentrate on energy-intensive exports. On the other hand, one of the government's highest priorities in industrial policy should be the development of a coal-based chemical industry in which the United States would have a permanent comparative advantage because of the nation's huge reserves of that energy source.

Energy

Of course, the government must subsidize the development of alternative energy sources. But it is also important to foster the development of the oil-field equipment industry. It is already a major exporter, shipping more than half its output abroad. Its prospects will be enhanced by intensive exploration efforts that are expected to get under way in many developing countries.

Energy conservation is both an urgent national need and a possible basis for a new set of export-oriented industries. Research and development efforts to improve the efficiency of power production and transmission—efforts such as superconducting generators, fuel cells, and amorphous materials for transformers—have huge potential payoffs and deserve strong public support. When such developments reach a commercial stage, a case could be made for some sort of subsidy arrangement that would speed up the process of replacing equipment.

Machinery

Here is an industry with unused potential. It is still a very strong international competitor, but some sectors are rapidly losing ground. In Germany, a big competitor of the United States, the government pays 25 percent of the industry's research bill. A case can be made, for example, that the farm-machinery industry has become overspecialized and that by concentrating on the production of the huge and expensive machines that are appropriate only for U.S.-style farming, it is opting out of foreign markets. Nobel laureate Lawrence Klein of the University of Pennsylvania points to the possibility of U.S. production of small tractors more suitable to the needs of developing countries. Although the farm-equipment manufacturers will probably have little interest in this, the existence of a "guaranteed market"—the strategy Klein favors for fostering new industries—might produce some new entrants. A guaranteed market may take the form of a government commitment to purchase part of a company's output.

Machine Tools

The industry's problem is the reluctance or inability of its companies to build sufficient capacity, and it may need government assistance to gain access to capital for expansion. Faster depreciation and more supportive export policies would help, and the fragmented industry might also benefit from further consolidation. The industry's rapid growth and technological development are important not just for their own sake but because the industry could become a major bottleneck for the whole process of reindustrialization. The next few years will be critical, since the 1981 economic slowdown will only temporarily ease the pressure on the industry's overtaxed capacity.

Coupled with the shortage of capacity in machine tools is a shortage of skilled labor. The cyclical and fragmented nature of the industry probably discourages the in-house training of workers, since individual companies are less likely to earn an adequate return on their "human capital" investments. Public support, in the form of training grants and similar mechanisms, could be of some help in increasing the future supply of labor.

Automobiles

The industry's urgent campaign to remake itself in a style consistent with an age influenced by OPEC should not be allowed to slacken. Although the next few years are bound to be difficult, the industry's long-term prospects are actually rather good. Its Japanese and European competitors no longer have a labor-cost advantage, and the problem of product design can easily be solved in time. Indeed, there is even a chance that the United States can once again become an auto exporter. The big U.S. car had no chance in a world where roads were narrow and gasoline was increasingly expensive, but the smaller cars that are now on the road and those on the drawing boards have no such problems.

Steel

Here lies one of the most difficult problems of industrial policy. Many of steel's problems are of its own making, but it is difficult for an industry to compete head-on against heavily subsidized foreign producers. There is also a need to maintain a healthy domestic steel industry for national security, although its role as a direct supplier to defense industries appears small. Lawrence Klein points out: "We found ourselves with our pants down because we were energy-dependent; we better not find ourselves steel-dependent."

This does not mean, however, that Washington should embrace the industry's protectionist program, which would lead to further inefficiencies and a considerably higher price for U.S. steel users. This would actually inhibit the solution of steel's longer-term problem, which is its aged and outmoded capital plant. A rational steel program calls for shrinking the industry somewhat through policies that encourage the elimination of the least efficient mills. This is what the Europeans are doing, and it will make them strong competitors even without public subsidies.

Apparel

This is another target for selective shrinkage. For the United States to produce, as it does, 90 percent of its apparel is an economic absurdity sustained only by the strongest of protectionist measures. This is not to say that the apparel industry has no place in the U.S. economy. Such labor-intensive pursuits make more sense in the United States, with its large and growing supply of unskilled workers, than in Europe and Japan, where labor shortages are in the cards.

But the attempt to compete head-on with the newly industrializing nations is ultimately self-defeating; rather than protectionism, what economists call "positive adjustment" is needed. The industry should be encouraged to consolidate, to upgrade its technology, and to specialize in high-quality products. And although hiring will be reduced, apparel makers should be given financial aid to automate as much as possible when the microprocessor revolution finally arrives.

Industrial Textiles

This industry gives evidence that the positive adjustment that is needed in apparel is, in fact, possible. In the last decade, industrial textiles have not only held their own in the domestic market but have been successfully exported. In 1979 more than $3 billion worth of textile products was shipped abroad, a 46 percent increase that was accomplished in part because of the devaluation of the dollar. Capital expenditure amounted to $1.5 billion, nearly three times that of the apparel industry, which had about the same value of total shipments.

Looking to the Future

It will not be easy, of course, to modernize a shrinking or declining industry. Not only do profits tend to be low, making it difficult to attract additional capital, but young aggressive management talent tends to go elsewhere. Thus one of the key requirements for a new industrial policy is to develop a long-run strategy for older industries to take the place of the current ad hoc approach. This will necessitate a policy framework in which government itself is able to undertake commitments that investors can depend on.

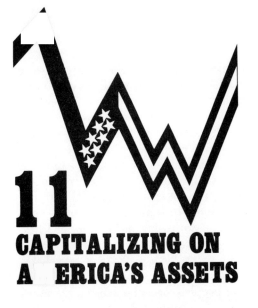

11
CAPITALIZING ON
A ERICA'S ASSETS

If the United States can forge a new social consensus centered on growth, increased competitiveness in both domestic and world markets is an achievable goal. This country possesses many rich resources—in technology, energy reserves, and labor power—that can be better exploited to bolster trade. Its multinational corporations are still the most dynamic element in the world economy. With the proper government policies and business initiatives, many industries and products have enormous potential for growth.

Preserving the Lead in Technology

To the extent that America's vaunted industrial machine may be running at half speed, it is not primarily for want of technological oil. Other industrial nations are closing the gap and in certain areas even surpassing the United States in innovation, applying new technologies to develop new products. But this does not mean that American ingenuity and inventiveness have been crippled in the process. Many foreign innovations continue to be built on technological breakthroughs made in this country, on concepts that American companies have, for various reasons, failed to exploit.

Remove some economic and political impediments to make the U.S. business environment more comparable with that in Japan or Germany and get U.S. companies to take more risks, and American technology can contribute to a rapid revitalization of manufacturing. Such a change would also help the United States maintain its lead in today's high-technology areas as well as give America a leg up in such emerging technologies as bioengineering.

However, any government policy aimed at reindustrialization must be grounded on a clear appreciation of what modern technology is about and its implications for growth and productivity.

Numerous studies have documented that the United States has been in the throes of historic transition for the past two decades. The old industrial society that generated wealth in the form of capital goods and manufactured products is giving way to a different society valued more in terms of intangible assets, such as knowledge and information processing. And the new information-based society cannot easily be gauged with the economic yardstick formulated for the old. For example, Vincent E. Giuliano, senior consultant on information processing at Arthur D. Little (ADL), points to the data processing and aerospace industries. "What those industries are really selling," he notes, "is a package of knowledge in hardware form." In such industries, he adds, "human capital—the investment in skills and knowledge of people—becomes ever more important, but the [economic] measures we use simply ignore the vast current rate of investment in human resources."

A workable strategy for reindustrialization must therefore recognize two things: first, that the country's economic health is increasingly determined by "invisible" investments in human capital, and second, that high technology is a key element to increasing productivity and spurring economic growth. The National Science Foundation, in a 1977 study, estimated that technological innovation was responsible for 45 percent of the nation's economic growth from 1929 to 1969. When NSF compared low- and high-technology industries, it found a big edge for high technology: twice the productivity growth rate, triple the real growth rate, one-sixth the price increases, and nine times more growth in employment.

New technology will be even more crucial in the years ahead. By 1990, for example, experts at Texas Instruments forecast that electronics will become the world's fourth largest industry.

A Revolution in Microelectronics

Barring some spectacular breakthrough, the most significant driving force in high technology for the balance of this decade will be the continuation of two current trends in electronics. First is the steep decline in the price of computing power. Second, and linked to the first, is the growth of microelectronics, especially the microprocessor. Together, these two trends will profoundly affect every aspect of daily life—and virtually every commercial and consumer product that runs on electricity. Indeed, computers and microprocessor chips soon will be ubiquitous so that any electrical product without one or the other will have about as much sales appeal as an antiquated "cat's whisker" crystal radio.

Microelectronics is the world's fastest-growing industry. And because of the continual development of new semiconductor components that are more powerful and cheaper, the trend toward digital solid-state products is certain to gather momentum. The companies that turn out chips seem almost contemptuous of the gears, cams, limit switches, and other mechanical doodads that are the guts of preelectronic products. Electronic engineers are reducing more and more mechanical functions to digital circuits set on a cornflake-size silicon chip. Once that has been done for a given type of product, chances are good that the mechanical predecessor will be at a serious cost and performance disadvantage, as many former makers of mechanical adding machines and watches can testify.

Using the latest chips, a small company can develop a superior product that can cut into the business of a corporate giant. Likewise, the products of any company—or country—without microelectronics expertise become increasingly vulnerable as each new generation of chips comes along. The computing power of chips continues to double every 2 to 3 years so that it becomes possible to build solid-state versions of products whose complexity had defied digitization just a short time earlier. Given the rapid progress in packing more and more intelligence onto smaller and cheaper chips, the act of remaining competitive will require that the electronics content of the products be continually updated. In addition, the increasing capabilities of microprocessors will mean that more and more know-how and functionalism will reside in the chip. Thus it will become easier for a company to jump into a market by simply buying the proper semiconductors or copying a competitor's electronics hardware. The company or country that makes the best chips thus sets the technological pace for a host of user industries. That realization is behind the urgent drive in Japan and Europe to develop indigenous semiconductor industries that can challenge the U.S. lead in microelectronics.

This process of continual innovation places a premium on research—and on being the first to market. After a year or perhaps two, imitators and "second sources" enter the market, and prices and margins drop rapidly.

Thanks to computerization in two other activities, computer-aided design (CAD) and computer-aided manufacturing (CAM), it will be progressively less expensive for companies to practice ongoing innovation. "CAD-CAM will begin an industrial revolution of its own," says Guy L. Fougere, a vice president at ADL. A company that uses an integrated CAD-CAM system not only can turn out new product designs much faster, it also can program the computer to make sure that the designs provide quality and reliability as well as the lowest possible manufacturing costs. And the digital output from the CAD computer can simply be plugged into the CAM system to reprogram that plant's manufacturing computers. "If you are not pretty well steeped in CAD-CAM, in 10 years you have a pretty good chance of being nonexistent," asserts Walter L. Abel, vice president of research and development at Emhart.

All signs thus point to a churning acceleration in product life cycles, paced by developments in microelectronics. The implications are staggering. Except for commodity-type items, many mature industries will be forced to march to a faster drummer. "We are talking about a product cycle that is 3 to 4 years, not the 10 to 12 we were getting a decade ago," notes J. Roy Henry, executive vice president of Burroughs. "And it could narrow further."

Under such conditions, an incremental improvement in a product will give a manufacturer an edge for no more than a couple of years before another manufacturer makes a one-up change. Any country that does not have thriving semiconductor and computer industries will be at a severe disadvantage. The Japanese, in particular, are determined not to allow that to happen.

The Robots Are Coming

One outgrowth of the microelectronic revolution has been the development of industrial robots. Despite the prospects for increased productivity and improved job performance, however, U.S. corporations have been slow to install robots in their plants. It has been the Japanese, rather, who have embraced that technology in order to improve productivity and cut costs in manufacturing industries. Even the most conservative estimates put half the world's robots in Japanese factories, and the Japanese intend to keep this lead for as long as possible.

U.S. companies are finally beginning to recognize the gravity of Japan's challenge. "There is a growing perception that increasing productivity is a do-or-die issue," comments Philippe Villers, president of Automatix, one of the newest U.S. robot makers.

During the past two decades only about 3500 industrial robots were installed in the United States. But in 1979 the pace quickened dramatically, and some suppliers were unable to promise delivery for 6 to 12 months. Shipments in 1980 alone about equaled half of all previous robot sales in the country. Several of the largest U.S. corporations are making major commitments to the use of industrial robots. General Electric, in perhaps the most ambitious undertaking, is about to launch a sweeping automation program that some experts say could eventually replace nearly half its 37,000 assembly workers with robots. GE already figures that it can eliminate 2000 blue-collar positions in relatively short order.

New robot technology is being introduced at a rapid clip. The latest computer-controlled robots are considerably more versatile than their simple-minded predecessors of just 2 years ago. And a new generation of robots that "see" and "feel" and even "think" is emerging from the laboratories. "We are at the bottom of a market explosion," asserts Brian R. Ford, manager of robot systems at ASEA Inc., the White Plains (N.Y.) arm of Sweden's ASEA. "The growth of this market," he adds, is starting to resemble "what happened in transistors and pocket calculators." Despite the fact that ASEA makes some of the most expensive robotic equipment—prices typically run higher than $100,000—the company sold out its entire 1980 production capacity by March of that year.

At West Germany's Keller & Knappich, sales director Joachim Nodlbichler says that demand for his company's robots "is growing by leaps and bounds." Revenues of Italy's robot makers will jump fivefold over the next 2 years, predicts Pietro Varvello, an economist at the Italian Federation of Scientific and Technical Associations. And the Japan Industrial Robot Association (JIRA) reports that the production value of its members' robots in 1979 climbed 37 percent to $148 million, and in 1980 production value more than doubled. By 1985 JIRA figures that Japanese robot makers will produce equipment worth $1.3 billion. Japan's manufacturing is among the world's most highly automated. To encourage even wider use of robots, Japan's Ministry of International Trade and Industry in April unveiled a government-supported program to lease robots to small- and medium-size companies that cannot afford to buy such equipment.

In the United States, the automotive and die-casting industries historically have been the biggest boosters of robots. The 150 units installed at General Motors' Lordstown (Ohio) plant have made millions of spot welds since the facility opened in 1966. Chrysler is now installing 116 spot-welding robots—the biggest single order by a U.S. company—for its new K-body compact cars. But Detroit's current downturn has curbed most of its robot purchases, in contrast to Volvo's recent $8 million purchase of 100 robots from Cincinnati Milacron and a 500- to 750-unit order reportedly in the offing from Japan's Toyota Motor Company. GM says, however, that it expects to double its robot population to 470 units by 1983. And the company will soon start up a vision-equipped unit for painting cars that can recognize thirty different body styles and adjust its spray painting accordingly.

Japanese competition seems to be a primary reason why so many U.S. companies are now switching to robots. Robert E. Fowler, a GE vice president and general manager of its Major Appliance Manufacturing Division, worries that the Japanese seem to be enlarging their lead in robotization.

To remain competitive, GE figures that it must improve its productivity by a 6 percent annual rate—in all its businesses, not just appliances. The strategic plan for achieving this goal calls for the wholesale installation of robots wherever possible over the next 5 years.

Not to be outclassed by GE, its rival, Westinghouse, has recently set up a Robotics Division to implement a decision by its Management Council, composed of representatives from all five Westinghouse companies, which has decreed that improved productivity is the company's primary objective. Anthony A. Massaro, director of the new division, says that he has a multimillion-dollar mandate to apply robots in "any and all manufacturing areas—anything that will make the factory of the future more productive."

In the meantime, U.S. robot manufacturers are bracing for a new wave of competition. Several Japanese companies in recent months have been quietly establishing beachheads in the United States to get in position to grab a major share of a United States market for industrial robots. Sales are expected to grow 35 percent annually during this decade and hit $2 billion in 1990.

For U.S. robot makers, keenly aware of the carnage wrought by Japanese competition in autos and machine tools, the lesson is clear. "The longer we delay a response, the tougher it is going to be," says a worried Michael Radeke, manager of Cincinnati Milacron's Industrial Robot Division. But responding to the Japanese threat will be difficult. While U.S. manufacturers are essentially small- to medium-size companies straining to keep up with growing domestic demand, many of their new competitors from Japan are corporate giants, able to invest the huge sums of money necessary for developing new products and large-volume production. Japan's 135 robot builders already turn out as many units annually as the rest of the world combined.

But granting the Japanese successes, there are questions even in Japan as to whether that country can ever displace the United States as the world's pacesetter in technology. "For years, we set our targets by following the United States," says Hiroshi Watanabe, executive managing director for research and development at Hitachi. "But lately we've come close to America, if not up to her level. That means we must now become a creative leader by ourselves." But that is proving difficult, he concedes, and many Japanese frankly worry whether their culture's groupthink mentality is conducive to breaking new ground.

That may explain why U.S. semiconductor companies are almost universally confident of maintaining their lead. J. Fred Bucy, president of Texas Instruments, maintains that semiconductors are not going to go the way of cars, steel, and consumer electronics. "There is a big difference in awareness today of the capabilities of the Japanese," he points out, "unlike the attitude that existed here 15 to 20 years ago, [when] U.S.

industry was caught napping." Yet U.S. auto executives only a decade ago were equally sure about their industry.

England, France, Germany, and other Western European nations are anxious to build their own semiconductor industries, too, if only for reasons of national pride. So far, though inroads are being made, none of these countries shows signs of overtaking the United States. Germany, for example, has problems much deeper than Japan's when it comes to electronics, although in other areas it is a world-class leader. "German exports consist of three pillars—autos, chemicals, and machine tools," notes Hermann Schunck, a director at the federal Ministry for Research and Technology. "We can't afford to let one of those pillars crumble." The Germans have thus concentrated on fine-tuning their technology in these areas. But in recent years they have begun to approach the point of diminishing returns in their penchant for reengineering—at the same time that mechanical processes everywhere are giving way to electronics. The German government has poured millions into the development of microprocessors, but the companies it supports have been unable to close the gap with the United States.

"Basic innovation is lacking," admits Klaus Luft, vice chairman of Nexdorf Computer. The Ministry for Research and Technology is now considering proposals to rectify the lag, because some officials there believe that Germany's machine-tool exports will face a crisis by 1985 if Germany does not keep pace with developments in microelectronics.

American machine-tool builders are also looking over their shoulders. Imports now account for more than twice as big a slice of the domestic market as in 1973. "The gap has been closing in technology," says James A. D. Geier, president of Cincinnati Milacron, in part because "it's always easier for the number two person to catch up." Some experts say that the technology for improving the competitive position of such industries as appliances, aircraft, steel, and even textiles and shoes is not lacking. The know-how that is needed exists. However, U.S. companies cannot raise the capital necessary to put the technology to work. Says Robert M. Dunn Jr., an economics professor at George Washington University: "Investment in plant and equipment that increases capital stock is critically tied to technological advance. Very few new inventions or productive improvements can be used with old machinery."

Harold T. Barraclough, program manager for advance development at SRI International, agrees that "high technology by itself can't save low-technology industries. If U.S. Steel has no profits," he explains, "it cannot afford a new process to improve productivity."

If capital is essential to applying technologies that already exist, it is even more crucial to nurture the emerging technologies that will form the new innovations and industrial foundation of the 1990s and beyond. Of particular importance to the future are new sources of energy, bioengineering, and "supermaterials." Most work in these fields is still concentrated in research laboratories, and funding has not been a major problem, although federal funds are being pruned somewhat.

For instance, while Atlantic Richfield (ARCO) may be tight-fisted in spending for most of its businesses, when it comes to photovoltaics—electricity from the sun—the company maintains an open checkbook. Photovoltaics, explains Robert O. Anderson, chairman of ARCO, "comes as close to being a Daddy Warbucks solution (to the energy crisis) as anything you can find." ARCO will not divulge its budget or investment to date in solar energy—insiders say privately that total spending over the next 5 years will be more than $200 million—but one recent example of its largesse occurred in 1980, when ARCO signed a $25 million licensing agreement with Energy Conversion Devices (ECD).

ECD is the company founded by controversial inventor Stanford R. Ovshinsky, who believes that more efficient photovoltaic cells can be made from amorphous silicon, a material that is much cheaper to produce than the silicon crystals now used for semiconductors. ARCO hopes that such a development will reduce the price of solar cells, now running about $7 per watt, to 70 cents a watt set by the Energy Department as a target for the mid-1980s.

And if the cost is cut further with volume production, the sun could furnish a good portion of our energy needs by 2000. Researchers at Argonne National Laboratory, Brookhaven National Laboratory, and a couple of university labs even foresee the development of artificial silicon leaves that could be more efficient at utilizing the energy of sunlight than natural plants.

A 1979 study by the Harvard Business School's energy project notes that solar energy—defined as including all sun-dependent sources, from wind to wood burned in stoves—could account for 20 percent of turn-of-the-century supply. And with innovations in such areas as orbiting solar-power satellites and ocean-temperature energy conversion (OTEC), Peter E. Glaser, an ADL vice president and solar-energy expert, predicts that solar energy's contributions 50 years hence could amount to 80 percent of U.S. electricity and 50 percent of nonelectrical energy.

Proponents of other emerging sources of energy are equally enthusiastic. Melvin B. Gottlieb, director of Princeton University's Plasma Physics Laboratory, believes that in the twenty-first century "the majority of our power could be generated through fusion." The process liberates more energy than present nuclear fission techniques and does not create long-term radioactive pollution.

Magnetohydrodynamics (MHD) is another source of future energy that should reach the demonstration-plant stage in the 1990s. Meanwhile, MHD research may pay off later this decade in improved methods of burning coal. Bett Zauderer, a manager of General Electric's MHD program, says that he expects "a tremendous spin-off in coal-combustion technology that will benefit the country a lot sooner than MHD will."

Perhaps the most exciting new technology on the horizon is biological, or genetic, engineering on what is sometimes referred to as "biotechnology." Some enthusiasts hail it as the semiconductor industry of the 1980s and 1990s. However, it is unlikely that biotechnology will create a concentrated industry of its own, like semiconductors. Instead, it will diffuse into such industries as chemicals, drugs, food, and energy. The first commercial applications should begin appearing soon, and by the late 1980s, according to a study by International Resource Development (IRD), biotechnology will be producing several drugs, including insulin, interferon, and perhaps morphine, in sufficient bulk to avert worldwide shortages that would otherwise occur. Biotechnology is the "ace card for the 1980s," says IRD's Ruth Lipsitz.

Fundamentally, then, America's technological base is still diverse, progressive, and vital. Warning signals have cropped up, but they are not symptomatic of inherent weaknesses in the science and technology communities; rather, they reflect problems in corporate management and government policy.

Capitalizing on Energy Assets

Compared with its major industrial competitors, the United States is rich in energy resources. It has more oil, more natural gas, and more coal than any other country in the Organization for Economic Cooperation and Development. More important, the United States is a world leader in the technologies needed to exploit these resources: oil-field equipment (both onshore and offshore), coal-mining methods, and synthetic-fuels know-how. But transforming this potential into reality—producing more of the country's domestic resources while spurring new growth in its energy-related industries—depends heavily on U.S. willingness to pay the full price of energy.

The notion of freeing oil prices is traumatic for a society that flourished on cheap energy for more than a century, but it is only by allowing prices to rise that the full adaptation to the energy crisis can proceed. Allowing prices to reach the levels actually prevailing in world markets is the most efficient arbiter of which industries should flourish and which should wither. Says Henry Lee, director of the Energy and Environment Policy Center at Harvard University: "The government has got to make sure that the prices industry sees are the actual, marginal costs of that energy. If not, industry is never going to make investments on the basis of reality."

That is finally beginning to happen. Controls on oil prices were to have been phased out by October 1981, but President Reagan lifted them just 8 days after his inauguration. Natural gas prices are scheduled to be decontrolled in 1985, but the Reagan administration may speed that up too. In the short run, these steps cause more of the same kinds of problems that the United States has suffered since energy prices began their upward spiral. They will mean a reduced standard of living for consumers and lower productivity growth for industry. A U.S. effort to cut its reliance on oil imports—still cheaper than domestic resources if the cost of possible interruptions is ignored—will only exacerbate those problems in the short run.

It will take a massive effort for this country simply to hold oil imports at their present level while beginning the long, arduous shift from reliance on imported oil to production of domestic coal and synthetic fuels. As much investment—some $500 billion—as was made in the last decade to meet a growth in energy demand of about 2 percent a year will be required in the next 10 years to achieve an energy growth of half that rate.

But domestic production of conventional oil and gas, which together account for nearly two-thirds of U.S. energy consumption, is also slowing. Oil production, for example, is expected to fall from 8 million barrels a day now to 6 million barrels in 1990. Thus, even if oil demand remains level over the next 10 years, more than half the U.S. requirement will still have to be imported. "The United States will remain extremely vulnerable on oil for the next 10 years," warns Sheldon M. Lambert, a Shell Oil corporate planner. So it must run hard just to stay in place.

The United States has only three real choices to produce significant amounts of new energy in the next 10 years: coal, synthetics derived from coal, and conservation (or, as its proponents call it, improved energy efficiency). For the next 20 years at least, alternative sources such as solar power are not expected to play a major role in U.S. energy supplies. At the same time, nuclear power is becoming less attractive for both environmental and economic reasons.

The drive for new energy sources will make energy one of the U.S. growth industries of the 1980s. There will be a greatly expanded search for oil and gas. Coal, after years in the doldrums, finally seems poised for rapid growth. Some of the more ambitious projections for the production of large amounts of synfuels have faded, but starts are certain on dozens of projects. And a massive new energy-efficiency industry is springing up to supply the services, equipment, and technology to improve the energy productivity of American industry.

With reserves of 150 billion tons, the nation possesses nearly a quarter of the world's coal. For the first time in years, analysts are optimistic that this vast resource will be exploited. Most are now projecting that coal consumption will grow from the present 740 million tons per year to about 1.2 billion tons in 1985.

Price is the main reason for the expected jump. Thanks to the latest OPEC increase, coal is a bargain. Coal delivered to utilities today costs between $1.25 and $2.50 per million Btu, compared with about $4 per million Btu for residual fuel oil. Moreover, coal prices are not likely to increase rapidly. There is plenty of production capacity now, and much more is expected in the next 10 years. "I wish there were a relationship between coal and oil prices," says William G. Karis, director of planning for Consolidation Coal. "But coal is a cost-based fuel."

The price of coal is certainly attractive, but the fuel still faces many problems. Most of them relate to the government. Environmental regulations continue to prevent Western coal facilities from expanding as rapidly as the industry would like. That could squeeze coal demand in the late 1980s. Another problem is the railroads. Many coal users feel that rail rates are too high and discourage coal use. "I feel like I'm paying for the whole damn railroad," says one Midwestern utility executive.

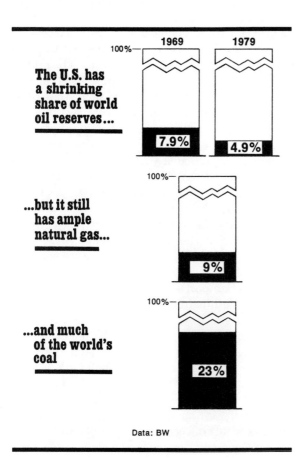

The U.S. has a shrinking share of world oil reserves...

...but it still has ample natural gas...

...and much of the world's coal

1969: 7.9%
1979: 4.9%

9%

23%

Data: BW

The problem of rail rates is just one of several that could stand in the way of a potentially lucrative coal export market. The National Coal Association projects that by 1990 the United States could export as much as 90 million tons a year of steam coal, up from only 10 million tons a year in 1979. "We don't have the port facilities," says J. Michael Gallagher, technical director of the World Coal Study, which is headquartered at the Massachusetts Institute of Technology. "And we'll need the cooperation of the producers, the railroads, and the shippers. It doesn't exist now."

At home, another problem in expanding coal output is the poor financial condition of electric utilities, which will be the main market for the new coal. In 1979 utilities consumed 528 million tons of coal. That figure is projected to rise nearly a billion tons by 1990. Again, the government will be the key factor. Congress is considering voting $10 billion to help utilities make conversions. That would not, however, help to overcome the objections of local governments to the increased air pollution that could result from the greater use of coal. Moreover, these expenditures appear less likely to occur in the Reagan administration.

President Reagan's decision not to press ahead with his predecessor's $88 billion program for developing synthetic fuels is expected to bring about a shake-out and restructuring of the fledgling industry. The retreat from a government-backed program of synfuels-developing liquid or gaseous substitutes for oil or gas from coal, oil shale, or tar sand—has come as a major blow to scores of oil companies, coal producers, gas pipeline companies, energy technology manufacturers, equipment suppliers, and construction companies that had been counting on government subsidies. But development of some synfuels, particularly shale oil and some coal gas, is expected to continue. In the end, say the experts, the industry will be smaller, with fewer companies, but it will be a lot stronger.

"We expect that a substantial synthetic fuels industry will be developed by the private sector regardless of government support," says Bruce R. Bockmann, a managing director of the investment bank of Morgan Stanley in New York. "Economic projects with strong sponsors will proceed. There are a good number of these projects."

Without massive government support—the Reagan administration does not intend to withdraw all Washington aid—only the commercially viable projects are expected to survive. However, with the steep rise in the costs of oil and natural gas, some synfuel projects have become commercially viable. "The question has always been, At what point have we reached the threshold where the prices are in the same ball park as oil?" says Mel Horwitch of the Sloan School of Management at MIT. "There are numbers that say it is now." Horwich may indeed be right. The estimated cost of producing a barrel of oil from shale ranges between $30 and $45, about the same as the market cost of conventional crude. And certain grades of coal gas can be produced at under $30 for what is the energy equivalent of a barrel of oil.

The improved economics of synfuels versus conventional energy sources is expected to encourage the big oil companies, such as Exxon, Union Oil, and Standard Oil of Indiana, to further increase their already substantial stake in the industry. Many oil company officials believe that the continued price increases for oil and natural gas make the development of some substitutes inevitable. Economists at Exxon, for example, are predicting that by the year 2000 substitutes ranging from wood chips to shale oil will replace more than 10 million barrels of oil per day.

The critical assumption of the industry optimists is, of course, that oil and gas prices will continue to rise. The biggest risk facing synfuel investments is that OPEC will cut prices if alternatives become too competitive. But synfuel supporters argue that such a threat from OPEC affects all expensive energy projects, including oil. "When you're talking about going into 2000 feet of water or putting a platform in the Gulf of Alaska to produce 50 million barrels of oil during its lifetime, you might as well build a synthetic plant," says an Exxon executive.

Synfuel advocates are also convinced that OPEC will not embark on a costly price war as alternative fuels come on stream. They believe that if a price war with OPEC became vicious or market forces drove prices down so far that it threatened the investments of major U.S. oil companies, the government would step in on national security grounds to help.

Other experts—many of whom favor conservation—are less sanguine about the prospects for synfuels. "We could save more oil for less money than we'll get from the synfuel plants by giving away small cars," claims Roger W. Sant, director of the Energy Productivity Center of the Mellon Institute, a division of the Carnegie-Mellon University. Sant estimates that by installing the most energy-efficient equipment available today, including automobiles, the United States could save up to 4 million barrels of oil per day. "There is a tremendous market in improving energy efficiency," says Sant. "It could be as much as $50 billion a year for the next 10 years."

Sant believes that many such investments—from simple improvements in existing equipment to installation of such things as cogeneration—are now so appealing that they can attract capital without the need for government incentives. Yet most energy experts think that over the long run some form of tax incentives will be necessary both to encourage energy efficiency and to develop a bigger synthetic fuels industry. In any event, everyone agrees that there must be new incentives for capital formation. Otherwise, much of the capital will simply be drained off into investments that improve energy efficiency without attacking the more fundamental problem of increasing productivity.

Trading Up on Population Growth

As the United States strives to reclaim its status as an economic superpower, the force that experts call "human resources" and that people call "workers" belongs emphatically under the heading of assets.

We have more workers than our competitors, we will have even more during the next decade (as our competitors' populations increase more slowly than ours), we have a better mix for industrial purposes, and we have a social climate that permits better use of their talents. Even our current immigration pattern is helpful. It was beneficial before and immediately after World War II, when talented European refugees headed for the United States. Now although large numbers of unskilled workers, many of them illegal aliens, are arriving, another stream is made up of managers, professionals, and technicians who come to escape high taxes, unstable governments, terrorist gangs, and the threat of communism.

The demographics are the easiest to chart. According to the Organization for Economic Cooperation and Development's projections for 1990,

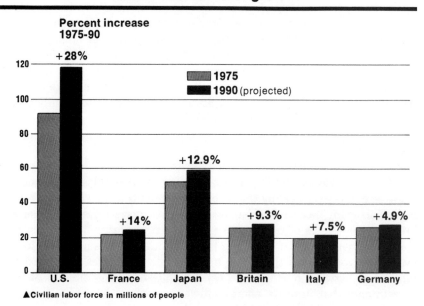

The U.S. will lead the industrial world in labor force growth

Percent increase
1975-90

1975
1990 (projected)

+28%   +14%   +12.9%   +9.3%   +7.5%   +4.9%

U.S.   France   Japan   Britain   Italy   Germany

▲Civilian labor force in millions of people

Data: Organization for Economic Cooperation & Development

which use 1975 as the base year, the civilian labor force will grow from 92.6 million to 118.5 million, a 28 percent increase. This compares with the two next largest increases—for France, from 21.7 million to 24.7 million, a 14 percent increase; and for Japan, from 52.2 million to 58.9 million, a 12.9 percent increase. The lowest projection is for West Germany—from 25.9 million to 27.2 million, a 4.9 percent increase.

Although growing faster than its overseas rivals, the U.S. labor force will increase at a slower rate than it has in the recent past. Growing at about 2 million workers a year instead of recent 3 million, the labor force of the 1980s will draw fewer of its entrants from young workers as the bulge created by the post-World War II baby boom finally passes into the workplace and history. As a result, says Paul O. Flaim, director of Labor Force Studies at the Bureau of Labor Standards, the country will be less preoccupied with youth unemployment than it has been, and the resources that have been spent in that area can be earmarked for training, retraining, and the improvement of productivity generally. As a result, predicts Flaim: "Our work force of 20- to 25-year-olds should be more productive."

Overall, the new work force will be usable for a greater variety of jobs because it will be better educated, says Dennis Johnston, an expert on social indicators at the U.S. Census Bureau. He observes that only 9 percent of today's work force has 8 or fewer years of schooling, compared with 30 percent in 1959, and that nearly 18 percent has had 4 years of college or more, compared with less than 10 percent in 1959. Flaim notes that "the trends are up, particularly among minorities, and that has to be helpful."

Moreover, says Eli Ginzberg, the Columbia University economics professor who heads the U.S. Commission on Employment Policy, "We are further ahead in knowing how to use the half of the population known as women, and I cannot overemphasize the importance of that fact." Some 51.1 percent of all U.S. women are in the labor force, but that is not entirely the point, says Ginzberg. Among other major industrial countries, Britain has 47.2 percent of its women in the labor force, and Japan has 46.4 percent, both fairly close to the U.S. percentage. In neither country, however, do women have the extent and kinds of education they have here, in neither do they hold the variety of jobs they hold here, in neither are they moving upward as steadily as they are here, and in neither does the government aid actively in their progress.

Add to this the fact that women entered the U.S. labor force in exceptionally large numbers only in recent years (in fact, the process is still under way), and the situation becomes unique. These women are labor force recruits from a brand-new source, and—unlike the farm workers who swarmed into factories during the industrial revolution or the poor immigrants whose heavy labor helped build the United States at the turn of the century—these recruits are highly diversified. They are capable of filling niches throughout the country's industrial structure, present and future.

The same social milieu that let women flood into the labor force allows the economy to gain more from individual talents than most countries do, Ginzberg believes. "This is still the most open society in the Western world," he says. Social mobility may not be as high as it once was, but a blue-collar worker can still rise into a managerial or other specialized job, giving the economy access to talents that would be stifled in a more class-conscious society.

Moreover, the labor force benefits of an open society do not end here. Despite the increasingly formal organization of the U.S. corporation, there is an easier flow of ideas among people at different levels than in any other major industrial country, Ginzberg insists, and therefore less risk that a good idea will be lost in the mumble of a lower-class accent.

Working together, the government and private industry produce excellent predictions of changing occupational patterns in the 10-year job forecasts of the Bureau of Labor Statistics, says Leonard Greenhalgh of Dartmouth College. The problem has been that neither schools nor companies paid much attention to the forecasts in designing training programs, he says. This must change if the country is to take full advantage of its human resources, Greenhalgh insists. He envisages a system under which government funds encourage schools to teach students the core requirements of new types of jobs implicit in the new technology, and the company that hires the graduates trains and retrains them in its specific needs.

Greenhalgh joins most labor force experts in predicting that workers of all levels will have several careers in the course of a working lifetime in the very near future. In fact, the future may be here; census data suggest that in one 5-year period in the 1970s, a full third of the labor force moved not simply into different jobs but different careers.

Some companies have already come to grips with this situation, says James W. Walker, a principal at Towers, Perrin, Forster & Crosby, management consultants, and president of the Human Resource Planning Society. He names Weyerhaeuser, Corning Glass, TRW, and Texas Instruments as among those who are taking a "strong, business-oriented" approach to human resources by planning ahead and teaching new technologies to avoid obsolescence.

Even more striking, says Van M. Evans, president of Deutsch, Shea & Evans, human resource consultants, is the development of career awareness among ordinary people. "People are buying the fact that they must accept change, that technology is moving fast, obsoleting many positions, creating new ones," he says. He cites the sale of millions of copies of books about jobs and the widespread readership of a College Board study, "Forty Million Americans in Career Transition," by Solomon Arbeiter. Psychologically, he says, the labor force may be readier for the new technology than many theorists believe.

Using Multinationals to Push Exports

U.S. multinational investment—a $200 billion stake that U.S. companies have built up in factories, mines, oil fields, banks, merchandising networks, and other businesses abroad—is yielding economic benefits both to the U.S. economy and to the foreign countries where the investments were made.

In 1980 U.S.-controlled companies overseas produced an estimated $500 billion worth of goods and services, an amount equal to the gross national product of France. Most of that stayed abroad in the form of wages paid to millions of local employees; purchases of materials, components, and services from local suppliers; and taxes paid to foreign governments. But more than $25 billion flowed back to the United States as profits and fee payments to U.S. parent companies.

Far more important for the revitalization of the U.S. economy, though, is the crucial role of U.S. multinational companies as exporters of American-made products and importers of foreign-made goods, some of which come from their own factories abroad. Some 2000 U.S. companies, led by the multinationals, accounted for 80 percent of the $220 billion worth of U.S. exports in 1980. One-fourth of those exports were "intracompany" transactions—sales of equipment, components, materials, and finished products by U.S. parent companies to their foreign affiliates. Beyond that, the more than 20,000 foreign subsidiaries, affiliates, and branch offices of U.S. multinational companies are a formidable marketing network for U.S.-made, as well as foreign-made, products.

Those figures refute the idea, advanced by some, that one way to cure the U.S. industrial malaise is by curbing investments of U.S. companies abroad. "The really successful U.S. multinationals like Caterpillar, IBM, and Texas Instruments are not the companies that are suffering," says William V. Rapp, a vice president of Morgan Guaranty Trust. "The erosion of the U.S. industrial base is more serious among companies that have been primarily national." Adds political scientist Stephen Blank of the Conference Board: "The business equivalent of Fortress America hasn't worked. [Companies] holding their own and even adding to U.S. employment and exports are companies that have taken advantage of global investing." Any attempt to confine U.S. companies to investment and technical development in this country alone would weaken their ability to meet Japanese and European competition by costing them global market share and cutting their access to foreign labor, raw materials, or land.

Nevertheless, the United States should tilt the balance of benefits from multinational investment, and from the trading role of American multinational companies, more sharply toward this country. To do this, what is required is the same mix of policies—aimed at stimulating investment and raising productivity—that are needed to strengthen the U.S. domestic economy. The managers of multinational companies have the option of reinvesting the profits that flow back from their foreign operations either in the United States or abroad. U.S. policies should be designed to make decisions to invest in the United States the more attractive alternative. The resulting increases in efficiency, lower costs, improved quality, and innovative products, in turn, would make it profitable for multinational companies to produce more goods in the United States for export both to their own affiliates and other customers. Expanded Export-Import Bank financing, export tax incentives, and other aids to exports will make it even more attractive for them to do so.

The multinationals have a unique capacity for adapting their production and distribution patterns rapidly to such changes in the relative advantages of producing in the United States rather than abroad. They are flexible in locating new facilities or expanding plants at alternative sites around the globe. And they employ sophisticated strategies for "sourcing" products, materials, and components from different points within their global organizations for use or sale by their affiliates worldwide. Thus the multinationals can be powerful instruments for translating the effects of increased U.S. competitiveness into rapid gains in trade and jobs for U.S. workers.

By contrast, it would be futile to try to keep jobs in the United States, as some labor unions advocate, by restricting investment outflows to prevent alleged attempts by U.S. multinationals to shift operations overseas to "runaway shops" that use cheap foreign labor. With or without such restrictions, U.S. plants that cannot compete with foreign costs will have to shut down and be replaced by overseas production, whether U.S.-owned or foreign-owned. When U.S. companies began to invest heavily overseas in the 1960s, they were impelled, in good part, by just such pressures: rising costs in the United States made it more and more difficult to compete in foreign markets with U.S.-made goods, and the artificially high exchange rate of the dollar made it cheaper to build plants or buy out existing companies abroad than in the United States.

Now, steps to revitalize U.S. industry could also spur a reverse flow of multinational private capital by making the United States a powerful magnet for more corporate investments from abroad. European, Canadian, and Japanese companies have already boosted their stake in the United States in recent years, to an estimated $60 billion at the end of 1980. This tide of incoming investment should be encouraged, because the U.S. economy will receive from it many of the same kinds of benefits that foreign countries have derived from U.S. multinational operations. In past decades, U.S. foreign investments spread American know-how around the globe. Now foreign companies that invest successfully in the United States are bringing valuable technology amd managerial know-how as well as capital. They have to do so in order to survive in the fiercely competitive U.S. business environment.

What managers of U.S. multinationals must do, for their part, to help revive U.S. economic strength is develop the full range of corporate synergisms that are created by operations on a worldwide scale. To keep their own companies and U.S. industry as a whole in the forefront, they must exploit the "feedbacks" from their global networks in order to reinforce the parent company's technological leadership and competitive strength. Thus computer manufacturer IBM and pharmaceutical maker Pfizer, for example, have set up major research facilities in Europe and Japan to tap pools of scientific and technical talent. These worldwide research efforts are closely coordinated with those of the parent company in the United States. Machinery and equipment maker Ingersoll-Rand (I-R), like other successful U.S. exporters, uses its manufacturing subsidiaries abroad as the cutting edge for I-R exports from the United States as well. The foreign plants make standard I-R products but also serve as marketing and service bases for sales of more costly and technologically advanced equipment that is made in the company's U.S. plants.

By such strategies, U.S. corporate managers must become more rather than less multinational in their outlook, even though their approaches to world markets vary widely in different industries. For oil and mining companies, which have little choice but to invest wherever oil and minerals are located, flexibility in adapting operations to fast-changing political conditions around the world is a necessity. For semiconductor makers, maintaining U.S. leadership in the face of mounting worldwide competition will probably require even greater use of plants in countries such as Taiwan and the Philippines, where wages are low, to manufacture components. The cost advantage of using such components in finished products enables the semiconductor makers to keep their U.S. operations competitive as well, and this saves U.S. jobs.

The penalty for not developing the full potential of multinational operations is illustrated by the disastrous consequences for the auto industry and indeed for the entire U.S. economy of the Detroit auto makers' failure to evolve global market strategies to match those of their rivals. Although General Motors, Ford, and Chrysler have been among the biggest multinational investors since World War II, they made the crucial error of segmenting the world market by designing and building different cars in North America, Europe, and even Australia. In doing so, they sacrificed economies of scale, diluted their research and development efforts, and lost the benefits to the U.S. parent companies of marketing and design feedbacks from the rest of the world.

Japanese and European rivals, even though they invested much less in overseas plants, nevertheless became more international in outlook because they developed integrated product lines to supply markets throughout the world, mainly by exports. Thus, when the energy crisis accelerated the creation of a single global market, the Europeans and Japanese were already making "world cars" that they could sell everywhere, including the United States, while Detroit was still scrambling to produce competitive models.

U.S. tire makers' troubles are another warning to American corporate managers that they must think globally. The rubber companies are major overseas investors, but the scores of plants that they replicated around the world in the 1950s and 1960s simply turned out the same U.S.-style tires for a series of national markets. Thibaut de Saint Phalle, of the Georgetown Center for Strategic and International Studies, points out that the U.S. companies failed to adapt their product to foreign-made autos and driving conditions, while France's Michelin, by contrast, invested heavily in research and development of the radial tire. The result was that the U.S. companies not only lost markets abroad but also left the way open for an invasion of the United States by foreign tires and the loss of tens of thousands of U.S. jobs.

What such fiascos show is that the impressive multinational networks that U.S. companies have built up abroad could quickly crumble if the U.S. parent companies fail to use them to maintain their own competitive strength. Japanese multinationals do this very effectively by means of a global investment strategy that is designed to maximize exports by the parent company from Japan. Apart from overseas investments in minerals, timber, and other resources that are needed by Japanese factories, most Japanese foreign investment, until recently, has been in assembly plants and in installations, such as textile mills, that use Japanese-made components and materials. As industry in Japan shifts toward new high-technology products and manufacturing methods, Japanese multinationals will have to transfer more low-technology, labor-intensive production to overseas plants. But Japanese investments in the United States in TV plants, and possibly in automobile plants in the future, are basically defensive moves to head off U.S. restrictions on imports of finished products from Japan. Leading auto makers Toyota and Nissan make it clear that they hope to export from Japan as long as possible if they can resist political pressures from the United States to start full-scale manufacturing in this country.

At the same time, U.S. negotiators in international forums will have to resist policies of foreign governments that are designed to distort normal market flows of trade and investment. Foreign countries try to extract for themselves an unfair share of the economic benefits from operations of U.S. multinationals. Latin American countries, especially, have adopted "import substitution" policies that require multinationals to set up local manufacturing subsidiaries or be excluded from their markets by import restrictions. Gradually, they are squeezing down imports from the United States for operations of such plants by requiring more and more local manufacture of materials and components under "local content" rules. Now, countries such as Brazil and Mexico are pushing multinational companies to export more products from those countries by offering export incentives and by linking investment approvals to export commitments. Other countries, such as France, also pressure prospective investors from abroad to include plans for exports in their investment proposals. And Canada prods multinational investors, mostly American, to concentrate all production of certain products in Canadian subsidiaries to supply global markets under worldwide "export mandates." C. Fred Bergsten, former Assistant Treasury Secretary for International Affairs in the Carter administration and now senior associate at the Carnegie Endowment for International Peace, calls such tactics "investment wars." Many of the exports spurred by such pressures, including practically all the automotive components that U.S. companies and Volkswagen must export from plants in Mexico, are likely to come to the United States, where they could displace U.S.-made goods.

Investment patterns are also being distorted by lush subsidies and other incentives offered to multinational companies by European as well as developing countries to attract industrial plants. Such practices, too, are likely to divert investment away from the United States, and the output of such plants may displace American-made goods in global markets. As an important part of the effort to revitalize the U.S. economy, the Reagan administration must push for agreements to curb these practices in international groupings such as the Organization for Economic Cooperation and Development and the General Agreement on Tariffs and Trade.

The United States needs to establish better access to world markets, not only for U.S. multinational giants but for thousands of small and medium-size American manufacturers. In Europe and in Japan especially, giant trading companies with global distribution networks and strong financial resources, such as Denmark's East Asiatic Company and Japan's Mitsubishi Corporation, provide the bridge between numerous small companies and export markets. The U.S. Congress should enact legislation, introduced in 1980, to authorize the creation of export trading companies in the United States. A crucial provision of the bill would allow U.S. multinational banks to own minority shareholdings, thus providing a link between the trading companies and the banks' worldwide information-gathering networks, financial resources, and international business expertise. By opening global markets for many of the estimated 20,000 U.S. companies that are potentially competitive in international trade but have never sold their products abroad, such trading companies should give an important boost to U.S. industry.

12
TWO STAGES OF
AN INDUSTRIAL POLICY

How far will President Reagan's economic program go toward solving the problems confronting the American economy in the 1980s? What will it do to enhance the competitiveness of U.S. industries? Will it generate a lot more capital investment and reverse the alarming decline in productivity? What about unemployment in the nation's industrial heartland? To put it more inclusively, with Ronald Reagan in the White House, do we really need a reindustrialization policy? Unfortunately, the answer is yes.

In a certain sense, the Reagan economic policy can be thought of as a weak form of reindustrialization, for one important aspect of the President's economic program calls for getting government off the back of business. And less than 6 weeks after taking office, the Reagan administration began to march in that direction. The administration wants not only to continue the deregulation of industries such as airlines, trucking, and railroads—which began under Presidents Ford and Carter—but to remove the pervasive social regulation that affects businesses large and small, such as environmental and safety and health regulations. The core of the administration's regulatory philosophy is much the same as that held by most economists: government intrusion in the private sector is justified if—and only if—it produces benefits to the nation as a whole that outweigh the costs and if regulation is the least expensive of the possible alternatives.

The Reagan administration believes that most regulations can be shown to be a burden to society—that is, their costs more than offset their benefits—but it would take too much valuable time to demonstrate this by means of economic analyses. President Reagan's strategy for easing regulation is to appoint regulators who support his resolve to reduce government intervention, use the power of executive order to rescind some regulations, cut the budgets of regulatory agencies under his control, and subject proposed new regulations to cost-benefit analyses. It may require congressional action in some cases, in light of the June 1981 Supreme Court decision rejecting cost-benefit analysis where worker health is concerned.

Getting rid of regulations that inhibit business, retard growth, and offer few benefits is an important step in the process of reindustrialization. And President Reagan gets good marks here. The Reagan administration, of course, is not proposing to return to the days when a factory could blow what it liked up the stack and dump what it liked into the river. The basic idea is to retain the objectives—clean air, safe products, honest labeling— but give business wide latitude in determining how to achieve them. Unless business executives can demonstrate that the results can be accomplished without burdensome rules and thousands of precise regulations, the President's deregulation drive will stall.

When it comes to the essence of the administration's economic policy— broad-based cuts in personal income taxes to stimulate growth—the Reagan program is found wanting, however. Supply-side economics lies at the heart of President Reagan's economic program. While "supply-side economics" have turned into buzzwords, the term has come to mean different things to different people. To most economists it means shifting resources from consumer spending to capital investment in order to increase productivity. The primary way to do this is to tilt tax cuts away from stimulating consumption and toward spurring investment.

But the ideas underlying President Reagan's economic program go well beyond that notion. They draw on the theories developed by economist Arthur B. Laffer of the University of Southern California, who believes that tax rates have grown so high that they have weakened the incentives to work, to save, and to invest. Laffer maintains that sharp cuts in personal taxes, such as those incorporated in the Kemp-Roth bill, which called for a 10 percent tax cut for each of 3 years, would increase work effort and savings, and generate so much economic growth that the government would be able to recapture the initial loss in tax revenues.

There are three problems in relying on the Kemp-Roth tax cuts to spur economic growth. For one thing, increases in social security taxes coupled with "bracket creep" (which occurs when inflation pushes taxpayers into higher tax brackets, even though their real incomes don't rise) mean that the rates that most Americans would actually be paying in 1984 after Kemp-Roth would be only slightly lower than the rates paid in 1980. For example, assume no increase in real wages and an 8 percent average inflation rate from 1980 to 1984—not unreasonable assumptions in today's economic environment. A family of four, earning $25,000 in 1980, paid on the average an effective tax rate, including social security taxes, of 17.7 percent. In 1984 the rate under Kemp-Roth would decline a minuscule 0.2 percent—to 17.5 percent. For a family earning $50,000 a year the rate would fall from 21.8 percent in 1980 to 21.1 percent in 1984. The only meaningful reduction occurs in the $200,000 bracket, where rates would fall from 35.9 percent in 1980 to 31.4 percent in 1984.

The reductions in the marginal tax rates—the rate at which the taxpayer gets hit on an additional dollar of income—are somewhat larger, at least at the upper end of the income scale. The family earning $50,000 a year in 1980, for example, paid 43 percent on any additional dollar of income; under Kemp-Roth that rate declines to 36 percent. (The marginal tax rate for the family earning $30,000 declines only from 28 percent to 27 percent.) By and large, however, continued inflation and increased social security taxes mean that the tax rates that the public will be paying in 1984 with Kemp-Roth will not vary very much from the 1980 rates. So it is hard to see how these cuts in taxes will get people to work and invest more. Indeed, the bill that finally passed cut the rates by 25 percent, making the impact more uncertain.

Even if taxpayers were to pay substantially lower tax rates, most economists—from liberal-leaning Nobel laureate Paul Samuelson to archconservative Nobelist Friedrich von Hayek—remain extremely skeptical that personal income tax cuts will generate the kind of supply-side effects that their proponents claim. The money would go predominantly into buying more consumer goods rather than increase the incentives to work and invest more, say the critics. In other words, the supply-side tax cut is, in effect, a demand-side cut which could exacerbate inflation.

Furthermore, across-the-board tax cuts would not reverse the devastating effect that the decline of U.S. industrial power has had on the industrial regions of the North and Midwest. Those industrial areas are faced with an accelerating exodus of people, companies, and jobs which has left in its wake urban decay and cities and states on the verge of bankruptcy. Even if a Kemp-Roth type of tax cut were to generate more savings and thus investment, it is unlikely that much of it would find its way to the nation's heartland to rebuild its rotting plants so that American industry can once again compete with its international rivals.

President Reagan has made a significant step toward alleviating the tax burden on capital-intensive companies through his version of the so-called 10-5-3 depreciation proposal. But there is no guarantee that the profit-starved industrial companies—so vital to America's revival—will benefit. And the plan might actually worsen the allocation of capital because it favors companies whose current profits are already high.

To revive American industry will require a strong dose of reindustrialization. It will require not across-the-board tax cuts but targeted cuts aimed at getting business executives to invest more. It will require a federal corporation to channel investment to ailing industries. It will require a policy that discourages current consumption and encourages current investment. This will, of course, be unpopular with the American public, but it will ensure that the cars and refrigerators and TV sets and computers we buy in the future will be produced in American factories by American workers and not in Japan and Taiwan.

Reindustrialization requires an industrial policy that chooses which industries, sectors, and product lines should be encouraged because they have a good chance in international competition and which should be abandoned as likely failures. Yet the large number of Edsels that both economic forecasters and business planning departments have produced demonstrates how easily the forecasts that must inevitably underlie industrial policy can go awry. But there is no alternative to social agreement on those sectors of the economy which must be encouraged. As Arnold H. Packer, former Assistant Secretary of Labor for Policy, Evaluation, and Research, puts it: "We must think about what our traditional economic sectors will look like a decade out and what the potential future sectors might be. If we simply watch while the rest of the world pursues active industrial policies, we will wind up making what Germany and Japan leave over."

Reindustrialization must be carefully explained to the American public; otherwise, it can conceivably accelerate the decline in the U.S. economy rather than arrest it. The danger is that the U.S. political system will translate reindustrialization into some brand of lemon socialism, whose main focus will be to save the lemons—obsolete jobs and companies—that are going bankrupt because they are too inefficient to compete in world markets. That's what happened in Britain and Italy.

Instead, rebuilding our industry will require a total reprogramming of the way Americans—including politicians—think about their economy. U.S. economic growth in the century between the end of the Civil War in 1865 and the beginning of the war in Vietnam in 1965 was the eighth wonder of the world. That growth occurred because basic U.S. institutions and attitudes were ideally suited to taking advantage of the growth opportunities available in that century. Those opportunities were presented by a great internal frontier crying to be exploited. Virtually every aspect of economic policy showed sheer genius in allowing the United States to grow rapidly—from Lincoln's Homestead Act of 1862, which ensured access to new land by the broad majority, to the Sherman Antitrust Act of 1890, which ensured that small owners would not be gobbled up by the powerful.

The rapid growth in productive capacity that developed from exploiting that frontier also put a distinctive stamp on U.S. social policy and labor relations. "Our job," said the United Auto Workers' most vigorous president, Walter P. Reuther, "is to carve the fat" off the companies. And he wanted to give that fat to the workers to make sure they had enough income to buy the products that industry could produce. A competitive advantage in world markets was not a major issue. Reflecting the same attitudes, U.S. social policy focused on redistributing income rather than training to increase productivity and growth. And for good reason— growth was easy to come by. But it is not anymore. The United States finds itself engaged in a battle for economic survival against powerful growth-oriented international rivals.

In the final analysis, whether America will reindustrialize depends on whether the business, labor, and political elites can get together to provide the necessary leadership. And that, in turn, depends on whether they can break out of their ideological shells to adopt a program that appears to rub, at certain seams, against the idea of a free market. Yet the great danger to the free market is in doing nothing. An enormous amount has to be done, and time is running short. America must make a start.

INDEX

Abel, Walter L., 57, 106, 162
Abernathy, William J., 20
Absenteeism, effects of quality-of-
worklife programs on, 93, 94, 97
Accelerated Cost Recovery System
(ACRS), 124
Adams, Walter, 13
ADR (asset depreciation range) system,
124, 125
Advancement policies (see Promotion of
executives)
Aerospace industry, 154–155
Affluence:
post-World War II, 7–8
psychology of, 69–71
(See also Standard of living)
Agriculture, 132
Aho, C. Michael, 146
Aircraft industry, 11, 14, 144
Airlines, 32, 80, 128, 181
Alperovitz, Gar, 133
Alternative energy sources, 144,
166–168, 170–171
Aluminum industry, 22, 133, 146
Ames, Charles B., 52
Antitrust policy, 35, 37, 82–85, 138, 139,
155, 182–185
Apparel and footwear industry, 2, 14, 15,
144, 145, 158
Arab countries, 136, 138
Arbeiter, Solomon, 175
Asian countries, 15, 154
(See also specific Asian countries)
Asset depreciation range (ADR) system,
124, 125
Auerbach, Alan J., 122, 124
Authoritarian management, 68–69, 88,
93

Automation (technological change), 68,
69, 98
with robots, 162–164
Automobile industry, 2, 26, 80, 142, 148,
154, 157
effects of automobile imports on, 48
failure to develop multinational
operations by, 177–178
labor-management relations in, 63, 67,
87
loss of competitiveness of, 14
near depression in, 16
production in (see Production,
automobile)
plants closed by, 50
quality-of-worklife programs in, 93–95
resistance to change in, 60
retaining lead of, 164
robots in, 163
short-term planning in, 48–49
(See also Fuel-efficient automobiles)
Ayres, James B., 55

Baker, Charles D., 109–110
Balanced budget, 34, 119, 120, 134–135
Bale, Harvey, 136
Balogh, Thomas, 75
Banks:
German, 148
U.S., 17, 32
as shareholders in proposed export
companies, 180
Barbash, Jack, 66, 68, 88, 91
Barraclough, Harold T., 165
Bechtel, Stephen D., Jr., 32
Bentsen, Lloyd M., Jr., 30, 52, 119, 123,
132

Berger, Roland, 61
Bergsten, C. Fred, 179
Bioengineering (genetic engineering), 11, 19, 128, 149, 159, 166, 167
Blacks, 2, 18, 70, 76, 77, 79
Blake, David H., 61
Blank, Stephen, 175
Bluestone, Barry, 98
Bluestone, Irving, 93
Bluhdorn, Charles, 54
Boards of directors:
    labor leaders on, 65, 88, 147
    and short-term planning, 52
    (*See also* Management)
Bockmann, Bruce R., 170
Bolling, Richard, 78
Bonus systems, executive, 59, 102–103
Borrowing from government, 130–133
Boskin, Michael J., 24, 42–44, 115, 116
Boycotts, Arab, 136, 138
Bradford, David F., 116
Brannon, Gerard M., 116, 128
Brazil, 179
Brill, Daniel H., 132
Britain, 12, 132, 135, 142, 151, 165, 172, 184
Brophy, Theodore, F., 59
Brovedani, Bruno, 153
Bucy, J. Fred, 164
Budget, federal, balanced, 34, 119, 120, 134–135
Burke, James E., 23, 53, 108
Business, role of, in loss of economic power, 47–61
    lack of risk-taking managers, 53–59
    (*See also* Risk taking)
    resistance to change and, 59–61
    and short-term planning (*see* Short-term planning)
Business schools, need to overhaul, 108–111
Byrom, Fletcher L., 47, 52–53

CAD-CAM (computer-aided design/computer-aided manufacturing) system, 161–162
Calore, Raymond, 93, 94
Canada, 12, 176–177, 179
Capital cost accounting, effects of inflation on, 43
Capital formation, 29, 79, 115
    (*See also* Profit; Savings)
Capital gains, taxation of, 118, 119
Capital investments (*see* Investments)
Capital/labor ratio, productivity, and, 24
Career awareness, need to develop, 174–175

Carli, Guido, 152
Carlson, Donald G., 102
Carter, Jimmy, 64, 68, 79, 90, 127, 133, 135, 141, 179
    economic revitalization board proposed by, 1, 88–89
    electoral defeat of, 7
    exports policy under, 36
    regulatory reform envisaged by, 32, 181
    tax reform program of, 119
Change:
    resistance to: by business, 59–61
        by unions, 65, 67
    technological 68, 69, 98
    with robots, 162–164
Chemicals industry, 14, 144, 145, 152, 155–156
Cities:
    1980 riots in, 77
    plight of, 17–19
    rebuilding, 70
Civil rights laws (1960s), 78
Clare, David R., 108
Clayton Antitrust Act (1914), 82
Coal, 155–156, 167–170
Codetermination, 65, 88, 147, 148
COLA (cost-of-living adjustment) clauses, 67
Cole, Robert E., 95
Coleman, Robert E., 29
Collaborative labor-management relations (*see* Labor-management relations, building collaborative)
Collective bargaining (*see* Labor-management relations)
Commons, John R., 66
Communist countries, exports to, 136
Company loyalty, 57–58
Comparative Advantage, Law of, 153
Compensation systems (*see* Executives, compensation systems for; Worker compensation systems)
Competitiveness, 30, 36, 181
    business role in loss (*see* Business role in loss of economic power)
    capital formation and reestablishing, 115
    effects of dollar depreciation on, 11
    effects of labor-management relations on (*see* Labor-management relations)
    effects of outdated antitrust policy on, 82–84
    effects of tax structure on, 30
        (*See also* Tax structure)
    failure to keep up plants and, 50
        (*See also* Modernization)

Competitiveness (*Cont.*):
  government credit to increase, 133
  loss of, 2, 10–15
    internal solutions to, 101
    skewed economy and, 16
  multinationals and, 175–176
  new kind of world, 25–27
  new values and, 72
  savings and (*see* Savings)
  (*See also* Exports; World market;
    specific foreign countries)
Computer-aided design/computer-aided
  manufacturing (CAD-CAM) system,
  161–162
Computer and computer-related
  industries, 16, 27, 54, 128, 144, 145,
  149, 151
  capitalizing on assets in, 160–167
  innovation in, 19–20
  loss of competitiveness, 2, 12–15
  oligopolies in, 83
  research in, 106
  support for, 155
Conable, Barker B. Jr., 119, 123, 132
Conable-Hance (formerly Kemp-Roth)
  bill, 30, 117, 118, 120, 122, 182–183
Conable-Jones bill, 123, 124
Concentration (*see* Mergers and
  acquisitions)
Congress, 29, 30, 115
  and antitrust laws, 35, 84
  and creation of export trading
    companies, 180
  government credit and, 132, 133
  and government help for utilities
    converting to coal, 170
  labor unions and, 63
  regulation and, 31–32
  social consensus and, 78–80, 85
  tax reform and, 118–120, 123–125,
    127–129
  trade policy and, 36, 134, 137, 139
  (*See also specific acts and bills*)
Congressional committees (*see* Congress)
Construction and housing industry, 22,
  67–68, 70, 132
Consumer safety (*see* Health and safety
  regulations)
Consumption:
  effects of high, on savings, 39, 42
  need to discourage, 76, 184
  taxing, 116–117
Coquillete, Robert M., 19
Corporate income tax, cutting,
  125–126
Cost-of-living adjustment (COLA)
  clauses, 67
Cost:
  of antitrust suits, 83–84

Cost (*Cont.*):
  of exports restrictions, 36
  of health insurance and pension plans,
    67
  of modernization, 50
  production, 27
    (*See also* Labor costs; Wages)
  of regulation, 31–32, 81, 82
Creative destruction, defined, 15
Credit, channeling, to business, 130–133
Currency:
  Japanese, 26
  and 1970s dollar depreciation, 11, 59

Data processing equipment industry, 144
Davison, Joseph W., 105
Decentralization of bargaining structure,
  67
Declining industries, 132
  abandoning, 184
  Japanese policy on, 142
Defense spending, R&D budgets and, 21
Denison, Edward, 23
Depreciation, 30, 44, 46, 49, 122–125,
  127, 131, 156, 183
  of dollar (1970s), 11, 59
Depressed industries, 145–146
Depression, The, 7, 19, 42, 69, 71, 130
Deregulation, 122, 167, 168, 181–182
  social consensus and, 80–81
  (*See also* Regulation)
Diebold, John, 103
Disposable income:
  1966–1973, 10
  1970s, 9
  personal savings as percentage of, 39
Dividends:
  paid by steel industry, 49, 50
  taxation of, 126
Dole, Robert, 118, 119
Dollar, depreciation of (1970s), 11, 59
Domestic market:
  automobile, 48, 49
  decline in U.S. share of, 8, 10–13
  effects of focus on, 27
  Japanese, 28
  (*See also* Imports)
Doyle, Frank P., 87, 91
Drucker, Peter F., 43, 59
Drug industry, 11–12, 20
Dunn, Robert M., Jr., 34, 40–42, 165

ECD (Energy Conversion Devices), 166
Economic growth:
  business decisions and (*see* Long-term
    planning; Short-term planning)
  declining, 7–28, 63

Economic growth, declining (*Cont.*):
and declining payoff from
innovation, 19–21
effects on industries, 10–15
shrinking standard of living
expressing, 7–10
skewed economy and, 15–19
and stunted growth of productivity,
21–24
export-led (*see* Export-led growth;
Exports)
labor-management relations and (*see*
Labor-management relations,
building collaborative)
modernization and, 78
(*See also* Modernization)
and need for new national policy,
77–78
(*See also* National policy)
post-World War II, 8
as process of creative destruction, 15
rate of (1862–1965), 184
social betterment and, 70
(*See also* Standard of living)
social consensus and, 75–76
(*See also* Social consensus)
stifling effect of government on (*see*
Government)
(*See also* Competitiveness; *specific
aspects of economic growth, for
example:* Exports; Gross National
Product)
Economic revitalization board, proposal
for, 1, 88–89
Economic well-being:
public view of, 72
(*See also* Standard of living)
Economies of scale, 83, 85
Education, 69, 70
of labor force, 87
of projected labor force, 173
of management, 60–61, 107, 108, 110
(*See also* Universities)
Electrical equipment industry, 87
Electronics industry (*see* Computer and
computer-related industries)
Employee development, 58, 60–61
Employee differences, need to encourage,
103–105
Employee stock ownership, 65
Employment:
effects of multinationals on, 176
full, 75
in high-technology industries, 160
in electronics industry, 15
increase: in 1960–1970, 24
in 1970s, in service industries, 22
regional statistics on, 17

Employment (*Cont.*):
in skewed economy, 15–18
social consensus and, 79
(*See also* Jobs; Unemployment)
Employment Act of 1949, 78
Energy Conversion Devices (ECD), 166
Energy crisis, 152, 178
Energy and energy industry, 16, 144,
145, 149, 156, 177
and capitalizing on energy assets,
167–171
conservation of, 158, 168
and developing alternative energy
sources, 144, 166–168, 170–171
legislation on, 49
prices of energy (*see* Prices, energy)
(*See also* Coal; Fusion energy; Natural
gas; Nuclear energy; Oil; Solar
energy; Synthetic fuels)
Energy Tax Act (1978), 129
Entitlement, concept of, 70
Environmental policy, 60, 70, 80, 81
coal use and, 169
exports and, 138
nuclear energy and, 168
productivity and, 22–23
steel and automobile industry affected
by, 49
Equal opportunity legislation, 70, 80
Erhard, Ludwig, 147
Etzioni, Amitai, 79, 80
European countries, 3, 36, 157, 158, 161,
178
automobile production in, 11
exports policy of, 136, 137
GNP of, 25
investments in U.S. by, 176
labor-management relations in, 65
post-World War II reconstruction of,
10
(*See also* France; Germany; Great
Britain; Italy)
Evans, Van M., 174
Executives:
compensation systems for, 48
bonus system in, 59, 102–103
promotion of, 57–59, 104
of young executives, 107–108
"Export Caucus" of the Senate, 35
Export-led growth, 25–27
core concept of, 26
defined, 25
Export trading companies, proposed
creation of, 180
Exports:
coal, 170
to communist countries, 136
to developing countries, 155

Exports (*Cont.*):
  effects of 1970s dollar depreciation on, 11
  importance of, 135–139
  by multinationals, 175, 177
  need for new national policy on, 134
    (*See also* National policy, cornerstones of new U.S.)
  1962–1979, 10–14
  political curbs on, 35–37, 136–138
    (*See also* Competitiveness; Trade policy; World market)

Failing businesses, 80, 133, 152, 184
Farley, James B., 55, 104, 107
Federal budget, balanced, 34, 119, 120, 134–135
Federal spending, 30, 34
  on defense, 21
  on job training, 79, 174
  on transfer payments, 42
Feldstein, Martin, 42
Fellner, William, 41
Field, Tom 119
Financial accounting, inflation and, 43, 44
Financial assets, inflation and move from, to tangible assets, 41–42
    (*See also* Consumption)
Firing of workers, 68
Fiscal crisis in cities, 19
Fisher, Irving, 117
Flaim, Paul O., 173
Footwear and apparel industry, 2, 14, 15, 144, 145, 158
Ford, Brian R., 163
Ford, Gerald, 181
Ford, Henry, 13
Foreign aid, 28, 137
Foreign Corrupt Practices Act, 34, 37
Foreign high-technology industries, 27, 144, 145, 148, 149, 151
Foreign policy curbs on exports, 35–37, 136–138
Foreign trade (*see* Competitiveness; Exports; Imports; Trade policy; World market)
Forrester, Jay W., 20
Fougere, Guy L., 161
Fowler, Robert E., 163
Foy, Lewis W., 49
France, 37, 84, 132, 135, 136, 165, 179
  growth of labor force in, 172, 173
  multinationals of, 178
  policy of, 141, 142, 148, 151
  productivity growth in, 22
Franko, Lawrence, 134

Fraser, Douglas A., 87, 88
Freedman, Audrey, 66, 67
Fringe benefits, 70
  (*See also* Health insurance plans; Pension plans)
Fuel-efficient automobiles, 48, 57, 171
  effects of failure to build, 13, 48–49, 60
Full employment, 75
  Employment Act (1946) for, 78
Fukushima, Kiyohiko, 143, 145, 146
Fuller, Donald W., 52
Funds:
  for research, 105–107
    as percentage of GNP (1964), 21
    slump in, 16
  (*See also* Federal spending)
Furniture industry, 22
Fusion energy, 166

Gallagher, J. Michael, 170
Gas prices, 48
Geier, James A. D., 165
Geneen, Harold S., 54
General Agreement on Tariffs and Trade talks, 36, 179
Genetic engineering (bioengineering), 11, 19, 128, 149, 159, 166, 167
Geneva round of multinational trade negotiations, 136
Germany, 12, 13, 49, 50, 159, 165
  credit allocation to industry in, 132
  innovation in, 21, 165
  investments by, 23, 40, 147
  labor force growth in, 172, 173
  labor-management relations in, 64, 68
    codetermination, 147, 148
  national policy of, 142, 147–148
  oligopolies of, 84
  productivity in, 22, 24, 147
  responses to change in, 61
  robot technology in, 163
  savings in, 40
  social consensus in, 77, 78, 147
  worker compensation in, 59
Gertler, Mark, 43, 44
Ginzberg, Eli, 173, 174
Giuliano, Vincent E., 160
Glaser, Peter E., 166
Global markets (*see* World market)
Gluck, Frederick W., 103
GNP (*see* Gross National Product)
Goldman, Jacob E., 19, 20
Goodman, Paul S., 97
Gottlieb, Melvin B., 166
Government:
  growth stifled by, 29–37
  regulation and (*see* Regulation)

Government, growth stifled by (*Cont.*):
  and trade policy vacuum, 35–37
  inability of, to meet expectations, 71
  role of, in forging social consensus,
    75–85
    (*See also* Social consensus)
  as source of savings, 42
    (*See also* Congress; Federal spending;
      National policy)
Gray, Harry, 31, 47
Great Britain, 12, 132, 135, 142, 151,
  165, 172, 184
Great Depression, 7, 19, 42, 69, 71, 130
Greenhalg, Leonard, 174
Greenspan, Alan, 42
Grievance and arbitration procedures
  (*see* Labor-management relations)
Gross National Product (GNP), 56, 141
  per employee (1963–1973), 24
  fourth quarter 1980, 16
  investments as percentage of (1970s),
    23
  investments in plants and equipment
    as percentage of, 40
  Japanese, 25, 26
  percentage of, spent on R&D (1964), 21
  size of U.S. and Japanese, compared,
    25
Grossed-up dividend credit, 126

Hambro, Rupert N., 142
Hammer, Armand, 107
Harrison, Bennett, 98
Hartland-Thumberg, Penelope, 25–26
Hayek, Friedrich von, 173
Hayes, Robert H., 54, 55, 58
Health insurance plans, 70
  cost of, 67
  maintenance of, following plant
    shutdowns, 99
Health and safety regulations:
  effects of: on foreign trade, 36, 37
    on productivity, 22–23
    on steel and automobile industry, 49
  profit taking precedent over, 71
  and public distrust of business on
    health and safety matters, 77
Henry, J. Roy, 162
Hessler, Curtis A., 130
High-technology industries, 11, 16–17,
  128, 136, 153, 160
  concentration in, 83
  foreign, 27, 144, 145, 148, 149, 151
  trade policy and, 36–37
  (*See also specific high-technology
    industries, for example:* Computer
    and computer-related industries)

Hispanics (*see* Minorities)
Hobgood, William P., 68
Homestead Act (1862), 184
Horizontal mergers, antitrust legislation
  preventing, 83
Horwitch, Mel, 170
House of Representatives (*see* Congress)
Households, net financial worth of, 41
Housing and construction industry, 22,
  67–68, 70, 132
Houthakker, Hendriks, 83
Human rights policy, 36, 37, 136

Imports:
  effects of 1970s dollar depreciation on,
    11
  and import substitution policy, 179
  Japanese policy on, 146
  by multinationals, 175
  U.S., 12–15
    automobile, 13, 48, 84
    machinery, 12–14
    oil, 5, 10, 168
    steel, 49
  wage increases favoring, 64
Incentive compensation plans for risk-
    taking executives, 102
Income:
  based on achievement, social consensus
    and, 76
  disposable: 1966–1973, 10
    1970s, 9
    personal savings as percentage of,
      39
  nation's total discretionary (1980), 10
  (*See also* Dividends; Profit; Wages)
Income maintenance programs, 42, 79
Income redistribution, 70, 72, 76, 185
  failure of, 77–78
  taxation and, 117, 119
Income tax (*see* Corporate income tax;
  Tax structure)
Indexation of personal income tax,
  117–118
Indicative planning, French, 148, 150
Individual retirement accounts (IRAs),
  118–119
Industrial promotion, 35
Industrial relations (*see* Labor-
  management relations)
Industry (*see* High-technology industry;
  see specific industry, for example:
  Aerospace industry; Automobile
  industry)
Inflation, 30
  balanced budget to fight, 120
  and cost of regulation, 32

Inflation (*Cont.*):
  effects of: on depreciation, 122–123
    on R&D spending, 21
    on standard of living, 8, 10
    on tax cuts, 183
  effects of Kemp-Roth (Conable-Hance)
    bill on, 120
  investments and, 23
    (*See also* Investments)
  savings (*see* Savings, inflation and)
  wages and, 63, 64, 67–68
Innovation, 2, 30, 155, 165
  declining payoff from, 19–21
  in Germany, 21, 165
  in high-technology industries, 83
  triggering, 119–130
    (*See also* Research and development;
    Technology)
Intellectual community:
  social consensus and, 79
    (*See also* Universities)
Interest rate on savings, effects of
    inflation on, 40
International competition (*see*
    Competitiveness)
International trade (*see* Exports; Imports;
    Trade policy; World market)
International Trade and Investment,
    Department of, proposal for, 135
Inventory, effects of inflation on, 43
Inventory accounting, 44
Investment tax credit (ITC), 49, 122, 125,
    126, 128–129, 131
Investments, 29, 53, 59–60, 69, 181
  collaborative policies on, 89
  effects of inflation on, 39–46
  effects of tax structure on, 2, 30, 42, 43
  and export-led growth, 26, 27
  foreign, in U.S., 176–177
  German, 23, 40, 147
  Japanese, 23, 40, 143, 177
  long-term, 50–51
  to meet energy demands, 168
  by multinationals, 175, 176, 179
  productivity and, 23, 24
    (*See also* Productivity)
  reindustrialization and need to
    encourage, 184
  social consensus and increased, 76
  tax cuts as incentives to, 30, 119–120,
    183
  transfer payments as sources of capital
    for, 76
  triggering, 119–130
Iran, 136
IRAs (Individual Retirement Accounts),
    118–119
Israel, 136, 138
Italy, 142, 152–153, 163, 172, 184

ITC (investment tax credit), 125, 126,
    128–129, 131

Jacobi, Herbert H., 148
Japan, 3, 37, 49, 50, 148, 157, 159, 161
  capital/labor ratio in, 24
  credit allocation to industry in, 132
  export-led growth in, 25–28
  innovation in, 21
  investments in, 23, 40, 143, 177
  job security in, 98
  labor force growth in, 172, 173
  labor-management relations in, 64
  multinationals of, 178–179
  national policy of, 36, 141–147
  oligopolies of, 84
  productivity growth in, 22
  quality control circles in, 95
  robot technology in, 162–164
  savings in, 40
  social consensus in, 77, 78, 142, 143
  U.S. and Japanese managers
    compared, 57–58
  worker compensation in, 59
  world market share held by, 10–15
    exports, 135, 136, 139
Jasinowski, Jerry J., 127, 141
Job enrichment, 56
Job rotation for managers, 107–108
Job satisfaction:
  worker participation and, 88
    (*See also* Quality-of-worklife programs)
Job security, 58, 98
Job training, 79–80
  following plant shutdowns, 99
  need for government spending on, 79,
    174
Jobs:
  creating, for excluded social groups, 76
  in high-technology industries, 17
  inability to meet expectations on
    creation of, 70
  1970s loss of industrial. 11
    (*See also* Employment;
    Unemployment)
Johnston, Dennis, 173
Joint ventures:
  in aerospace industry, 155
  in computer industry, 155
  with small firms, 106
Jones, Cardell, 95
Jones, James R., 123
Jones, Reginald H., 29, 30, 72, 105, 126,
    135
Jones, Thomas V., 53, 101
Jordan, Barbara, 85
Jorgenson, Dale, 23, 122, 124

Juster, F. Thomas, 41, 116

Karis, William G., 169
Katz, Abraham, 36
Katzell, Raymond A., 71, 77
Kemp, Jack, 30, 120
Kemp-Roth (renamed Conable-Hance)
    bill, 30, 117, 118, 120, 122, 182–183
Kennedy, John F., 90
Keogh plans, 118–119
Kerr, Clark, 71
Keynes, John Maynard, 39
Keynesian economics, 30, 120
Kirby, Robert E., 101
Kirkland, Lane, 79, 88, 89
Klein, Lawrence, 39, 156, 157
Knowledge workers, productivity of, 56
Kochan, Thomas A., 89, 90
Kodama, Yukiharu, 143
Korea, 24

Labor costs:
  Japanese, 14
  manufacturing unit, 22
  (See also Productivity; Wages)
Labor force, 158
  education of, 87
  of projected labor force, 173
  effects of plant closings on, 98
  growth of (1975–1990), by nation,
    172–173
  robots and, 162
  U.S., 21, 154
    in machine tools industry, 157
    women in, 173–174
  (See also Workers)
Labor law reform bill, defeated (1978),
    65, 89
Labor laws, violation of, 64
Labor-management relations, 2, 63–72
  building collaborative, 87–99
    at national level, 90–91
    and plant closings issue, 97–99
    and quality control circles, 95–97
    by reforming work practices, 92–93
    signs of progress toward, 88–92
    Tarrytown experiment as example
      of, 93–95
  conflictual: and inability to meet
    expectations, 69–72
    increased conflict in, 64–65
    and nature of collective bargaining
      system, 66–69
  French, 151
  German, 148
    codetermination, 147, 148

Labor-management relations (Cont.):
  social consensus and, 76
Labor unions, 29, 48
  British, 151
  drop in membership of, 65
  German, 147
  Japanese, 146
  leaders of, on boards of directors, 65,
    88, 147, 148
  multinationals and, 176
  reindustrialization supported by, 1, 2
  role of, in forging social consensus, 3,
    75, 78–79
  (See also Labor-management relations:
    Workers)
Laffer, Arthur B., 182
La Force, J. Clayburne, 31, 58
Lambert, Sheldon M., 168
Land, Edwin H., 54
Landen, Delmar L., Jr., 88, 92
Latin American countries, 15, 154, 179
Lear, Robert W., 61, 104
Lee, Henry, 167
Leisure time, 69
Leveraging of bonuses, 102
Levinson, Harry, 104
Lincoln, Abraham, 184
Lipsitz, Ruth, 167
Loans:
  and channeling government credit to
    industry, 130–133
  governmental guarantees on, 80
Long, Russell, 127
Long-range risk taking, rewarding,
    101–103
Long-term decisions, 101–111
  in collective bargaining, 68
    (See also Labor-management
      relations)
  encouraging employee differences and,
    103–105
  overhauling of business schools as,
    108–111
  promotion of young executives as,
    107–108
  research funding as, 105–107
  rewarding risk taking as, 101–103
Lordstown plant (General Motors), 163
Luft, Klaus, 165

MacAuley, Patrick, 154
MacAvoy, Paul, 84
MacDougal, Gary E., 107
Machine tools industry, 13, 14, 144,
    156–157, 164, 165
Machinery industry, 12–14, 145, 156
Macroeconomic policies, 147, 150, 151

Magnetohydrodynamics (MHD), 166–167
Management:
  authoritarian, 68–69, 88, 93
  education of, 60–61, 107, 108, 110
  Japanese, 14, 26–27
  participatory, 56, 88, 92, 146
  shortsighted, effects on innovation, 20, 21
  and social consensus, 76, 78–79
  (See also Boards of directors;
    Executives; Labor-management
    relations; Long-term decisions;
    Risk taking; Short-term planning)
Management by objectives (MBO), 48, 57
Mann, H. Michael, 85
Manning, Bayless, 31
Manufacturing industries:
  losses of, on domestic and world
    markets, 10–11
  productivity growth in, 22
  (See also specific manufacturing
    industries)
Mark, Jerome E., 166
Marolda, Anthony J., 55, 61
Marshal, Ray, 90
Marshal Plan, 78
Massaro, Anthony A., 164
Masse, Pierre, 150
May, William F., 111
MBO (management by objectives), 48, 57
Meany, H. Jack, 31, 47
Mendenhall, John R., 127, 128
Mergers and acquisitions, 52, 59, 83, 98, 157
  cost of, 54–55
  in high-technology industries, 83
Mettler, Ruben F., 79, 101
Mexico, 179
MHD (magnetohydrodynamics), 166–167
Microelectronics industry (see Computer
    and computer-related industries)
Midwestern United States, 2, 15, 17, 18, 65, 183
Military power:
  effects of stunted growth on, 28
  use of, 137
Mill, John Stuart, 117
Mining industry, 22, 133, 177
Minority groups:
  blacks, 2, 18, 70, 76, 77, 79
  role of, in forging social consensus, 3, 75, 79
  (See also Poverty)
Mitchell, Donald W., 48
Mitchell, Parren J., 131
Modernization, 30, 39, 49, 50
  economic growth and, 78

Modernization (Cont.):
  and investments in new plants and
    equipment, 43
  German, 40, 147
  1965–1980, 40
Monopoly and oligopoly, 82–84
Morgan, Richard, 51
Morral, John F., 81
Multilateral trade agreements, 136, 137
Multinationals, 159
  using, to push exports, 175–180
Murphy, Thomas A., 48
Murrin, Thomas J., 95, 96

Nader, Ralph, 60
National Labor Relations Act, 89
National policy, 48, 142
  British, 151
  cornerstones of new U.S., 115–139
    channeling credit to business as, 130–133
    new trade policy as, 134–139
    reviving savings as, 115–119
    triggering investment and
      innovation as, 119–130
  French, 141, 142, 148–151
  German, 141, 142, 147–148
  Italian, 152–153
  Japanese MITI, 141–147
  U.S., 48, 77–78
    on antitrust, 35, 37, 138, 139, 155, 182–185
    basic tenets of, needed for
      reindustrialization, 183–184
    under Carter (see Carter, Jimmy)
    contradictory aspects of, 32–34
    on industrial promotion, 35
    toward multinationals, 175, 176
    on resource development, 30, 34–35
    under Reagan (see Reagan, Ronald)
    on spending (see Federal spending)
    targeting of industries and, 153–158
    on trade (see Trade policy)
  (See also specific aspects of national
      policy, for example: Environmental
      policy; Tax structure)
Nationalizations, 132
Natural gas, 167, 168, 170, 171
Natural resources, 30, 34–35
Nesheim, John L., 37
Net worth of households, 41
Nixon, Richard M., 67, 85, 132
Nodbichler, Joachim, 163
Nonsupervisory personnel, disposable
    income of (1979, 1980), 10
Nontariff barriers, 136

Nonunion companies (open shops), 65,
68, 69, 89
Norris, William C., 105
Norsworthy, J. Randall, 23
Northern and Northeastern United
States, 2, 15–19, 65, 97, 98, 183
Nuclear power, 144, 168
Nuclear proliferation issues, 36, 37, 136,
138

Ocean-temperature energy conversion
(OTEC), 166
Occupational safety, 68, 80
Office equipment industry, 144, 151
Oil, 16
imports of, 10, 168
prices of, 10, 26, 167–171
shale, 170–171
Oil industry (see Energy and energy
industry)
Oligopoly and monopoly, 82–84
Omnibus National Export Policy Act
(1980), 137
Ong, John D., 35, 79, 89
Open shops (nonunion companies), 65,
68, 69, 89
Organized labor (see Labor unions)
OTEC (ocean-temperature energy
conversion), 166
Output per worker-hour (see
Productivity)
Ovshinsky, Stanford R., 166

Packard, David, 106
Packer, Arnold H., 78, 184
Participatory management (worker
participation), 56, 88, 92, 146
Patents, decline in number of
(1970–1975), 21
Pension plans, 65, 67, 70, 99
Personal income tax (see Income tax)
Peterson, Peter G., 27
Petrochemicals industry, 155–156
Phipps, Charles H., 105
Planning, 26, 27, 101, 102
for export-led growth, 26–27
governmental, dangers of, 80
(See also National policy)
short-term, 47–52
innovation and, 20, 21
(See also Long-term decisions)
Plant shutdowns, 49–50, 65, 97–99,
102
Plants and equipment (see Depreciation;
Modernization)
Plastics industry, 11, 14, 67, 155–156

Political influence:
loss of economic power and loss of,
28
means for exerting, 137
Pollution (see Environmental policy;
Health and safety regulations)
Population growth:
in Southern and Western U.S., 15–17
trading up, 172–175
Posner, Richard A., 35
Potter, Robert J., 105
Poverty, 70, 76, 77
(See also Income redistribution;
Minority groups; Unemployment)
Price-fixing, 35, 82
Prices:
effects of monopolies on, 82, 83
effects of regulation on, 32
(See also Regulation)
energy, 22, 145
coal, 169
gas, 48
natural gas, 168, 170, 171
oil, 10, 26, 167–171
wages and, 75
(See also Wages)
(See also Inflation)
Printing industry, 68
Prodi, Romano, 153
Product safety (see Health and safety
regulations)
Production, 69
automobile: drop in, 11
General Motors—1980, 84
1980—Tarrytown, 95
domestic oil, 168
effects of monopoly on, 82
Japanese, 12, 163
sagging (1970s), 11–13, 15, 30
social consensus and renewed emphasis
on, 76
unions and changes in process of, 68
Productivity, 30
countrywide, factors affecting, 56
effects of deregulated energy prices on,
168
faltering, 18, 19, 21–24, 63, 70
German, 22, 24, 147
growth of, annual adjustments to
wages and (1975–1979), 63–64
in high-technology industries, 160
job satisfaction and, 97
labor-management relations and, 63
new values affecting, 72
potential effects of Kemp-Roth
(Conable-Hance) bill on, 120
and Reagan economic program, 181
with robots, 162

Productivity (*Cont.*):
  social consensus and: as focus of social
      consensus, 142
    renewed emphasis on productivity,
      76
  standard of living and, 8
  worker participation and, 88
Profit, 49
  in concentrated industries, 83
  effects of COLAs on, 67
  effects of inflation on, 39, 43–46
  maximization of short-term, 49–52
  as measure of performance, 81
  public view of, 71
Promotion of executives, 57–59, 104
  of young executives, 107–108
Protectionism, 136, 142, 146, 150, 157,
      158
Public attitudes:
  toward institutions, 70–71, 77
    corporations, 81
  toward new industrial plan, 76, 77
  (*See also* Social consensus)
Public-interest groups, role of, in forging
      social consensus, 3, 75

Quality control circles, 95–97, 147
Quality-of-worklife programs, 77, 96–97
  effects on absenteeism of, 93, 94, 97
  Tarrytown plant experiment with,
      93–95
  and work practices reform, 92
Quotas, 15

Radeke, Michael, 164
Railroad industry, 32–34, 68, 127, 128,
      169–170, 181
Rapp, William V., 175
Rapping, Leonard A., 10
Rates of return, 52
  on investments, 42
  on savings, 115
  (*See also* Dividends; Profit)
Rawls, John, 70
R&D (*see* Research and development)
Reagan, Ronald, 7, 29–35, 42, 80,
      117–120, 129, 168, 183
  deregulation and, 32–33, 181
  energy problems and, 170
  federal spending and, 34
  industrial promotion and, 35
  labor-management relations and, 89
  multinationals and, 179
  and resource development, 34–35
  supply-side economics and, 120, 122
  tax reform and, 2, 30, 115, 117–118,
      123–124, 183

Reagan, Ronald (*Cont.*):
  trade policy and, 134–135
Recession, 1980, 18
Regulation, 2, 29–34, 42
  contradictory, 32–34
  cost of, 31–32
  effects of, on R&D, 11, 21
  growth of, 81
  productivity and, 22
  reindustrialization and need for
      farsighted policy on, 80
  (*See also* Deregulation; Environmental
      policy; Health and safety
      regulations)
Research and development (R&D), 50,
      55, 101, 155, 166
  in alternative energy sources, 144,
      166–168
  effects of regulation on, 11, 21
  funds for, 105–107
    as percentage of GNP, 21
  slump in, 16
  Japanese, 145
  joint: in aerospace industry, 155
    in computer industry, 155
    with small firms, 106
  sag in (since 1960s), 20–21
  (*See also* Innovation; Technology)
Resistance to change:
  by business, 59–61
  by unions, 65, 67
Retail trade, 17
Retirement programs, 42
  IRAs, 118–119
Reuss, Henry S., 78
Reuther, Walther P., 185
Rewards:
  for long-range risk taking,
      101–103
  (*See also* Promotion of execu-
      tives)
Ricardo, David, 153
Risk taking, 47, 53–59
  education and, 110
  rewards for, 101–103
Robot industry (*see* Computer and
      computer-related industries)
Rohatyn, Felix G., 78, 133
Rosow, Jerome M., 93
Roth, William V., 30, 35, 120
Rousseau, Jean Jacques, 75, 87
Rubber and tire industry, 16, 49, 50, 63,
      67, 87, 91, 133, 178

Safety regulations (*see* Health and safety
      regulations)
Saint Phalle, Thibaut de, 148, 178

Sales representatives, productivity of, 56–57
Samuels, Michael A., 137
Samuelson, Paul, 183
Sant, Roger W., 171
Sarnoff, David, 54
Savings, 2, 30, 69, 182
  inflation and, 115
    adjusting taxation of savings to, 117–118
  effects of inflation on, 39–46
  taxation of: effects on savings, 2, 30, 40
  reviving, with tax reform, 115–119
Schmidt, Helmuth, 64
Schoenfeldt, Lyle F., 109
Schools (see Education; Universities)
Schroeder, Friedrich W., 53
Schumpeter, Joseph A., 15
Schunck, Hermann, 165
Schwartzman, David, 83
Scotese, Peter G., 52
Scott, Bruce R., 25
Semiconductor industry (see Computer and computer-related industries)
Senate and Senate committees (see Congress)
Service industries, 17, 22, 25, 56
  (See also Banks)
Severance pay for plant shutdowns, 99
Shale oil, 170–171
Shapiro, Irving S., 29, 64, 123
Shenton, Ronald, 95
Sherman Antitrust Act (1890), 81, 85, 184
Shipbuilding industry, 146, 152
Short-term planning, 2, 47–52
  innovation and, 20, 21
Short-term profit, maximization of, 49–52
Short-term research, 20
Simeral, William G., 102
Simon, Herbert, 106
Skaggs, Allen H., 19
Skewed economy, 15–19
Small cars (see Fuel-efficient automobiles)
Small firms, 80
  effects of corporate income tax cut on, 126
  innovation by, 20
  joint venture with, 106
Smith, Adam, 82
Social change, resistance to, 60
Social consensus, 3, 72, 75–85, 90, 159
  in France, 150–151
  government and, 80–85
  primary focus of, 142
  (See also Productivity)

Social consensus (Cont.):
  requirements for, 75–77
Social problems, social consensus and, 77
Social security, 42
Social unrest, 69, 71, 76, 77
Solar energy, 166, 168
Southern and Southwestern United States, 15–18, 65
Spaventa, Luigi, 153
Spencer, Edson W., 52
Standard of living:
  inability to meet expectations of, 69, 70
  shrinking, 7–10, 15
State laws on plant shutdowns, 97–98
Steel industry, 2, 26, 80, 83, 145, 146, 152, 157–158
  domestic market share of, 13
  labor-management relations in, 63, 64, 67, 69, 87, 91
  near depression in, 16
  near-profit maximization in, 49–50
  productivity in, 22
  promotion of, 35
  world market share of, 14
Stevenson, Adlai, 35
Stieber, Jack, 68
Stock market, 52–53, 107
Stock ownership by employees, 65
Stockman, David A., 132
Strikes, 26, 63, 69, 70, 91
Subsidies (see Government)
Sugges, Peter R., 53
Supply-side economics, 30, 120–122, 182, 183
Sussman, John A., 55
Synthetic fuels (synfuels), 167, 168, 170–171

Tangible assets, inflation and move away from financial assets to, 41–42
  (See also Consumption)
Tariff barriers (protectionism), 136, 142, 146, 150, 157, 158
Tarrytown experiment (General Motors), 93–95
Taylor, Charles, 43, 44
Tax credits, 126–130
  to boost innovation, 128–130
  employment, 80
  grossed-up dividend, 126
  investment, 49, 122, 125, 126, 128–129, 131
  refundable, 127
  targeting industries for, 127–129
Tax cuts, 117–120, 122–124, 126–130, 182–183

Tax cuts (*Cont.*):
  for Americans working abroad, 138
  as boost to innovation, 128–130
  effects of inflation on, 183
  investments and, 30, 119–120, 183
  Reagan and, 30, 115, 117–118,
      123–124, 183
Tax-deferred pension plans, 118–119
Tax structure, 3, 79, 138, 153
  effects of, on investments, 2, 30, 42,
      43
  need for reform in (*see* Kemp-Roth bill;
      Tax credits; Tax cuts)
  profit and, 44, 46
  reindustrialization and need for
      farsighted tax policy, 80
  savings and (*see* Savings, taxation of)
Technological change (*see* Automation)
Technology, 15, 19
  dangers of excessive reliance on,
      153–154
  to develop energy assets, 167
  preserving lead in, 3, 159–162
  transfer of, 155
  (*See also* Innovation; Research and
      development)
Telecommunications industry (*see*
      Computer and computer-related
      industries)
Textile industry, 89, 146, 154, 158
Thatcher, Margaret, 151
Thuronyi, Victor, 116, 118
Thurow, Lester C., 82, 84, 119
Time-motion studies, 56
Tire and rubber industry, 16, 49, 50, 63,
      67, 87, 91, 133, 178
Tobacco industry, 69
Trade adjustment assistance, 146
Trade agreements, multilateral, 136, 137
Trade Agreements Act (1979), 134
Trade embargoes, 36, 37
Trade policy, 35–37
  need for new, 134–139
  reindustrialization and need for
      farsighted, 80
  social consensus and, 78
  (*See also* Exports; Imports)
Training (*see* Job training)
Transfer payments:
  as source of investment capital, 76
  (*See also* Income maintenance
      programs; Retirement programs)
Tripartite committee concept, 90
Trowbridge, Alexander B., 34
Trucking industry, 32, 80, 91, 181
Turnover, effects of quality-of-worklife
      programs on, 93, 97
Typists, productivity of, 56

Ullman, Al, 123, 127
Ulman, Carter, 64
Unemployment, 16–19, 41, 181
  among blacks, 2, 18
  in cities, 17–19
  high wages vs., 91
      (*See also* Wages)
  in Italy, 152–153
  and loss of competitiveness, 2
Unemployment benefits, 70
Unions (*see* Labor unions)
Universities:
  and need to overhaul business schools,
      108–111
  role of, in research, 106
  (*See also* Education; Intellectual
      community)
Urban problems (*see* Cities)
Usery, W. J., Jr., 68, 69
Utilities industry, 22, 69, 170

Vaccara, Beatrice N., 154
Value-added tax (VAT), 116, 127
Values, changed societal, 71–72
Vietnam war, 78, 184
Villers, Philippe, 162
Voluntary compliance, hostile business-
      government relations and decline in,
      31

Wages, 88, 133
  and COLAs, 67
  German, 147
  growth of productivity and adjustments
      of (1975–1979), 63–64
  high: as entitlement, 70
      unemployment vs., 91
  industrywide patterns of, 67
  inflation and, 63, 64, 67–68
  Japanese, 1980 increases in, 143–144
  multinationals and, 176
  and severance pay for plant
      shutdowns, 99
  social consensus and limits on, 79
Walker, Charls E., 2, 119, 120, 128, 133
Walker, James W., 174
Wall Street, 52–53, 107
Walton, Richard E., 97
Watanabe, Hiroshi, 142, 145, 164
Watson, Thomas, Jr., 54
Wealth redistribution (*see* Income
      redistribution)
Webb-Pomerene Act (1918), 84
Weber, Arnold R., 65, 67, 91
Weidenbaum, Murray L., 31, 80, 82
West Germany (*see* Germany)

Western United States, 15–18
White-collar crime, 35, 36
Wimpisinger, William, 65
Women in labor force, 173–174
Woodson, Robert L., 76
Work, changed attitudes toward, 71
Worker compensation systems, 59,
    67
    (*See also* Health insurance plans;
        Pension plans; Wages)
Worker participation, 56, 88, 92, 146
Workers:
    and company loyalty, 57–58
    disposable income of (1979; 1980),
        10
    effects of short-term planning on,
        56
    firing of, 68
    GNP per (1963–1973), 24
    Japanese, 57–58
    and MBO, 48, 57
    strikes by, 26, 63, 69, 70, 91

Workers (*Cont.*):
    (*See also* Employment; Jobs;
        Productivity; Unemployment;
        Wages *and entries beginning with*
        terms: Job; Labor)
Workers' councils, German, 148
World cars, 178
World market:
    need to provide better access to,
        179–180
    U.S. share of, 8–15
    (*See also* Competitiveness; Exports)

Yankelovich, Daniel, 69–72, 77
Young, Lewis H., 1
Youth:
    bringing, into social consensus, 76
    unemployment among black, 18

Zanderer, Bett, 167

The Business Week Team

The Reindustrialization of America was prepared by a special *Business Week* team headed by senior editor SEYMOUR ZUCKER. Zucker supervises economic coverage of the U.S. and world economies for *Business Week*. Prior to joining the magazine in 1973 as economics editor, he was a staff economist for the National Broadcasting Company. Before that, he was an economist for the Port of New York Authority, specializing in regional analysis. Zucker, a native New Yorker, received his B.A. and M.A. degrees in economics from Brooklyn College and earned his Ph.D. in economics from the New School for Social Research. In 1976 he was awarded the Poynter Fellowship in economic journalism by Yale University.

CLAUDIA H. DEUTSCH is *Business Week*'s management editor. Deutsch has been a business journalist for thirteen years, seven of those years with *Business Week*. She covered such diverse fields as retailing, purchasing, technology, and environment before assuming her current position in January 1978. Born in New York, she holds a B.S. degree in child psychology from Cornell University.

JOHN HOERR, an associate editor of *Business Week,* began specializing as a labor reporter when he first joined *Business Week* in 1960. He has spent most of the last twenty years reporting on and writing about labor in Detroit, Pittsburgh, and New York. Hoerr left the magazine in 1969 and went to WQED-TV, Pittsburgh's public television station, where he wrote and produced film documentaries and served as an on-air correspondent for a nightly news program. Hoerr returned to *Business Week* as labor editor in 1975 and became associate editor in 1979. Born in McKeesport, Pennsylvania, he is a graduate of the Pennsylvania State University.

NORMAN JONAS is senior economic correspondent based in Washington, D.C. Born in the Bronx, New York, he was graduated Phi Beta Kappa from the City College of New York. After working for a number of New York newspapers, primarily the *Times* and *Wall Street Journal,* Jonas came to *Business Week* in 1966. Since 1973 he has been analyzing and writing about economic policy, with special emphasis on tax and spending programs from the nation's capital.

JOHN E. PEARSON is a senior writer for *Business Week* who focuses on international trade and investment and writes in-depth reports on economic, political, and business developments overseas. A graduate of Harvard University with a B.S. in electronic physics, he worked on newspapers in Minnesota and Mexico and served as correspondent in Latin America for *Business Week* and other McGraw-Hill publications. During two decades at *Business Week,* Pearson has been the recipient of awards from the Overseas Press Club of America for excellence in reporting and writing on foreign affairs.

JAMES C. COOPER joined *Business Week* in 1980 as an associate in the economics department, where he writes mainly for the magazine's Business Outlook section. Prior to coming to *Business Week,* Cooper was an economist with the American Paper Institute, where he served as director of special studies. He holds B.S. and M.A. degrees in economics from North Carolina State University.